CONTINUING PROFESSIONAL DEVELOPMENT IN SOCIAL WORK

Carmel Halton, Fred Powell and Margaret Scanlon

First published in Great Britain in 2015 by

Policy Press
University of Bristol
1-9 Old Park Hill
Bristol BS2 8BB
UK
t: +44 (0)117 954 5940
e-mail pp-info@bristol.ac.uk
www.policypress.co.uk

North American office:
Policy Press
c/o The University of Chicago Press
1427 East 60th Street
Chicago, IL 60637, USA
t: +1 773 702 7700
f: +1 773-702-9756
e:sales@press.uchicago.edu
www.press.uchicago.edu

British Library Cataloguing in Publication Data
A catalogue record for this book is available from the British Library

Library of Congress Cataloging-in-Publication Data
A catalog record for this book has been requested

ISBN 978-1-4473-0738-9 paperback

Cover design by Policy Press
Front cover: image kindly supplied by Yogesh Arora (www.yogesharora.com)
Printed and bound in Great Britain by CMP, Poole

Contents

Acknowledgements

We would like to thank the Irish Association of Social Workers (IASW) for their cooperation in the administration of the online survey; their help was invaluable. We would also like to sincerely thank all of those IASW members who participated in the research. We would also like to thank the members of the School of Applied Social Studies' Practice Advisory Board (PAB) for their assistance in developing the questionnaire. We are grateful to our colleagues in the Institute of Social Science in the 21st Century (ISS21) at University College Cork for their interest and support.

List of abbreviations

AASW	Australian Association of Social Workers
CPD	Continuing professional development
DCYA	Department of Children and Youth Affairs
HCPC	Health and Care Professions Council (England)
HSE	Health Service Executive
IASW	Irish Association of Social Workers
NSQWB	National Social Work Qualifications Board
OMCYA	Office of the Minister for Children and Youth Affairs
PQ	Post-qualifying
RAE	Research Assessment Exercise
SSSC	Scottish Social Services Council
SWRB	Social Workers Registration Board (New Zealand)
SWTF	Social Work Task Force

Preface

Continuing professional development (CPD) is broadly understood as the education of professionals after they have completed their formal training; but there the complexity begins. As we will see in this groundbreaking book, CPD takes many and diverse forms. It is underpinned by the idea that professionals need to renew and enhance their knowledge, skills and competencies throughout their professional life cycles. CPD embraces formal learning activities – such as courses, conferences, seminars, workshops – and informal learning through supervision, reading, reflection and peer support. It is located at the interface between professional practice and ongoing professional development.

Social work, like many other professions (law, medicine, teaching, nursing, etc), is in the process of incorporating CPD into its professional domain. Our study is about 'CPD and social work'. We ask: what exactly is CPD? How is it impacting on social workers' practice? Can it be made more relevant to social workers' professional lives? Who benefits? In an era when deprofessionalisation threatens social workers' role and task, does CPD help to put professionalisation back into social work? Or, is CPD simply a management tool to promote proceduralism and uniformity in social work practice – globally, in the age of austerity? Can social workers utilise the reflective space offered by CPD to redefine themselves in challenging times? In a knowledge society, is CPD the key to social work's future? Will CPD help social work practitioners remain relevant to the needs of service users?

While a substantial international literature has emerged about CPD over several decades, precious little research attention has been paid to what social workers want from CPD and what they think about it. Furthermore, while the literature often leads those interested or involved in CPD to assert that 'we know what it is', much of the knowledge is speculative, at best. Can we even answer with certainty straightforward questions such as: who engages with CPD? What do they think about CPD? What motivates them to engage in CPD? What are the barriers to participation in CPD? What are the most common forms of CPD? What is CPD's contribution to professional development? What do practitioners want from CPD? Are there diverse CPD agendas, reflecting differing value orientations between practitioners, managers, agencies and the state? We need to find answers to these questions. That is the purpose of this book.

The slogan 'think global, act local' summarises the contemporary context of CPD. It is internationally promoted and debated but largely practised in local contexts. Our study surveys members of the Irish Association of Social Workers (IASW), locating their experiences within wider international debates and practices that define the discursive arena of CPD in social work. Ireland is one of the most globalised countries in the world. It is culturally located within the Anglo-Saxon tradition of social work. Its welfare state is based on a liberal market model, which it shares with Britain, the US, Australia, New Zealand and Canada. Like other advanced democracies, Ireland has been transformed into a multicultural society. Social work is challenged to reflexively respond to the scale and pace of global change as experienced locally. CPD will play a vital role in interpreting this change and reframing social work practice in post-modernity.

This international study is comprised of eight chapters. In Chapter One we set out to define and explain the international context of CPD. We look in particular at its emergence within social work and consider the implications for social work education and practice in a number of countries across the world. While we focus primarily on the debate within the English-speaking world, our analysis is relevant to social work globally. Asian countries, such as India, Singapore and, more recently, China, experience many of the same challenges that social work faces in the West, and, in this respect, professionals in these countries may find this book very helpful. In the 21st century, Latin America has been at the forefront of the debate on social justice. European social work has a largely shared agenda with the English-speaking world.

Chapter Two sets CPD within contemporary international debates about social work education. In Chapter Three, we analyse a national study of Irish social workers in the context of their expressed needs for CPD and preferences in terms of course choices, ranging from popular therapeutic and counselling courses, through significant interest in management and administration, down to empowerment and social justice, which is very much a minority interest. The important contextual issue of barriers to participation is taken up in Chapter Four, in which we juxtapose the opinions of practitioners and managers.

For many social workers, their most common experience of CPD is through supervision, but does it meet practitioners' needs or agency needs? We pose this question. Chapter Five explores the complex issue of supervision, which is much the most common experience of CPD for social work practitioners, but maybe does not always meet the professed needs of the supervisee. The relationship between learning and reflection is addressed in Chapter Six as an overarching theme. We move on in Chapter Seven to considerations of the wider policy and epistemological issues that frame CPD. Finally, in Chapter Eight, we seek to provide conclusions within the challenging times we live in that provide the context in which social workers practice, and seek to map out the futurescapes of social work practice.

This has been an exciting and revealing piece of research. We have set our survey within a broad international context of social work. We hope the study will make a valuable and challenging contribution to the debate about CPD in social work.

ONE

Continuing professional development: the international context

Many of the ideas that underpin continuing professional development (CPD) can be traced to the 1960s and 1970s, a period when economic prosperity and productivity were increasingly linked to education. In the following decades, there was sustained political support for whole societies to become engaged in continual learning and development (Beddoe, 2009: 723). Initial education was no longer seen as sufficient for a professional lifetime, particularly in the context of rapidly changing societies, globalisation and new technologies. Terms such as 'lifelong learning', the 'learning society' and the 'learning organisation' encapsulate the idea that learning is an ongoing process that is not confined to schools, universities or other educational institutions.

While the idea of CPD (in one form or another) has been in circulation for some time, it has undoubtedly gained momentum in the social work sector over the last decade, particularly with the move towards greater regulation of the profession. In this introductory chapter, we will outline the concept of CPD, explore why it has assumed such significance in social work and other professions, and identify the different models of CPD currently in operation. We will also consider some of the concerns and criticisms raised in the literature, particularly in relation to: the lack of research on the impact of CPD; the dominance of certain CPD formats and objectives; and the implications of a shift from voluntary to mandatory systems of CPD.

What is continuing professional development?

There are a variety of definitions used for CPD across different professions and jurisdictions, but most of these definitions share a set of common characteristics. CPD is generally described in terms of an ongoing process of education and development that continues throughout the professional's career, and which includes both 'formal' and 'informal' elements. Thus, Bubb and Earley (2007: 4) describe CPD as 'an on-going process encompassing all formal and informal learning experiences' that enable staff 'to think about what they are doing, enhance their knowledge and skills and improve ways of working'. Similarly, Alsop (2000: 1) defines CPD as a process of ongoing education and development of professionals, 'from initial qualifying education and for the duration of professional life, in order to maintain competence to practice and increase professional proficiency and expertise'. One of the most commonly used definitions is that of Madden and Mitchell (1993: 12), who describe CPD as 'The maintenance and enhancement of the knowledge, expertise and competence of professionals throughout their careers according to a plan formulated with regard to the needs of the professional, the employer, the profession and society'.

Over the last few decades, regulatory organisations have come to play an important role in defining what constitutes CPD for different professions. In countries where a system of registration is in operation, practitioners are generally required to undertake CPD in order to maintain their registration. A review of the frameworks used by organisations in three countries (the Health and Care Professions Council [HCPC][1] in England, the Social Workers Registration Board in New Zealand, and the Scottish Social Services Council [SSSC][2] in Scotland) suggests that a broad range of activities can be categorised as CPD, including work-based learning, professional activity, attending courses and self-directed study (for examples, see Table 1.1). The SSSC, for instance, emphasises the fact that CPD is a wide-ranging concept that encompasses 'academic and practice development and, equally importantly, informal learning and learning and development in the workplace and any development which contributes directly to improving the quality of care received by service users' (SSSC, 2004: 6). A later discussion paper, commissioned by the SSSC and published by the Scottish Institute for Excellence in Social Work Education, reiterates the point that CPD should not be defined solely in terms of 'training and qualifications' and identifies a range of opportunities for learning within the workplace, including peer discussion, mentoring, staff development days, job shadowing and so on (see Skinner, 2005: 8). Similarly, the HCPC in England and the Social Workers Registration Board in New Zealand identify a variety of learning activities (see Table 1.1) and recognise the importance of flexibility in meeting the needs of practitioners who are at different stages of their careers and who work in various settings.

Informal and work-based learning is also central to the notion of the 'learning organisation', a concept that originated in the business sector but has gained ground within social work in recent years. According to Gould (2004: 4), what is implied in learning organisation approaches is a:

shift from seeing learning in the workplace as something only derived from going on a course or taking a distance learning module, to recognising that most workplace learning is non-formal and unplanned where learning happens all the time but is often not identified as learning because what people learn is their practice.

Professional supervision is considered to be one of the most fundamental mechanisms through which the CPD needs of social workers are met in the workplace. In recent years, the importance of regular supervision for practice has been reiterated in a series of policy reports and child abuse inquiries, both in the UK (Laming, 2003, 2009; SWTF, 2009; Munro,

Table 1.1: Examples of continuing professional development

Health and Care Professions Council (HCPC, 2012: 8–9) (England)
• work-based learning, for example, learning by doing, case studies, reflective practice, peer review, work shadowing, secondments, journal club, in-service training, supervising staff or students
• professional activity, for example, involvement in a professional body, lecturing or teaching, mentoring, being an examiner or tutor, presenting at conferences
• formal/educational, for example, courses, further education, research, attending conferences, writing articles or papers, distance learning, running a course
• self-directed learning, for example, reading journals/articles, reviewing books or articles, updating knowledge through the internet or TV
• other, for example, public service, voluntary work
Scottish Social Services Council (SSSC, 2004: 6) (Scotland)
• qualifications required for registration
• PRTL [Post Registration Training and Learning] requirements necessary to maintain registration status[a]
• formal learning, normally leading to a recognised award within the SCQF [Scottish Credit and Qualifications Framework]
• informal and work-based learning, often provided by or supported by employers, such as induction and in-house courses, job shadowing and secondment
• experiential learning, which takes place through life and work experiences, and is often, but not always, unintentional learning
Social Workers Registration Board (2010: 3) (New Zealand)
• work-based activities, for example, peer review, journal club, in-service training
• professional activities, for example, involvement in a professional body, mentoring
• formal education, for example, further education, distance learning, seminars
• self-directed learning, for example, reading or reviewing books and articles

Note: [a] For details, see SSSC (2011).

2011) and Ireland (McGuinness, 1993; OMCYA, 2009: 42; Gibbons, 2010; HSE, 2010a; Department of Children and Youth Affairs, 2011). Ideally, supervision combines professional accountability with support and development (Blewett, 2011), although, as we shall see in Chapter Five, this is not always the case in practice.

While CPD is generally described as a process of learning undertaken *after* the completion of initial qualifying education (see Alsop, 2000: 1; Higham, 2009: 1), there are some exceptions. As indicated in Table 1.1, the SSSC includes 'qualifications required for registration' in its definition of CPD (SSSC, 2004: 6). This is because many social services managers and front-line workers employed in day care and residential services in Scotland had no relevant qualification. Therefore, the process of registering the workforce and enabling them to achieve the required qualifications within the given timescales was seen as a priority for the social services sector (SSSC, 2004: 10).

What is the nature and purpose of continuing professional development?

Definitions of CPD generally incorporate some notion that the professional will be better able to perform his/her role, and that the quality of services to the client group will consequently be maintained or improved. From the 1960s onwards, there was a growing realisation that initial education does not equip professionals for all of their working lives (Houle et al, 1987; Cervero, 2000). With rapid social change, the explosion of research-based knowledge and technological innovation, many leaders in the professions recognised the need for continuing professional education (CPE) in order to prepare people for practice (Cervero, 2000: 4). Organised and comprehensive programmes of continuing education started to develop in many professions, including engineering, accounting, law, medicine, pharmacy, veterinary medicine, social work, librarianship, architecture and nursing. Professional associations, in particular, took systematic steps to ensure that their members continued their development on an ongoing basis (Lester, 1999: 111). By the early 1990s, Gear et al could comment that the:

> inadequacy of initial professional education as a preparation for one's entire working life is now well recognised by professional bodies. It is not just that knowledge dates, but that the very concept and interpretation of professional tasks and roles change over time. (Cited in Lester, 1999: 111)

The idea that CPD can be a means of dealing with changing roles and expectations is a recurring theme in the literature on social work education (see, eg, Postle et al, 2002). According to Williams (2007), social workers currently practise in an environment that is constantly changing: globalisation, privatisation and neo-conservatism have converged to change the issues, populations and impediments that they face in delivering services. One of the ways that social work has responded to these challenges is by instituting expectations that professionals will maintain competence though CPD. For example, cultural competence training programmes have been introduced in Canada for social workers and other professionals working in areas where there have been significant changes in the population and, as a consequence, the service user group (Williams, 2007).

While CPD may have been constructed as a means of addressing professional and societal change, it is not concerned with simply *updating* knowledge on the latest issues, policies and approaches (Cervero, 2000: 8–9). A number of studies have suggested that knowledge gained from formal learning often has surprisingly little effect on enhancing practice unless it is developed alongside experiential learning and becomes integrated with the practitioner's tacit repertoire of knowledge-in-use (see Lester, 1999: 5). One of the main objections to the 'update' model of learning is that it underestimates the intricacy and unpredictability of everyday practice. In a much-cited passage, Schön (1987: 3) observes that the most important issues facing professional practice are located in 'the swampy lowland' where 'messy, confusing problems defy technical solution'. It is perhaps for this reason that the idea of reflective learning and practice has had a particular resonance within social work education, at both the qualifying and post-qualifying stages (Blewett, 2011). Proponents argue that a reflective approach is better suited to working with service users, where each individual situation is unique and complexity of practice is not amenable to a mechanical 'tick-box' approach (Wilson and Kelly, 2010: 2443). The concept of reflective learning in social work is explored in detail in Chapters Two and Six.

Although reflective learning has gained ground in the last few decades, there is by no means a consensus on how CPD – particularly at the post-qualifying higher education level – should progress (Postle et al, 2002: 159). In the UK, a number of commentators have argued, for example, that social work education has been unduly influenced by managerialist agendas and narrowly defined organisational priorities (Lymbery, 2003; Dominelli, 2007). On the other hand, employers sometimes claim that social work education is out of touch with practice, and does not prepare students for the realities of work (see

Parsloe, 2001: 11). As for any profession, there are multiple stakeholders within continuing education for social workers, and therefore the building of a coordinated system of continuing education will be characterised by struggles over the educational agenda (Cervero, 2000: 11). Debates concerning the future of post-qualifying social work education are considered in detail in Chapter Two.

While the ultimate purpose of CPD is to improve social work practice, the orientation and objectives of specific CPD programmes can vary considerably. In this context, it is useful to refer to Beddoe's (2006) typology of the 'modes and focus of continuing education', which identifies five broad categories of educational focus and outcomes (see Table 1.2). The first two categories – *compliance* and *performance* modes – are organisationally generated and often represent the employer's minimum expectations of staff development. This might include, for example, induction and other forms of 'in-house' training designed to familiarise staff with the organisation's procedures and policies, or to train them in particular methods or approaches to practice. In this instance, it is the organisation that determines what knowledge is to be utilised by the practitioner: 'The organisation, in the form of a service unit responsible for training, decides what knowledge is to be offered to social workers, packages it and delivers it' (Beddoe, 2006: 104).

In the *knowledge updates* mode, the focus of CPE begins to shift from the narrowly defined 'utilitarian approaches' described earlier, towards the exploration and application of new theoretical understandings or research evidence to practice. *Knowledge updates* may be organisationally generated or may include some individual investment. In the next mode of CPE – *reflective/reflexive practice* – practitioners begins to take greater ownership of their learning and its application to practice. CPE, in this instance, is concerned with professional renewal, reflexivity, change, innovation and even transformation. Thus, Beddoe (2006: 105) argues that:

> To be more than 'navel gazing', reflective approaches need to be change oriented and put all practices up for close scrutiny. Truly transformative learning requires, at the very least, that learners are supported to take off their expert mantle, admit that they often struggle to find answers to the really hard questions in practice and look for partnerships with service users and others.

Finally, the mode of *research/scholarship* is important in growing the knowledge base of the discipline. It might include, for example, practitioners undertaking doctoral studies, though in the current climate few employers would be able to find the resources to support this form of study. Beddoe (2006) concludes that it is generally at the level of 'compliance' and 'performance' (categories 1 and 2) that most investment in training occurs in the social services. However, in this form of training, there is often inadequate time to practise new skills and discuss and explore new information, and little opportunity for critical reflection (see also Ennis and Brodie, 1999: 10). Moreover, the focus on policy and compliance may be seen by social workers as an attempt 'to dress policy change up as training'. In our own research with social workers (discussed in Chapter Three), we found that in-service training was, as Beddoe (2006) suggests, often concerned with introducing the latest policy initiatives, particularly in relation to child protection.

Supporting social workers

While it is generally agreed that the purpose of CPD is to improve services to clients, there are also benefits for the professionals themselves. Personal growth, professional development, job satisfaction and fulfilling one's potential are just some of the rewards identified in the literature. A recent publication from the Chartered Institute of Personnel and Development, for example, maintains that the CPD process is 'empowering and exciting and can stimulate people to achieve their aspirations' (Megginson and Whitaker, 2007: 3).

In the social work profession, CPD is seen as a means of supporting and motivating practitioners who often work in stressful situations. This is important not only for the well-being of the practitioners themselves, but also for the quality of the service they provide, as Seden and McCormick (2011: 172) point out:

> In caring work, if you are not able to care for yourself and obtain the relevant support for your professional actions there will inevitably be repercussions for others. Service users are not best served by social workers who are near to burnout, too tired to care or who have become indifferent and cynical through overload, poor management or poor agency practices.... Therefore, a social worker's sense of personal well-being about occupying their role, together with necessary support, is critical for their service users' and for their own mental health.

Table 1.2: Modes and focus of continuing education

Modes of CPE	Focus of CPE	Outcomes
1. Compliance	• learning to perform specific new tasks • learning to implement policy change in practice	Adaptation and accommodation
2. Performance	• learning to solve problems defined within the work context • applying new information/ procedures	
3. Knowledge updates	• learning about research evidence for new practice • learning about new theoretical developments	Knowledge consumption
4. Reflective/ reflexive practice	• using new information to review and change practice • synthesising and utilising research findings • learning to be a reflective practitioner • learning to deconstruct and reconstruct expertise • learning to be a practice researcher • learning to utilise action research to solve problems or enhance practice	Innovation, challenge and change
5. Research/ scholarship	• conducting effective research • learning to theorise from analysis of research data • dissemination of findings and ideas • direct or indirect application of new knowledge to practice	New knowledge, theory-building

Supervision is seen as having a key role to play in this regard: providing support is regarded as one of the three main functions of the supervisory relationship. In addition, post-qualification education may help social workers to feel more confident in their role and in their work within multi-agency settings. Indeed, CPD has come to be seen by some policymakers as a means of increasing rates of recruitment and retention, and of boosting the morale of the workforce. The importance of training for a motivated and competent workforce is summed up in the following strategy report from the Scottish Executive (2005: 8):

> If staff do not feel well enough equipped for the job, are not sure what is expected of them and fear the consequences of getting it wrong, they will leave, or keep their heads down and fail to reach their potential. That is why it is so important to make sure staff get the training and development opportunities they need.

This view is reiterated in a discussion paper commissioned by the SSSC (Skinner, 2005), which maintains that there is long-standing evidence that staff development opportunities and accessible career pathways are critical factors in retaining staff. CPD is seen as having a role to play in professional renewal and career development, preparing social workers for different roles, for example, in management or in other areas of social work practice (Beddoe, 2006).

Professionalisation and continuing professional development

Professionalisation and education are inextricably linked. As Tovey (1994: 8) has argued: 'professions and professionals are socially constructed statuses; and education plays a key role in achieving and securing that status and marking off lines of differentiation from non-professionals'. Similarly, Madden and Mitchell (1993) point to occupations that are in the process of professionalisation using CPD schemes as part of their strategy to improve their credibility and status. In recent years, however, CPD has also come to be seen as a means of *defending* professional expertise in the face of criticism from the public, the media and the state. Houle et al (1987) trace this phenomenon to the late 1960s and 1970s, when the previously unassailable position of the professions came under attack. In the US, various professional groups faced a rising tide of distrust, hostility and litigiousness. Some of the attacks came from within the professions themselves: the Chief Justice of the US, for example, asserted that half the lawyers in the country were incompetent. Similarly, leading physicians did not remain silent on the deficiencies of the health professions. Meanwhile, rising litigation and insurance claims were proof of the public's dissatisfaction (Lester, 1999). The pressure induced by all of these attacks led to the proposal of many remedies, 'some calling for the use of a carrot and some for the sharp application of a stick' (Houle et al, 1987: 90). Continuing education appeared to be one of the more 'enlightened' responses:

continuing education seemed a direct benefit that was sure to help the situation. To the extent that deficiency exists, it can best be remedied by further study. Moreover, a professional who visibly puts himself or herself in a posture of learning has thereby built a defence against future attack and a profession that encourages such a posture is one that is obviously setting itself on the path of righteousness. (Houle et al, 1987: 90)

Houle's comments are particularly relevant in light of the various crises and scandals that have beset the social work profession in recent years, and the policy response. In the UK, the death of several children, following months or years of abuse, lead to widespread criticism, particularly from the media (Franklin and Parton, 1991; Fitzgerald, 2012). While a number of reforms to the child protection system were subsequently put in place, CPD was also posited as a means of better preparing social workers for their role in child protection. The Laming report[3] (Laming, 2009: 54) highlighted the importance of continuing education in enabling social workers 'to carry out their roles effectively'. Similarly, the Munro review of child protection in England (Munro, 2011: 116) 'places a premium on CPD', while in Ireland, the Roscommon Child Care Case Report[4] made the case for more effective supervision (Gibbons, 2010). These reports undoubtedly boosted the case for CPD, though some commentators have questioned whether they take sufficient account of the political and social context within which child protection systems operate. With regards to the Munro review, for example, Featherstone et al (2012: 14) argue that 'without a clear understanding of the likely impact of the wider political context within which recommendations are located, its analysis and recommendations for practice may be undermined'. Similarly, it could be argued that the Roscommon Report, which focuses almost entirely on the immediate circumstances of the child abuse case, ignores wider constitutional and political issues.

Continuing professional development models

Social work has increasingly moved towards greater regulation: Ireland, the UK, New Zealand, Hong Kong and South Africa, for instance, have national registration arrangements. Licensing is regulated within the various jurisdictions of the US and Canada (Beddoe and Duke, 2009: 786). In Australia, the Australian Association of Social Workers (AASW) is currently campaigning for the introduction of a regulatory system, on the grounds that this will be a 'means of enforcing safe and competent practice' (AASW, 2012).

In countries where a system of registration is in operation, social workers are generally required to undertake CPD in order to maintain their registration. In addition, many professional bodies, such as the AASW and the Irish Association of Social Workers (IASW), operate CPD programmes in which participants undertake a certain amount of CPD over a given period, for which they receive CPD points. Practitioners can usually choose from a wide range of learning activities in order to fulfil the requirements of registration bodies. However, debates continue as to the most appropriate model of CPD. Currently, there are two main models in operation, based on the notion of 'inputs' and 'outputs'.

An inputs-based model 'specifies how much CPD activity should be undertaken over a given period of time in terms of either hours spent or points collected and is linked to recognised learning activities' (O'Sullivan, 2006: 5). The advantage of this approach is that it provides the professional or regulatory organisation with a relatively straightforward means of gauging participation and, if necessary, taking sanctions against members (Lester, 1999: 112). On the other hand, critics argue that the inputs model is overly simplistic, failing to consider the quality of learning or its relevance (if any) to practice. Nonetheless, this approach – in some form – is used by a number of professional organisations and registration boards, including the Social Workers Registration Board (New Zealand), which specifies a minimum of 20 hours' CPD per year. The AASW CPE programme requires social workers to complete a minimum of 75 points over a 12-month period. As a general rule, one learning hour of CPE activity is equivalent to one CPE point; though some events accrue double points.

The 'outputs' model places more emphasis on practitioners identifying their CPD needs, evaluating the learning and demonstrating how this has impacted on their practice. In recent years, many professions have recognised the importance of the process and results of learning as opposed to quantitative inputs. The HCPC in England, for example, has eschewed the inputs approach, explaining to registrants that:

> We do not need you to undertake a certain amount of CPD (for example, to do a number of hours or days). This is because we believe that different people will be able to dedicate different amounts of time to CPD, and also because the time spent on an activity does not necessarily reflect the learning gained from it. (HCPC, 2012: 7)

According to the HCPC standards, registrants must: (a) maintain a record of their CPD; (b) undertake a mixture of learning activities; (c) seek to ensure that their CPD has contributed to the quality of their practice and service delivery; and (d) seek to ensure that their CPD benefits the service user (HCPC, 2012: 4). Those selected for audit will be expected to show how they have met these standards.

The registration system in Scotland is based on the inputs model, though there is also recognition of the importance of CPD outputs. Every social worker registered with the SSSC is required to complete 15 days (90 hours) of training and learning activities within the three-year registration period. Interestingly, the SSSC further stipulates that:

> at least 5 days (30 hours) of this training and learning activity shall focus on working effectively with colleagues and other professionals to identify, assess, and manage risk to vulnerable groups. This is in order to ensure that they are assisted to meet their primary responsibility of protecting children and adults from harm. (SSSC, 2011: 3)

It is somewhat unusual for a social work registration body to identify a particular *content* area, and it may reflect the current preoccupation with risk assessment and reduction within social work (see Buchanan, 2011). On the 'outputs' side, registrants are required to demonstrate in their 'record of achievement' how their learning has contributed to their professional development and informed their practice (SSSC, 2011: 8). According to the SSSC guidelines (SSSC, 2011: 8, emphasis in original):

> What we mean by this is that you need to demonstrate *how* what you have learned has helped you to put into practice, or has built on, or has reinforced your professional practice and *how* you have used that in working practice.

Critical perspectives

Professional associations, regulators and government departments tend to be optimistic about the potential of CPD to address a range of issues in social work, from low rates of recruitment and retention to improving systems of child protection. A more critical perspective is found in the academic literature. Ennis and Brodie (1999: 10), for example, note that while the profession aspires to a notion that CPD should be coherent, integrated and progressive, in practice, the attendance of staff on training programmes is often a matter of expediency, depending on the availability of places, funds in the training budget, short-term priorities and so on. It is therefore not surprising that 'going on a course' can be treated with some scepticism: unless attendance 'is placed in the context of an overall staff-development plan, their impact is likely to be limited and transitory' (Ennis and Brodie, 1999: 10). Commentators in other professions have also struck a cautionary note, including Houle et al (1987: 90), who question 'the uncritical acceptance of continuing professional education as a panacea for all of the ills of a profession'. Similarly, Coffield (2002) observes wryly that 'lifelong learning is a wonder drug or magic bullet that, on its own, will solve a wide range of educational, social and political ills' (cited in Beddoe, 2009: 724).

Commentators in a number of countries have noted that despite the increasing investment in CPD, there is a lack of evidence of the overall impact of CPD on practice (Preston-Shoot, 2007: 25: Ennis and Brodie, 1999: 10). Much of the research that has been carried out has focused on practitioners' satisfaction with courses or learning programmes, rather than on the outcomes for service users (Houle et al, 1987: 91; Williams, 2007: 123). In a review of the literature for studies published between 1974 and 1997, Clarke (2001) located only 20 evaluations of in-service training programmes within social services agencies, and most of these had methodological limitations, which included a focus on trainee satisfaction, dependence on self-reports and no follow-up research. Similarly, in the Canadian context, Williams (2007: 123) notes that a typical evaluation form asks the learner to assess the quality of learning material, perceptions of learning gains and satisfaction with instructions. Although answers to these questions are important, they do little to assess what the participant has learned, or how able that participant will be to transfer any new learning to the professional environment. Williams acknowledges that there are a number of reasons why more comprehensive evaluations are difficult to implement: for example, it is unclear when the effects of an educational programme will materialise and have an impact on professional conduct. In addition, social work is far from achieving a consensus on what measures will best evaluate the effectiveness of practice. Nonetheless, Williams argues, it is important to obtain more reliable information on programme effectiveness, and suggests a mixed-methods evaluation as one means of achieving this.

Despite the current enthusiasm for CPD in social work, there remain significant barriers to participation, including heavy workloads, lack of staff cover for those attending courses and a lack of funding (see Chapter Four). Concerns have also been raised in the literature that the development of CPD may be rather uneven, focusing on particular formats and functions, at the expense of others. In North America, Cervero (2000: 4) argues, CPD systems for different professional groups are dominated by the informational update:

> I would characterise them as devoted mainly to updating practitioners about the newest developments, which are transmitted in a didactic fashion and offered by a pluralistic group of providers (workplaces, for-profits, and universities) that do not work together in any coordinated fashion.

Moreover, the amount of continuing education offered by employers dwarfs that offered by any other type of provider, and surpasses that of all other providers combined (Cervero, 2000: 5). Similarly, Beddoe (2006) reports that most of the investment in training in the social services is for various forms of in-house training, which focus on 'compliance' and 'performance'. However, as noted earlier, this form of training does not allow sufficient time to practise new skills or discuss and explore new information, and there are few opportunities for critical reflection.

With the introduction of registration systems in a number of countries, CPD is increasingly becoming a matter of professional obligation rather than personal choice. This raises certain issues for the profession. It may, for example, change the spirit in which people decide to undertake CPD. As Marsh and Doel (2005: 65) point out: 'it will be interesting to see if learners' enthusiasm is affected when assessment is seen as a necessary chore for credits'. Similarly, Morgan et al (2008: 234) note that some professionals may see CPD as a 'points-gathering exercise' rather than an opportunity for learning – an issue that was also raised by social workers participating in our research (see Chapter Four). Alsop (2000: 4) warns that CPD will only be of real benefit if the learning takes place as a voluntary activity, as part of the process of lifelong learning and as part of a personal commitment to self development:

> No amount of legislation on CPD will ever ensure that learning will support competent practice unless the individual him or herself actually wishes to learn. This means that CPD activity needs to be meaningful for an individual if it is to be taken seriously and the benefits to the individual need to be clear and to be valued.

While CPD is part of a strategy to improve recruitment and retention in the workforce, it could become an onerous burden if social workers themselves do not feel engaged and committed to the process.

Conclusion

Over the last decade, CPD has come to be seen as an essential part of the professional life of social workers. Regulatory bodies have made it a condition for renewing registration while professional associations routinely promote it among their members. Policymakers claim that CPD has the potential to increase rates of recruitment and retention, boost the flagging morale of the workforce, and improve services. In-service training, supervision and other forms of work-based learning are seen as particularly important because social work qualifying courses are often generic in nature and do not necessarily equip graduates with the specialised skills they will need in practice. The complexity of the social work role has grown in a society that is increasingly conflicted about issues of human vulnerability in relation to dependent social groups: children, the elderly and disabled people. To meet the challenges of contemporary social work, practitioners are expected to constantly upskill.

As we have seen in the course of this chapter, there are a variety of definitions for CPD, most of which focus on the maintenance and enhancement of knowledge, expertise and competence. The ultimate objective of CPD is generally seen to be the improvement of services. However, there are differences of opinion as to how this is to be achieved, with different stakeholders pursuing their own educational agendas. Moreover, while there has undoubtedly been considerable investment in CPD, significant barriers to participation remain and some objectives and formats may have been favoured at the expense of others. The drift towards greater regulation of the profession will inevitably boost the numbers undertaking CPD, but, as we have seen, this also raises concerns that training and learning may come to be seen as a 'tick-box' exercise if practitioners themselves do not feel engaged in the process. These issues will be explored in detail in subsequent chapters, particularly in relation to debates concerning the future of post-qualifying higher education (Chapter Two) and to our own research with social workers in Ireland (Chapters Three to Five).

Notes

[1] The HCPC regulates 16 professions in England, including social work.

[2] The SSSC is responsible for registering those who work in the social services and regulating their education and training.

[3] Lord Laming was commissioned to report on the progress being made across England to implement 'effective arrangements for safeguarding children', following on from the statutory inquiry into the death of Victoria Climbié (Laming, 2009: 3).

[4] The Roscommon Child Care Inquiry considered the Health Service Executive/Western Health Board's management of a case in which six children were abused and neglected by their parents over several years.

TWO

Contemporary debates in social work education

> While social work may be heir to its own history, it is the
> child of contemporary politics. (Harris, 1997: 32)

Over the last few decades, major debates within social work have drawn attention to the impact of neoliberalism and globalisation on social work practice and, by extension, social work education. The formation of neoliberal governments in a number of Western countries – particularly the US and the UK – heralded a gradual rollback of the state, resulting in a residual welfare service. Some scholars have argued that rather than offering a critique of these developments, the social work profession has itself increasingly succumbed to neoliberal influences, loosing sight of its earlier social justice remit (Ferguson et al, 2005; Noble and Irwin, 2009). The emergence of 'manageralism' and competence-based learning approaches are seen as manifestations of a neoliberal agenda within the profession. In this chapter, we will outline some of these major debates within social work education, and consider the development of two contrasting approaches to learning, broadly described as reflective and competence-based.

In the second part of this chapter, we will look at a range of other issues that are pertinent to the development of social work education, including funding, course provision and the status of social work as an academic discipline. Our focus will be on the types of social work education undertaken by *qualified* practitioners and provided by universities and other higher education institutions (eg diploma courses, doctorates). For the sake of brevity, we will refer to these as post-qualifying (PQ) education.

Socio-political context of social work education

Over the last three decades, neoliberalism has had a major impact on the development of social work and other state-funded public services (Garrett, 2010: 341). A core tenet of neoliberal philosophy is the reduction of the role of the state, based on the argument that welfare constitutes both a burden to the taxpayer and a disincentive for people to better themselves (Lymbery, 2003: 101). From the 1980s onwards, there was a gradual return to fiscal restraint in the spending of public monies in most Western countries, and this had serious consequences in terms of the provision of health, welfare and community services (Noble and Irwin, 2009: 348). Current economic problems – which began with the banking crisis of 2008 – have led to even deeper cuts in public services, at a time when the numbers unemployed and living in poverty are on the increase. This reduced commitment to public services has been evident in increasingly selective, means-tested and conditional support (Featherstone et al, 2011: 13). It is argued that welfare services should be reserved only for those in greatest need, thereby transforming welfare into a residual service (Lymbery, 2003). However, critics point out that an increasingly selectivist approach to state support will result not only in economic hardships, but also divisions within society. As Noble and Irwin (2009: 350) argue, in the 'retreat to a form of residual welfare', social problems are regarded once again as the result of individual pathology. Consequently, the focus of social work tends to be on the individual, placing practitioners in a 'social control, policing and surveillance role' (Noble and Irwin, 2009: 350). Moreover, valuing the private over the public has gradually undermined any concept of the 'public good' or 'community' and replaced these concepts with the notion that individuals are seen as responsible for their own well-being (Noble and Irwin, 2009: 348).

Another important tenet of neoliberal philosophy is that public-sector institutions are inefficient and wasteful of resources, and that many welfare services would be more economically and efficiently provided by the private sector (Lymbery, 2003: 101; Garrett, 2010: 342). Consequently, services that were formerly part of direct state provision have, over time, been moved into the non-government sector (Hugman, 2001: 325; Dominelli, 2007: 31). In the UK, for example, the private sector's role in providing children's homes and related children's services is increasing (Garrett, 2010: 343), while private equity firms have entered the foster-care 'market' in significant numbers (Mathiason, 2007). Furthermore, those services that remained in the public sector began to incorporate private-sector practices in the belief that this would make them more efficient (Harris, 2005). Public services would also become more accountable to the government through a system of targets and audit; ironically, at a time when the private sector (particularly banking) enjoyed a sustained period of 'light-touch' regulation in most Western countries. The development of an audit culture within social work was further exacerbated by negative media coverage of the profession, particularly in the field of child protection (Buchanan, 2011: 12).

It was within this context – of private-sector influences coupled with demands for greater accountability – that a managerial elite and an ideology of 'managerialism' began to emerge within social work. It was believed that effective management would resolve the problems within the public sector, and that managers must be given the freedom to transform welfare organisations. In the UK, 'new managerialism' was to become a major vehicle for implementing government initiatives and monitoring their progress (Dominelli, 2007); thereby acting in the interests of the New Right reformers (Lymbery, 2001). In the process, social work practice became increasingly bureaucratised, target-driven and procedure-led. Social workers in many countries now work in organisations where adherence to an ever-expanding list of procedures is curtailing their scope for creative practice and the exercise of professional judgement (Dominelli, 2010: 41; Murphy et al, 2010). Moreover, the bureaucratisation of practice has reduced the amount of time social workers spend in developing relationships with service users, once thought to be central to social work practice (Parsloe, 2001: 15; Dominelli, 2010: 41; Munro, 2011). As Dominelli (2010: 45) argues, the relationship element is now virtually absent from state-based social work in the UK, 'as the norm for public-sector social workers is to commission services and manage budgets'. Similarly, Parsloe (2001: 14) notes that social workers are becoming 'resource managers' who arrange for others to do the hands-on work with service users – a development that she attributes to 'the creeping managerialism that is engulfing social work'. With an increasing focus on accountability, efficiency and compliance, some critics have also argued that social work is moving further away from its social justice remit. According to Noble and Irwin (2009: 350):

> This retreat from a welfare state is undermining social work's mission to fight for collectivist values of social justice, to engage in critical exploration and analyses of social problems and to draw attention to the new policy agenda that is denying human and democratic rights to some sections of the community. It also prevents social workers from providing a strong voice demanding a fair redistribution of wealth and societal resources (Dominelli, 2002, ...). In many instances social workers espousing these ideas are increasingly being regarded as dinosaurs of the past or out of touch with the new political correctness.

They conclude that 'lost in this post modern moment is any vision for the future, let alone a belief in social work's link with the broad social justice and human rights movements' (Noble and Irwin, 2009: 350). Similarly, Green (2006: 257) argues that social work's political potential for illuminating and challenging inequalities has been curtailed by the state, and that statutory social workers in particular have been 'redirected into a technical, statutory, behavioural role'.

What has been the impact of neoliberalism on social work education? As Garrett (2010: 349) points out, it might be expected that social work education would provide a bulwark 'against the encroachment of neoliberal hegemony within the profession' and that it would instil and defend a set of values that 'might counter the incursion of neoliberalism into social work'. This has not necessarily been the case; indeed, some critics argue that social work education itself is increasingly shaped by neoliberal and managerialist priorities (Dominelli, 2007), particularly with the introduction of a functional competencies approach to learning (Garrett, 2010: 349). Lymbery (2003: 104) argues, for example, that there is little doubt that the adoption of the competence framework in the Diploma of Social Work (in the UK) is intimately connected to the growth of managerialism. The notion of 'competence' derives from vocational qualifications and assumes the measurability of social workers' performance. It has explicit links with a managerialist agenda, 'where the complexity of social work activity is reduced to the simple following of procedures' (Lymbery, 2003: 100). In the following section, we will look more closely at the emergence of competence-based learning in social work.

Competence and social work education

Competence-based education and training, which originated in the US during the 1960s within teacher education, had considerable influence in the UK in the 1990s. According to Payne (2005a: 237–8):

> It was based on 'behaviourable' models of learning, which sought to define clearly what individuals should be able to do, enhanced by functional analyses of roles and tasks within jobs.... In the functional analysis of professional tasks, the job is broken down into clearly defined tasks, for which training can develop specific competences, and may be built up into a range of different job roles in which people may demonstrate personal competence.

In essence, competence-based approaches move the emphasis away from the specification of educational inputs (the training received) towards the assessment of outputs or 'competencies' (Barber and Cooper, 1997: 114).

Competence-based approaches have been the dominant paradigm in social work education in the UK since the early 1990s (Wilson and Kelly, 2010: 2432), particularly at the qualifying stage. Their influence has also been evident, to varying degrees, in the development of the PQ framework. Lymbery (2003), for example, notes that the PQ Award in Social Work was largely competence-driven, though the Advanced Award in Social Work (a higher-level award) was much less oriented towards a competence-based approach. However, Higham (2009: 16), commenting on the current PQ frameworks for England, Scotland and Northern Ireland, notes 'an apparent preoccupation with evidencing "competence"'. The competence approach has also influenced the development of social work education in Australia (Barber and Cooper, 1997; Hugman, 2001: 327) and New Zealand (Nash and Munford, 2001).

Proponents of the competence model argue that it results in much clearer specifications and more transparent assessment methods (Payne, 2005a: 238). According to O'Hagan (1996), competence-led training helps to ensure a greater uniformity of practice standards and less subjective assessments. He claims that before the introduction of the (competence-based) Social Work Diploma, teachers had 'enormous discretion and power' and could behave in 'an authoritarian, challenging, even threatening way' (O'Hagan, 1996: 16). Reform to social work education has helped to redress this power imbalance: 'Whatever challenges competence-led training poses, its concentration on evidence certainly minimised the possibilities of the abuse of power within the tutor, student, and PT relationship.' (O'Hagan, 1996: 16). Wilson et al (2005: 724) note that in Northern Ireland, competence-based approaches to social work training have been generally welcomed by both agencies and academic institutions. The authors identify a number of possible reasons for this, including a strong tradition of joint agency and university involvement in the management and delivery of social work education and training, which may have helped to create favourable conditions for competence-based learning. In the case of Approved Social Work (ASW) training, the introduction of a standardised form of assessment appeared to offer the prospect of greater levels of quality assurance for employers and higher status and greater security for Approved Social Workers (ASWs).[1] Finally, Wilson et al (2005: 725) suggest that it may be that 'the particular social and political context of practice in this part of the UK encourages educators and trainers to use competence-based learning'. By contrast, the emergence of the 'competence project' in Australia during the 1990s was strongly contested (Barber and Cooper, 1997). In its defence, Barber and Cooper (1997: 123) argue that social work education was at that time badly in need of new ideas, and output-based standards at least provided 'the freedom for experimentation to occur'. Like O'Hagan, the authors suggest that many of the concerns expressed regarding the competence approach are unfounded.

Critics, on the other hand, have dismissed the competence model as a reductionist, 'tick-box' approach to education and practice. One of the main concerns raised in the literature is that competence-based models of education fail to adequately prepare social workers for the complexities and uncertainties that characterise social work (Lymbery, 2003; Dominelli, 2007: 30; Murphy et al, 2010: 175). It is argued that social workers are constantly confronted with situations that are not amenable to set forms of resolution and that therefore require the application of professional judgement (Lymbery, 2003: 107). Competence-driven approaches to learning are unlikely to prepare social workers for the more unpredictable and challenging aspect of their practice. Such approaches tend to focus on the acquisition of mechanical skills and an adherence to agency policies and procedures, thereby leading to a formulaic and risk-averse style of practice:

> The end product of the competence approach is a functionary capable of working on the routines of practice according to specified procedures. Hence, the social worker that emerges would be at a loss to either innovate or think and act strategically in terms of the profession and its future development. (Dominelli, cited in Lymbery, 2003: 105)

Lymbery (2003: 108–9) argues that limitations of the competence model become even more explicit at the PQ stage, and that the education required at this level 'must be based on the need to prepare practitioners for the exercise of professional judgement in complex cases'. Similarly, Higham (2009: 8), in her review of the PQ frameworks in the UK, is critical of their focus on competence, arguing that education at this level 'should promote critical reflective practice and innovative thinking that move social workers towards capability and expertise'. The preoccupation with a narrow concept of 'competence', she suggests, does not allow development of practice expertise, and may even limit social workers' career opportunities (Higham, 2009: 16).

A second major criticism of competence-based education is that it is anti-intellectual, overlooks the political context of social work and focuses on the more prescriptive, regulatory and controlling aspects of the profession's role (Green, 2006; Wilson and Kelly, 2010: 2433). Significantly, it is not only service-users who are being 'regulated' and 'controlled' within competence models, but also professionals themselves. Eraut (1994: 159) argues that 'competence', initially a rationale for justifying professional examinations or assessments, has become a tool of governmental regulatory control over the professions. As Lymbery (2003: 104) suggests, in the social work context, the 'competent' practitioner may also be seen as a more compliant worker, and hence less troublesome in social service agencies. Similarly, Garrett (2010: 349) locates the emergence of competence-based education within a narrative of social control, in which 'the forces of neoliberalism have sought to "close down" the spaces for alternative ways of *perceiving* and *doing* social work'. One of the main ways of achieving this, he argues, has been to try to ensure that the professional training of social workers is compatible with, or does not unduly destabilise, neoliberal nostrums: 'Consequently, various governments, often aided by employers, have worked hard to inject into the profession more of an emphasis on vocational training' (Garrett, 2010: 349). The marginalisation of social sciences teaching and the imposition of a competence approach to learning have also played a key role in this process.

The struggle to ensure that social work education was committed to producing social workers with 'an appropriate ideological disposition' has been apparent since the foundation of social work in England, Garrett argues. In the late 1970s, it reached a critical point as social work education was seen as partly responsible 'for the increasing politicisation and radicalism of social workers' (Jones, cited in Garrett, 2010: 350). In the following decades – particularly with the emergence of neoliberal ideas – new attempts would be made to control and regulate social work education, at both qualifying and PQ stages. Competence-driven initiatives can be understood as part of this wider agenda.

Managerialism and learning in the workplace

Another concern raised in the literature is that competence-based practice and a managerialist culture may impede learning in the workplace. As we saw in Chapter One, work-based learning is seen as a key element of continuing professional development (CPD). However, an overzealous adherence to rules and procedures, and a preoccupation with accountability and risk management, may inhibit the development of a 'learning culture' within organisations. In the case of supervision, for example, a review of the international literature suggests that meetings are generally infrequent and focused on the managerial (case management) function (see Burns, 2012: 224). Noble and Irwin (2009: 352–3) argue that supervision is becoming increasingly concerned with evaluation and accountability, and is being used as a tool to enforce the new 'managerialism'. A series of influential reports published in England over the last decade also highlight concerns about the nature and frequency of supervision (Laming, 2003, 2009; SWTF, 2009; Munro, 2011). A common experience among social workers is that supervision is dominated by a managerial need to focus on performance, leaving little time for reflection (Munro, 2011: 115).

In Ireland, the vital role of supervision in social work has been emphasised in child abuse inquiries (McGuinness, 1993; Joint Committee on the Family, 1996; Gibbons, 2010) and policy documents (OMCYA, 2009: 42;[2] HSE, 2010a; Department of Children and Youth Affairs, 2011). The recently established regulatory body, CORU,[3] states in its *Professional code of conduct and ethics* that social workers 'should seek and engage in supervision in professional practice on an on-going and regular basis' (CORU, 2011: 11). Similarly, *Children first* (Department of Children and Youth Affairs, 2011: 43) recommends 'adequate and regular supervision of staff', though little guidance is provided on what this might mean in practice. The recent *Report of the Task Force for Children & Families Social Services* (HSE, 2010a) identifies four main functions of supervision – management, support, learning and development, and mediation – and maintains that the supervisor should ensure that there is equal emphasis on each of these four (HSE, 2010a: 64). However, research carried out with social workers employed by the Health Service Executive (HSE) suggest that supervision in Ireland, as in other countries, tends to be focused on the managerial/case management function (Burns, 2012: 224). We will return to the issue of supervision in more detail in Chapter Five.

Other impediments to learning in the workplace include a 'culture of blame' and a preoccupation with risk management, which have increasingly characterised social work. In a qualitative study of continuing education in New Zealand, Beddoe (2009) explored social workers' understanding of and attitudes towards the concept of the 'learning organisation'. Her findings suggest that while practitioners are positive about the ideals of the learning organisation, this is tempered by practical considerations and constraints. Participants expressed doubts that the essential conditions of the learning organisation were in place, particularly the conditions of trust that enabled practitioners, managers and policymakers to learn from mistakes (Beddoe, 2009: 734). One of the intended outcomes of the learning organisation is critical reflection, but this is difficult to achieve in the absence of trust: social workers are reluctant to admit to (and learn from) mistakes in the current 'culture of blame' (Beddoe, 2009: 729). This issue was also raised in a major review of the child protection system in England that was carried out by Eileen Munro during 2010–11.

The Munro report

The Munro report (Munro, 2011) is particularly pertinent to debates about learning in the workplace, connecting with several of the themes discussed so far in this chapter. One of Munro's main conclusions is that the child protection system has become over-bureaucratised and concerned with compliance, at the expense of flexibility and the exercise of professional judgement. This situation is, in part, due to the publication of a series of high-profile child abuse inquiry reports, which have focused 'too readily' on human error, rather than taking a broader view. While the subsequent reforms to the child protection system may have been well intentioned, Munro argues, they have inadvertently created obstacles to good practice. In the face of public outcry when mistakes are made, there has been a shift towards defensive practice, 'where a concern with protecting oneself or one's agency has competed, and sometimes overridden, a concern with protecting children' (Munro, 2011: 20). This in turn has reinforced the compliance culture: a strict adherence to procedures is seen as a means of defending the organisation and fending off criticism. In such a situation, procedures become an end in themselves.

Munro argues that there needs to be a move from a compliance culture to a *learning* culture, in which social workers are given more scope to exercise professional judgement. An important first step would be reducing the degree of central prescription. The review recommends 'stripping away much of the top-down bureaucracy that previous reforms have put in the way of frontline services' while retaining those procedures that are necessary to good practice (Munro, 2011: 135). The review also makes the case for radically improving the knowledge and skills of social workers from initial training through to CPD. A range of suggestions are made in this regard, including, for example, using research evidence to inform practice, treating serious case reviews as opportunities for learning (rather than simply blaming) social workers and providing time for reflection, particularly within the context of supervision. The review 'places a premium on CPD' and supports more co-working on cases and on-the-job practice coaching, as well as more formal local teaching programmes in particular areas of knowledge, skill sets and intervention methods. While the Munro review expresses the hope that managers and social workers will share its view on the importance of CPD, it also recognises that there are 'severe issues in relation to the quality of and access to social work CPD' (Munro, 2011: 117).[4] The social work regulator is seen as having a strong and important role in promoting CPD; and the need for investment in increasing the expertise of the workforce is also noted.

While the Munro review of child protection has been welcomed, concern has also been expressed that it largely ignores the political and social context of neoliberalism within which the current child protection system operates. Featherstone et al (2011: 14) argue that 'without a clear understanding of the likely impact of the wider political context within which recommendations are located, its analysis and recommendations for practice may be undermined'. Consequently, the Munro review offers only partial solutions. It is not just 'red tape' or target and audit systems that require reconsideration, there also needs to be a much more fundamental review of the impact of government policy (Featherstone et al, 2011: 8).

Reflective learning

Over the last few decades, reflective learning has come to be seen as a means of countering the managerialist, competence-based approaches to social work education and practice described so far in this chapter. Proponents argue that a reflective approach is better suited to working with service users where each individual situation is unique and complexity of practice is not amenable to a mechanical 'tick-box' approach (Wilson and Kelly, 2010: 2443). Thus, Ruch (2002: 202) observes: 'The essence of reflective practice involves acknowledging precisely that which the competency culture avoids – the uniqueness of each situation encountered, the extraordinary complexity of human functioning whether in relation to individual personality, family dynamics or inter-professional relationships'. Similarly, Winter et al (1999) argue that the reflective paradigm sets out 'to defend professional values, creativity, and autonomy in a context where they are generally felt to be under attack from political and economic forces which threaten to transform the professional from an artist into an operative' (Winter et al, 1999: 191). In spite of the shift towards competence-based approaches to social work education, reflective teaching and learning has gained increased ground in recent years and is a feature of social work programmes in a number of countries at both qualifying and PQ level (Wilson et al, 2005: 725; Murphy et al, 2010: 177).

The development of a reflective learning culture within social work owes much to the scholarship of Donald Schön and John Dewey, whose work we will consider in detail in Chapter Six. In the following definition, Lyons (2002: 99) encapsulates some of the key features of the reflective approach:

> Reflection [is] an intentional act of mind engaging a person alone, but especially in collaboration with others – students, other colleagues, researchers – in interrogating a compelling or puzzling situation of teaching or learning to construct an understanding of some aspect of it. Such an act looks both backwards and to the future. It is in the service of understanding that will shape action. It likely takes place over long stretches of time, involves narrative for it is the story of meaning, and often raises ethical issues for people involved.

While the value of reflective practice and learning is well documented, this approach is also open to criticism for not taking account of wider socio-political factors that have a major impact on both process and outcomes (Postle et al, 2002: 159). Some writers have made the case for *critical* reflection, which focuses on issues of power and control. According to Brookfield (2009: 294), critical reflection calls into question the power relationships that allow, or promote, one particular set of practices over others: 'Some one engaged in critical reflection always asks whose interests are served by particular codes of practice, and stays alert to the way they are embracing ideas and behaviours that are subtly harming them'. Given the pervasiveness of a managerial culture within social work, and the continuing rollback of the welfare state, the need for critical reflection has, arguably, never been greater.

Reconciling competency and reflective learning

Despite substantial differences, reflective and competency-based approaches should not be seen as mutually exclusive. Lymbery (2003: 100), in particular, has argued that some combination is necessary: 'social work practice should be located on a continuum encompassing both competence and creativity, the appropriate response being determined by the level of predictability and the complexity of the situation under investigation'. While some of the issues facing social workers are of a complex nature, others are amenable to more technical solutions. Consequently, it is important to consider how the elements of competency and creativity can be reconciled in practice. With regards to social work education, Lymbery (2003: 108) argues that at the qualifying level, competency can be defined as 'a necessary but insufficient element'. At the PQ level, the balance between competency and creativity should shift still further in the favour of creativity: 'professionals should aspire through processes of continuous professional development to move beyond competence to expertise' (Lymbery, 2003: 108).

Wilson et al (2005: 725) have also looked at ways in which the 'polarities' within social work education might be bridged. In the context of Northern Ireland – which favours competency-based learning – they suggest that there is a need to emphasise the importance of reflective practice as an integral component of social work education and training at qualifying and PQ levels. They argue that the nature of competency-based training is complex and changing, and that continued attention to the reflective nature of practice needs to be taken into account in the design and delivery of social work programmes.

Post-qualifying education, the university and public expenditure cuts

In the second part of this chapter, we will turn our attention to a number of other issues pertinent to the development of social work education, including: the funding of PQ social work education within the HE sector; debates about who should provide CPD; and concerns regarding the academic standing and research base of social work as an academic discipline.

From the 1960s onwards, governments in most Western countries funded the expansion of third-level education in the expectation that this would help to secure economic prosperity. Education came to be seen as part of the 'knowledge economy' and universities as part of the 'higher education market' (Galpin, 2009: 71). While state support undoubtedly contributed to the growth of higher education, it also shaped developments within the sector. In the Australian context, for example, Rosenman (2007: 16) notes that the universities are 'tied by funding strings to the Commonwealth Government's apron' and are consequently subject to constant changes in policy direction. With regards to social work education, he argues that 'the external policy and funding environment ultimately shapes who and what is taught in social work schools and the type of research that is performed there' (Rosenman, 2007: 16).

Universities are also vulnerable to changes in funding policy. Over the last few decades, in line with neoliberal philosophy, there have been attempts to shift the responsibility for paying for third-level education from the state to the individual. In the UK, this trend has been evident under both the New Labour and the Conservative–Liberal Democrat Coalition governments. Moreover, in periods of economic recession, state funding is liable to be reduced, particularly for PQ education. Yuen and Ho (2007) provide an interesting case study of this process in their analysis of education policy in Hong Kong following the economic and political upheavals of the late 1990s. The economic crisis prompted the government to re-examine public spending, there were widespread cutbacks and higher education was increasingly shaped by the forces of marketisation and managerialism. This would have far-reaching consequences for social work education, particularly at postgraduate level, where funding for all programmes was terminated from 2005/06 onwards. It was argued that postgraduate students should be engaged 'in gainful employment' and therefore able to support themselves financially. Those with financial difficulties would be eligible to apply for government loans to be repaid at a later date. In this way, postgraduate programmes in Hong Kong were turned into a self-financing mode on a full-cost recovery basis.

Cutbacks to postgraduate funding and supports for mature students have also been made in Western countries following the financial crisis that unfolded from 2008 onwards. In addition, while all disciplines are subject to the vagaries of state funding, some may be more vulnerable than others, particularly if education is seen primarily in terms of an economic investment. This perspective is exemplified by a report from the Organisation for Economic Co-operation and Development (OECD) on higher education in Ireland, which concentrates strongly on the role of education in servicing the economy to the neglect of its social and developmental responsibilities (Lynch, 2006). The OECD's focus on developing a skilled workforce for the economy disadvantages disciplines within the arts, humanities and social sciences because their work is clearly not defined as central to the national development agenda. As higher education becomes increasingly subject to market forces, the social sciences are in a vulnerable position.

While the importance of CPD for professional development in social work has been foregrounded in recent years, questions clearly remain as to how this is to be funded and supported during a period of economic austerity. This is particularly the case for PQ university courses, where the investment in money and time is typically much greater than for other forms of CPD, for example, workshops, conferences or short courses. Research in the UK suggests that limited funding is particularly detrimental to the development of CPD at an advanced level (see Galpin, 2009: 72). In our research with social workers in Ireland, we found that most of those who had undertaken PQ university courses either did so at their own expense or their employers paid part or all of the fees. However, in recent years, the funding for the HSE and other major public-sector employers has been cut and this in turn has reduced the availability of funding for social workers to undertake CPD. Respondents reported that it is now difficult (or, in some cases, impossible) to get funding from their employer to attend one-day courses, never mind those at third level, which typically cost thousands of euros. The issue of funding is therefore a huge concern for Irish social workers who will in the next few years be required to undertake CPD in order to retain their social work registration. Our research suggests that little or no consideration has been given to how CPD will be supported at a national, regional or local level (see Chapter Four).

Who should provide post-qualifying social work education?

Important questions have been raised in relation to who will provide PQ education and, more broadly, who drives its development (Galpin, 2009). In the US, Cervero (2000) found that there are an increasing number of collaborative arrangements among providers, especially between universities and workplaces. While the collaborative approach has advantages, it also raises questions about who controls the content of the programme and who decides its goals. The issue of collaboration has particular relevance for social work education, where employers are often involved, in some capacity, at the qualifying and PQ stage. In Northern Ireland, for example, there has been a strong tradition of joint agency and university involvement in the management and delivery of social work education, particularly through the PQ consortium (Higham, 2009: 9–11; Taylor et al, 2010; Wilson et al, 2005: 724).[5] The partnership philosophy was given a further boost in 2009 when the Social Work Task Force stated that the education and training of the next generation of social workers must be 'the joint responsibility of universities and employers' (SWTF, 2009: 4). Elsewhere, the report recommends collective action at national and local levels, including 'close collaboration between employers and educators' (SWTF, 2009: 9). The benefits of current collaboration in PQ education are outlined:

> Where there are strong partnerships and good collaboration between employers and HEI [higher education institutions] – for example in commissioning, planning and developing current PQ courses – this has led to a more strategic approach to ongoing learning and the exchange of knowledge, more sharing of resources; and positive steps to develop and update practice. (SWTF, 2009: 38)

Employers are encouraged to 'get more involved in devising and delivering local strategies and courses that will ensure the delivery of high quality education and training to produce the kinds of social workers they want and need' (SWTF, 2009: 17). This recommendation is set within the wider context of business–university partnerships: 'Active partnerships of this kind would reflect the aspiration that employers and businesses become "active partners with universities, not passive customers"' (SWTF, 2009: 17).

However, increased employer involvement in the education of social workers has given rise to a number of concerns. Collaborative arrangements may mean that social work education will be even more open to the type of managerialist agendas outlined earlier in the chapter. Moreover, employers and educators may have very different ideas on the purpose of social work education, and what their respective roles should be. Parsloe's recollections of her visits to students on placement illustrate this tension:

> I remember that on my annual visits to local directors and chief probation officers I was often told that my students did not know about rather specific procedural matters. This worried me because it suggested that neither of us had a clear idea of what the other should be doing. I do not think it is the job of the educational institution to teach students procedures to be followed in particular agencies. I thought they should either learn this on placements or as part of the induction to their first jobs. Arrogantly I used to wonder what these top managers thought education was. No doubt they thought I had no idea what working in their agency demanded. I do not mean to imply that I had bad relationships with agency heads. This was not the case; a fact that makes our lack of understanding harder to unravel. (Parsloe, 2001: 11)

Taylor et al's (2010) description of partnership arrangements in the provision of social work education in Northern Ireland also sheds light on the kinds of tensions that can emerge. They note that in the early days of the partnership, various perspectives from the university side could be identified, from those genuinely seeking partnership to those utterly opposed to it as an affront to university autonomy. On the agency side, similarly, there were various perspectives: those genuinely seeking partnership as a chance to make the curriculum more relevant; those who were ambivalent or hostile; and those who expressed a desire to be involved but were not prepared to commit resources. Some university staff were anxious that the outcomes might be too tied to 'training' rather than 'education'; on the other hand, some employer training staff were concerned that university staff might still have undue influence in creating learning that was too removed from the reality of practice (Taylor et al, 2010: 481). Despite these challenges, Taylor et al (2010: 486) conclude that the key to success in PQ education is clearly partnership: 'proactive and committed work between employers, candidates and educational bodies'. Green (2006: 249) provides a different perspective on the issue of collaborative arrangements by considering the implications for social work as a discipline. He argues that the involvement of various stakeholders in planning, evaluating and delivering social work education raises questions about the discipline's intellectual status and independence, and may further contribute to the low academic status of social work (an issue we return to later).

In Ireland, there is no tradition of collaborative working between universities and employers to provide PQ education along the lines described earlier. However, employers do play an important role in the provision of certain types of CPD: in a survey of Irish social workers, we found that almost all respondents had undertaken in-service training over the last two years – a far higher proportion that those undertaking academic or other external courses. Moreover, employers play a key role in providing (or withholding) time off and funding for social workers to attend external courses. Their decisions are based not only on the availability of resources, but also on the perceived relevance of the course to the applicant's work. In this context, it seems likely that employer policy will have an important – albeit indirect – influence on the future development of CPD, defining what is 'relevant' and appropriate for their workforce.

Developing the research and knowledge base

If PQ social work programmes are to be developed within universities, particularly at doctoral level, then the research and knowledge base of the discipline needs to grow. Commentators in a number of countries have noted social work's poor academic and research record in comparison with that of other disciplines. In a wide-ranging critique, Green (2006: 245) argues that one of the most important issues facing contemporary social work education is 'social work's subordinated academic status and its associated poor professional credibility'. Factors that have contributed to this situation include: low entry criteria; social work's applied and multidisciplinary status; and an overemphasis on practical skills and competencies as opposed to intellectual skills. A lack of clarity about what social workers can or should do and how that needs to be linked with higher education are other important factors, according to Green. Social work is 'perceived as needing lower entry qualifications and less training, as well as more state control and surveillance than the fully hallmarked professions such as law and medicine' (Green, 2006: 250). Moreover, social work's commitment to, and reputation for, research has historically been poor: in the UK, it was rated by the Research Assessment Exercise (RAE) as 68th out of 72 submitted subjects in 1992 and 57th out of 69 in 1996 (Green, 2006: 246). The number of submissions to the RAE panel also declined from 32 in the 1996 RAE to 30 in the 2001 RAE, though there was a significant improvement in the quality of submissions. Dominelli (2007) also comments on a research deficit in social work, which has damaged the discipline's standing in the academy, where it is seen as 'second-rate' for failing to attract research funding and produce the large numbers of refereed papers characteristic of other social professions.

Similarly, in the Australian context, Rosenman (2007: 10) has noted that social work as a discipline has traditionally performed fairly poorly on most measures of research performance. He outlines the challenges facing the discipline:

> Its record in achieving national competitive grants has been relatively poor due, in part, to the relative recency of the development of research expectations in university social work schools. Furthermore, social work lacks an agreed research paradigm or model and tends to be caught in often sterile debates about appropriate research methodologies. Social work also lacks a tradition of research publication and tends to be relatively parochial in its publishing, with few

journals being truly international or aspiring to be included in international citation indices. As a result, social work typically performs less well than the other social science disciplines ... in most measures of research performance, such as obtaining grants, graduating PhD students, and publishing in journals.... This will raise particular issues about how social work will fare in the RQF [Research Quality Framework] process that looms on the Australian higher education horizon. (Rosenman, 2007: 10)

Rosenman argues that it is critically important for the standing of social work in universities, as well as for the development of the field and the profession, that high-quality PhD students come through honours programmes and into postdoctoral and academic appointments. The heavy focus on undergraduate preparation for professional entry has meant that the need for research and knowledge-building that will take the field forward has had less focus. Significantly, a survey of Australian social work educators found that the majority (86%) thought that social work needed to improve its research capacity (Agbim and Ozanne, 2007: 78).[6] In New Zealand, Beddoe (2007: 48) notes that the majority of social work programmes are located in institutions in which research has not been a high priority and, therefore, the research base for social work education is very underdeveloped. The lack of a research tradition in social work is also a major challenge facing social work educators in the US, as Khinduka (2007: 20) points out:

Unlike other learned professions and academic disciplines, social workers as a group do not have a strong track record of conducting original scholarly work. Individual luminaries notwithstanding, perhaps it is not an exaggeration to say that the profession of social work as a whole is more comfortable with ideologies than with ideas, with advocacy than analysis, with basing its interventions on anecdotes and intuition rather than evidence and empirical data, and sometimes even with thinly veiled anti-intellectualism rather than a spirit of scientific inquiry and disciplined skepticism. Although the earliest programs of social work education in the US were founded with the mission to make philanthropy more 'scientific', many of our interventions are far from 'scientific'.

Khinduka argues that preparing graduates for building a systematic body of practice-relevant knowledge for the profession that is conceptually and methodologically sound must become a driving concern of doctoral education. He also suggests that social work programmes with the requisite institutional infrastructure should consider the development of post-doctoral programmes.

While there is general agreement that the research base for social work needs to grow, there are a number of challenges, not least in terms of funding (see Dominelli, 2007: 42). Questions have been raised in the UK, for example, as to whether the research funding for universities privileges the natural sciences over other disciplines, such as the social sciences (Galpin, 2009: 72). If this is the case, Galpin argues, it may further disadvantage subject areas such as PQ social work education. Similar issues were raised in Australia following the publication of a set of national research priorities in 2001. These priorities, when first announced, were completely science and technology-based and 'did much to confirm to the social sciences that their research was not valued' (Rosenman, 2007: 11). Moreover, funding is often dependent on a department's (or an institution's) *existing* research record. In New Zealand, Beddoe (2007: 53) notes that schools of social work are often caught in 'the vicious cycle' of struggling to find time and funds for research, while low research outputs limit their claim to contestable funds within their institution. It is difficult for academics to get 'buy-out' from teaching through funded research. Many social work educators have to teach four courses per semester and visit students on placement while trying to manage small research projects, apply for grants and write for publication (Beddoe, 2007: 53).

Beddoe suggests a number of ways forward, which include maintaining very strong relationships with major state-funded agencies, health boards and non-government organisations. In addition, secondments could help to meet shortfalls in teaching expertise and joint research projects could 'create stronger relationships between academic scholarship and practitioner research' (Beddoe, 2007: 53). In the UK, Green (2006) notes that the RAE and a general emphasis on research is improving social work's academic image, a point on which Parsloe (2001: 17) concurs. Further progress could be made by concentrating on social work's 'ability to understand and integrate theory and research from different disciplines and apply these to practice, presenting this as a particular disciplinary strength' (Green, 2006: 258). Another means of raising the status of social work could be by extending and standardising education and training, particularly at PQ level: 'Social work educators should invest in and emphasise the importance of a range of post-qualifying training and specialist, academic training as opposed to the intermittent, short, in-house, non-academic courses that social workers in the field tend to be offered' (Green, 2006: 258).

Conclusion

As we have seen in the course of this chapter, social work education faces a number of challenges. While the importance of CPD for professional development in social work has been acknowledged in recent years, questions remain as to how this is to be funded and supported, particularly in the current economic climate. There are debates over who should provide PQ education and what its purpose is. Partnerships between universities and employers have been heralded as a means of making social work more relevant; on the other hand, such partnerships may run the risk of perpetuating what Parsloe (2001: 14) describes as 'the creeping managerialism that is engulfing social work'.

Similar questions have been raised about the nature of social work education. The last few decades have seen the emergence of two competing approaches: reflective and competency-based. The latter has gained considerable ground, most notably in the UK. While proponents argue that the competency model results in much clearer specifications and more transparent assessment methods, critics have dismissed it as a reductionist, 'tick-box' approach to education and practice. Moreover, it tends to de-professionalise social workers and is politically conservative (see Postle et al, 2002: 159). Reflective learning has come to be seen as a means of countering managerialism and competency-based approaches. However, critics argue that this model also tends to overlook the political context of social work, focusing instead on the individual. A number of scholars have called for social work education and practice to adopt a more critical role and place greater emphasis on the values of social justice. According to Ferguson et al (2005: 8), this does not mean 'back to the 1970s', but forward to a new engaged social work practice. In Chapter Eight, we will consider how social work education, including CPD, can help social workers engage with the structural context of practice.

Notes
[1] ASWs are qualified social workers specially trained in mental health work. ASWs were given a number of duties and responsibilities under the Mental Health (NI) Order 1986 (see Wilson et al, 2005: 722).

[2] The *Report of the Commission to Inquire into Child Abuse, 2009: implementation plan* acknowledges the importance of supervision, particularly for newly qualified social workers. One of the 'actions to be taken' identified in the report states that: 'the HSE will establish a mandatory year of limited caseload, supervision and support for newly qualified social workers (*by January 2011*) and will consider the rotation of social workers across children in care, child protection and child welfare teams' (OMCYA, 2009: 44, italics in original).

[3] CORU is a multi-profession regulatory body that was set up under the Health and Social Care Professionals Act 2005. It is an umbrella body, made up of the Health and Social Care Professionals Council and 12 registration boards, one for each of the professions named in the Act, including social work. The word CORU is not an abbreviation, it 'originates from an Irish word, "cóir" meaning fair, just and proper' (CORU, 2013, 'Frequently Asked Questions', (Available at: http://www.coru.ie/en/faq, accessed 14/08/2013.)

[4] The barriers to participation in CPD are considered in more detail in the Social Work Task Force (SWTF, 2009: 38) report, which concludes that success in improving CPD will 'depend heavily on shared commitment from employers, educators and professionals'.

[5] Until recently, a UK-wide framework for PQ education and training was managed by regional PQ consortia, partnerships of employers and higher education institutions (Higham, 2009: 9). In Scotland, Wales and Northern Ireland, a single consortium was formed in each country; while in England, 17 consortia worked independently of each other (Higham, 2009: 10). The original PQ framework has now been superseded by new frameworks in each of the four countries that comprise the UK.

[6] Many gave their views on how this might be achieved, which included: '(a) improving productivity through "partnerships with agencies", (b) "partnership with other disciplines", (c) "promoting the profession", and (f) "broadening the concept of research resources between schools and increased cross-disciplinary research"' (Agbim and Ozanne, 2007: 78). Factors that inhibited research activity included: heavy teaching loads, administrative commitments, difficulties in obtaining funding, family commitments and a lack of support for research interests.

THREE

Continuing professional development: a national study

In Ireland, for much of the 20th century, getting a job was synonymous with the end of formal education for most people, including those working in social services. Employers and other organisations provided some in-service training, though courses were generally short-term, participation was optional and there was no overall strategy for continuing education. Over the last two decades, however, continuing professional development (CPD) has assumed far greater significance within the social work profession in Ireland. The vital role of supervision and ongoing training in child protection has been emphasised in child abuse inquiries (McGuinness, 1993; Joint Committee on the Family, 1996; Gibbons, 2010) and policy documents (OMCYA, 2009: 42; HSE, 2010a; Department of Children and Youth Affairs, 2011). The recent *Children first: national guidance for the protection and welfare of children* report (Department of Children and Youth Affairs, 2011: 62–4) identifies the objectives of child protection and welfare training and calls for the development of a training strategy in the Health Service Executive (HSE). Like the Munro (2011) and Laming (2009) reports, *Children first* emphasises the importance of multidisciplinary and inter-agency training in equipping practitioners for their role. As the number of social work managers expands, the need for specialist training in management has also been acknowledged in policy and inquiry reports (Gibbons, 2010; HSE, 2010a; Department of Children and Youth Affairs, 2011) and in the academic literature (Leinster, 2009, 2010).

The Irish Association of Social Workers (IASW) and the former National Social Work Qualifications Board (NSWQB) have for a number of years promoted and supported CPD. However, the setting up of the regulatory body, CORU,[1] in 2010 is particularly significant as social workers will henceforth be required to undertake CPD in order to renew their registration. While the recognition of CPD as an important part of professional life is to be welcomed, it also raises a number of important questions: 'What constitutes CPD?'; 'How is it to be provided?'; and 'Who should finance and support its development in the current climate of austerity?'.

Despite growing interest in the potential of CPD for the social work profession in Ireland, very little research has been carried out in this area. It is against this background that researchers at University College Cork initiated a two-year project that aimed to map the current provision and uptake of CPD opportunities among social workers, assess its contribution to professional life, and identify the barriers to participation. The project was based on an online survey and interviews with members of the professional association, the IASW. The findings of the research will be reported in Chapters Three to Five.

While the focus of our research is on Ireland, the issues raised are significant in an international context. There are, for example, a number of parallels between the barriers to participation experienced by social workers in Ireland and those in other countries (see Chapter Four). The research reported here may be of particular interest to countries that, like Ireland, are in the process of introducing regulatory systems that require professionals to undertake CPD. In the course of the project, we explored social workers' reactions to the establishment of the new regulatory system, and how they thought it would impact on the status and provision of CPD within the social work profession.

In this chapter, we provide an overview of: the different forms of CPD identified in the research; social workers' motives for undertaking CPD; and the perceived outcomes and impact on practice. This is followed by a discussion of social workers' preferred forms of CPD, and how it might be developed in the future. We will begin by setting the issue of CPD within the wider context of the development of the social work profession in Ireland.

Social work in Ireland

The origins of social work in Ireland can be traced to the 19th century, when a wide range of charitable activities relating to education, health and welfare were undertaken by volunteers, usually women. During the first half of the 20th century, the social work profession gradually began to take shape, though the numbers employed remained relatively insignificant, due in part to a lack of state support. Irish social policy during this period was guided by the Catholic principle of subsidiarity, which held that the state should not be responsible for providing supports or services that individuals, families and other associations were in a position to provide for themselves. Where families were considered unable to meet the needs of their members, it was believed that Church-run institutions and voluntary agencies were in the best position to provide assistance. As a result, much of Irish social provision was under the control of the Catholic Church or voluntary organisations (many of which had Church connections), with the state having a much lesser role. While religious principles underlined various aspects of social services and social work up to the 1960s, there is also evidence to suggest that Church leaders regarded the profession with a degree of suspicion, on the grounds that it intervened in the 'private' sphere of family life (Gaughan and Garrett, 2012). As John Charles McQuaid, the formidable Catholic Archbishop of Dublin, stated in a letter to the Director of the Family Welfare Agency in 1951: 'Our people do not want lady-analysts of their lives and motives. Trouble is certain to develop if almoners [hospital social workers] undertake psychological investigations in our homes or in our hospitals' (cited in Skehill, 1999: 132).

It was not until the 1970s, with the emergence of a comprehensive welfare state in Ireland alongside a lessening of the influence of the Catholic Church, that opportunities for professional social work began to develop, most notably, within the statutory services. In her history of social work in Ireland, Skehill (1999) notes that the expansion in employment of social workers reached a peak during the 1970s and early 1980s, but remained relatively stagnant for the following decade and a half. The one area that continued to grow 'at an accelerated and extensive rate' was that of child and family social work within community care (Skehill, 1999: 165). There are a number of possible reasons for this, including the 'discovery' of child abuse in the 1970s in most Western societies, followed by a series of scandals concerning child abuse (within families and Church-run institutions) in Ireland during the 1990s. With the publication of high-profile inquiry reports and increased media attention, child protection issues have become a major area of political and public concern in Ireland.

The social work profession in Ireland underwent a further period of expansion in the late 1990s and early years of the 21st century. Figures from the NSWQB (2006: 22) indicate that the number of posts grew from 1,390 in 1999 to 2,237 in 2005, representing a 61% increase over a six-year period. Despite recent cutbacks, the areas in which social workers practise are now more extensive than ever before. The profession has become 'much more recognised and recognisable' (Leinster, 2010: 74), particularly with the recent introduction of statutory registration for 12 health and social care professions, including social work. The term *social worker* has been designated a 'protected' title, and since 2012, social workers have been required to register with the Social Work Registration Board in order to practise (Health & Social Care Professionals Council, 2012a).

According to the most recent NSWQB (2006: 22) survey, social work is still a predominantly female occupation, with women accounting for 83% of the workforce. It is predicted that this gender imbalance is unlikely to change in the short term as the number of male entrants to professional training courses continues to be low. The HSE is the main employer of social workers in Ireland, with over half of all social work posts located there (NSWQB, 2006: 15). Other major employers include voluntary, community and private agencies (14% of posts), the probation service (13%), and hospitals (10%).

The social work profession has made significant strides over the past 40 years in establishing itself as a profession and in gaining recognition (Skehill, 1999: 171). However, as Skehill (1999) argues, while the context and nature of professional social work today is significantly distinct from earlier practices of voluntary and religious-based social work, it has also inherited key features from its past, including an 'individualistic' approach to social problems. Social work practice continues to be constructed within a consensus view of society that takes little account of factors such as structural inequalities, racism, sexism and classism, which affect many clients' lives. A wide range of individual and group-focused professional practices and therapies are increasingly occupying the space of social work – psychotherapy, solution-focused therapy and family therapy being some key examples (Skehill, 1999: 194). Discourses that are more radical have gained little space within Irish social work at any point in its history, and this remains the case to the present day (see also Gaughan and Garrett, 2012).

Social work education in Ireland

In order to qualify as a social worker in Ireland, candidates are required to complete a relevant primary degree, normally in the social sciences, followed by a postgraduate qualification in social work at Masters or diploma level. There are four two-year Masters-level (MSW) programmes at University College Dublin, University College Cork (UCC), Trinity College Dublin (TCD) and the National University of Ireland, Galway. Alternatively, a four-year undergraduate course can be undertaken at TCD or UCC (for details, see Health & Social Care Professionals Council, 2012b). While the TCD degree admits school-leavers, the UCC degree is targeted at mature students.

While qualifying programmes have become well-established in Ireland, the expansion of post-qualifying (PQ) education has moved at a much slower rate, with only a small number of courses targeted at social workers (Leinster, 2009: 36). The lack of PQ educational opportunities is all the more surprising given the rapid expansion in numbers and changing role of social workers over the last four decades. There is, according to Leinster, a growing disjunction between training needs and opportunities:

> While development in social work education has progressed at a relatively slow pace, the increasing demands on the social work profession as a whole have moved much more rapidly, increased responsibilities arising from the introduction of new legislation, a rapid growing multicultural society, more complex family structures and the increasing diversity of social problems has made the social work task more demanding. (Leinster, 2009: 42)

One of the most significant developments of recent years has been the setting up of the Social Work Registration Board, which has 'statutory responsibility for the assessment, approval and monitoring of training courses for the health and social care professions' under the Health and Social Care Professionals Act 2005. Social workers registered with the Board will be required to undertake CPD in order to maintain their registration, and thereby their right to practise. While CPD in one form or another appears to be well-established within the social work profession (eg through in-service training and short courses provided by the professional association), the introduction of registration is nonetheless highly significant in making CPD a matter of professional obligation rather than personal choice. Clearly, this has far-reaching implications for social workers and employers, particularly in terms of financial and time commitments.

The research project: methodology

As noted earlier, the project set out to map the current provision and uptake of CPD opportunities among social workers, assess its contribution to professional life, and identify the barriers to participation. The project was based on both quantitative and qualitative methods, details of which are provided in the following.

The research process fell into two parts: an online survey of members of the professional association, the IASW, followed by a series of interviews and a focus group discussion. The survey was intended to provide a broad overview of practitioners' experience of CPD while the interviews and focus group afforded the opportunity for a more in-depth analysis of specific issues, some of which emerged from the survey.

Online survey

The survey questionnaire was piloted with 15 social workers during May 2011 and revised in the light of their comments, most of which concerned the length of time necessary to complete the questionnaire. The final version consisted mainly of 'closed' questions, though a small number of open-ended questions allowed respondents to express their views on the outcomes of CPD. Questions were constructed to address issues under broad categories, such as: background information on the respondent (eg age, gender, employment status, social work qualifications); experience and outcomes of CPD; barriers to participation; and CPD needs.

The questionnaire was administered online (using 'survey monkey' technology) from June to July 2011. At the research team's request, the IASW forwarded an email to 750 of its members,[2] informing them of the research and inviting them to complete the questionnaire, which could be accessed through a web link. This initial email was followed up by three reminders, sent from late June to mid-July. Members were also given the option of completing a paper copy of the questionnaire in case of technical difficulties in accessing or completing the online version. While those completing the questionnaire were able to do so anonymously, they could provide their contact details for subsequent follow-up interviews.

Of the 750 IASW members contacted, 282 returned questionnaires, a response rate of 38%. The survey data was imported into SPSS for analysis. Responses to open-ended questions were coded and analysed.

Profile of survey respondents

The majority of survey respondents (82%) were female (a figure that reflects the gender imbalance within the profession overall[3]) and were spread across different age ranges, the two largest categories being the 26–35 and 46–55 age groups.[4] Nearly three quarters were employed on a permanent full-time basis, followed by permanent part-time (12%).[5] Those employed on a temporary, or job-share, basis made up a comparatively small proportion of the sample. In most cases, respondents were social workers employed by Community Care (HSE), hospitals and voluntary/community organisations (see Table 3.1). The probation service was comparatively under-represented: less than 3%

of respondents were employed in this sector, compared with the 13% figure recorded in the NSWQB (2006) workforce survey.

Table 3.1: Employer

Employer	Frequency	Per cent
Community Care (HSE)	109	39
Hospitals	57	20.5
Voluntary/community organisations	55	20
Private organisations	13	5
Probation service	7	2.5
Local authority	5	2
Hospice	5	2
Defence forces	2	1
Other	25	9
Total	**278**	**100%**

As Table 3.2 indicates, the sample included practitioners at different stages in their careers, ranging from newly qualified to principal social workers. About a quarter of respondents held management-level positions (ie head social workers, principal social workers and team leaders).

Table 3.2: Current position

	Frequency	Per cent
Newly qualified social worker (qualified within the last 2 years)	23	8
Social worker (basic grade)	101	36
Senior social worker	44	16
Head social worker	4	1
Principal social worker	36	13
Team leader	24	9
Senior practitioner	11	4
Probation officer (basic grade)	5	2
Senior probation officer	1	<1
Other	28	10
Total	**277**	**100**

Note: Examples in the 'Other' category included Guardian ad Litem, counsellor and training officer.

A range of different fields of practice were represented in the sample, the largest single category being statutory child protection and family support (21%), followed by medical (13%) and learning disability (13%) (see Table 3.3).

Table 3.3: Field of practice

	Frequency	Per cent
Child protection and family support (statutory)	59	21
Medical	37	13
Disability: learning	35	13
Mental health: adult	26	9
Fostering	14	5
Disability: physical/sensory	13	5
Adoption	12	4
Older people	11	4
Child and family work (non-statutory)	6	2
Mental health: child/adolescent	10	3
Primary care	7	2
Probation	7	2
Palliative	5	2
Community work	3	1
Travelling community	3	1
Addiction/substance misuse	2	<1
Homelessness	2	<1
Housing welfare	1	<1
Occupational health	1	<1
Other	28	10
Total	282	100

Note: 'Other' includes child sexual abuse assessment, residential childcare, training and consultancy, early intervention services, and so on. In addition, a few newly qualified social workers indicated that they did not yet have a main field of practice.

Interviews and focus group

Interviews were held with 16 IASW members who had indicated on their questionnaire that they were willing to take part in this stage of the research. In addition, a focus group was arranged with a further four IASW members, all of whom worked in the same organisation.

Interview participants were at various stages in their careers, from basic-grade social workers to team leaders, and were drawn from various areas of social work, including: child protection and family support; child sexual abuse assessment; fostering; hospital-based social work; mental health; occupational health; probation; homelessness; addiction/ substance abuse; community work; and social work education. The interviews and focus group discussions were taped, transcribed and analysed thematically.

Post-qualifying higher education

Post-qualifying higher education (HE) courses represent a considerable investment in time and money for the professional and (in many cases) their employer. In this section, we report on the numbers of survey respondents undertaking HE, their choice of courses and the supports available to them. The findings suggested that counselling and therapy remain popular choices among social workers (see also Leinster, 2009, 2010), and that post-qualifying courses, regardless of subject area, tend to be multidisciplinary.

A substantial proportion of survey respondents (41%) had completed, or were currently undertaking, post-qualification HE. Not surprisingly, Irish universities were found to be the main course providers. As Table 3.4 shows, 38% of courses were undertaken at universities, though a significant number were also provided by HE colleges (the Royal College of Surgeons and the National College of Ireland) and by a range of other institutions, including, for example, the Institute of Public Administration, the Irish Hospice Foundation and the Addiction Training Institute. In addition, some respondents had attended UK or other international institutions. Very few post-qualifying courses were taken at Institutes of Technology.[6] It should be noted, however, that in 30% of cases, respondents did not name the institution at which they had undertaken their post-qualifying course.

The majority of those who had undertaken post-qualifying HE indicated that they had received some form of support from their employer, mainly in the payment of fees or time off work (see Table 3.5). There was less evidence of support for additional costs, such as travel and subsistence. Some respondents elaborated on the form of support that they received, pointing out that their fees had been paid for one course but not another. In one instance, the respondent did not receive time off work or payment of fees, but was allowed to base their research on their workplace.

Although the figures in Table 3.5 indicate significant support, we must be cautious in interpretation: it is possible that others who might have *wanted* to undertake higher education did not do so because they did not receive support – and their views are not represented here. Moreover, comments in open-ended questions suggest that financial support for CPD (in general) was more readily available in the past, a topic that we will return to in Chapter Four on barriers to participation.

Table 3.4: Institutions at which courses were undertaken

	Number of courses undertaken at these institutions	% of courses undertaken at these institutions
Irish universities	51	38
Third-level colleges	7	5
Institutes of Technology	3	2
Other Irish institutions	18	13
UK universities and HE institutions	11	8
International universities and HE institutions	5	4
Unspecified	40	30
Total	**135**	100%

Table 3.5: Employer support for higher education

	Frequency	Per cent
Employer paid some or all of course fees	58	71
Employer contributed to other costs	14	17
Employer provided time off work	57	70

Notes: Based on 82 respondents: non-response (34); not applicable (166). Multiple response question; therefore, total may be greater than 100%.

Course choice

The majority of post-qualifying HE courses undertaken by participants were at either Masters (33%) or diploma (30%) level, followed by certificate (10%), PhD (7%), degree (3%) and foundation programmes (1%).[7] A diverse range of courses were reported by respondents, no doubt reflecting the different areas in which they work (see Table 3.6). The most popular course choices were in the fields of therapy and counselling, including, for example, psychotherapy, integrative counselling, gestalt therapy, cognitive behavioural therapy and so forth. Just over one fifth of HE courses undertaken by respondents were in management and administration, a significant finding given the increasing recognition of management training needs (HSE, 2010a).

Table 3.6: Course content

	No of courses	% of courses
Counselling and therapy	37	27
Management and administration	29	22
Child protection	11	8
Social science	10	7
Supervision	7	5
Bereavement	6	4
Mental health	6	4
Addiction	5	4
Mediation and dispute resolution	3	2
Post-qualifying social work	3	2
Equality studies and social justice studies	2	2
Eating disorders	1	<1
Other	12	9
Unspecified	3	2
Total	**135**	100%

The issue of course choice was explored further in the interviews and focus group discussion. The popularity of counselling and therapy courses is particularly significant in the context of ongoing debates about the nature of the social work profession, some of which were outlined in Chapter Two. Critics argue that contemporary social work tends to overlook the broader political and social context of issues such as poverty or addiction, focusing instead on working with the individual service user (see Skehill, 1999). A number of commentators have called for social work education and practice to adopt a more critical role and place greater emphasis on the values of social justice (see, eg, Ferguson et al, 2005). The dominance of counselling and therapy courses within post-qualifying education, as reported in our research, may be indicative of an individualised approach to social problems and raises questions as to the direction of social work education. In the course of the interviews and focus group, we had an opportunity to ask social workers themselves for their views on this issue.

For the most part, interviewees were not surprised that counselling and therapy were the main areas of post-qualifying study. Several participants noted that while they did not regard their role as that of a counsellor or therapist, there was nonetheless a therapeutic element to their work. As one child protection worker pointed out, practitioners work with people who have been "traumatised by some event in their life" and they therefore need certain skills in order "to communicate with people and even just recognise the signs". While clients might ultimately be referred on to counsellors for more specialist help, social workers made the initial contact. Moreover, social workers in certain areas of practice build ongoing relationships with their clients. In these instances, counselling skills were seen to be an advantage not only for understanding and communicating with clients, but also for developing greater self-awareness on the part of social workers. Alternatively, a qualification in counselling or therapy could be a means of moving into a different area of social work or of leaving the profession altogether in order to specialise in some aspect of therapy or counselling.

A few interview participants expressed a degree of ambivalence about the dominance of counselling and therapy within post-qualifying social work education. One principal social worker compared her experience as a manager in Ireland and the UK, noting that "we have identified ourselves very much with counselling and therapy in Ireland ... but there are lots of other areas that we need to develop", these included risk and needs assessment and inter-agency working. However, two other managers suggested that Irish social work has already begun to move away from 'therapeutic-type work' towards what might be seen as a more administrative or managerialist role. It was asserted that counsellors and other professionals are increasingly taking over roles that were originally performed by social workers. Meanwhile, social workers themselves are devoting more time to assessments, referrals and reviews, as 'therapeutic work' is outsourced to other professionals:

> "I can see compared to when I started social work that an awful lot of other people are doing what used to be the social work role. Childcare workers, family support workers, and the social workers are then doing the assessments, the referrals, the tick boxes, the review meetings and making sure everything is done according to the statutory requirements. And then maybe going to court, whatever the case may be. And the individual counselling, individual therapeutic work is now being done by other people." (Principal social worker)

Similarly, a childcare manager noted that the nature of her work was changing and predicted that over the coming years, therapy and counselling courses would assume far less importance in post-qualifying education. The process by which social workers have been gradually distanced from their client group has been documented in the UK (see Chapter Two).

Only one social worker, who had recently qualified, expressed the concern that a focus on therapy and counselling diverts attention away from the wider context in which social problems are located:

> "you are individualising the person and you're saying they're the problem, and you're trying to change them so they can live in the world they are in … and that to me is the exact opposite to what social work purports to be about."

While she was not surprised to find that counselling and therapy were the most popular course choices, she herself would not be enrolling:

> "A lot of the training doesn't really interest me in a way because I don't have any interest in learning one specific tool to use on a person [laughs], like a little experiment and see if it works on them … I don't really have a particular interest in a lot of that but unfortunately that's all there is."

Another noteworthy feature of the post-qualifying HE courses undertaken by survey respondents is that they are often multidisciplinary, rather than social-work-specific. In the case of management training, for example, the most popular choices were the Masters in Business Administration (MBA) and the Masters in Health Services Management, a programme offered to managers working generally in the health services. As noted earlier, the lack of management courses specifically for social workers has been documented by John Leinster (2009, 2010).

In the course of the interviews/focus group, we asked participants for their views on the multidisciplinary nature of current post-qualifying social work education. Several interviewees had themselves undertaken multidisciplinary courses and their remarks were generally quite favourable: they highlighted the fact that social workers are often part of inter-agency teams and that it is therefore appropriate for them to be trained within that context. Moreover, two managers (both of whom had undertaken Masters degrees in management) told us that there are many areas of common ground within management, regardless of the sector in which one works. They argued that multidisciplinary education should not be seen as a threat to social work values, but rather as an opportunity to promote these values to a wider community beyond the social work profession. According to a principal social worker in the HSE:

> "Well, part of social work values is to effect social change. And the only way we are going to effect social change is to get out there and mix with other people. And what better way to do that than through education. And to bring social work values into your education with others."

She went on to say that education was a means of promoting a better understanding of social work among the wider population:

> "And I think that one of the issues with social work is the isolation, and that people don't understand us; they have a fear of social workers; and we need to get out there more and education is one of the ways of doing that."

Given the negative representation of social workers, particularly in the UK media, it is perhaps understandable that this practitioner (who worked in London for several years) was concerned to dispel some of the myths and preconceptions surrounding the profession. Similarly, a number of other interviewees claimed that multidisciplinary training could promote mutual understanding between different professionals who sometimes work together (including social workers, police, nurses, doctors, teachers), particularly in the field of child protection.

Other forms of continuing professional development

Apart from post-qualifying HE, survey respondents participated in a wide range of CPD, both work-based and externally provided (see Table 3.7).

Table 3.7: Types of continuing professional development undertaken

	Per cent
In-service training	93
Courses/workshops (other than HE and in-service training)	68
Attending conferences, seminars and presentations	95
Supervision	86
Peer consultation	48
Mentoring	24

In-service training

In-service training is clearly one of the most widely available forms of CPD, with the vast majority (93%) of survey respondents having undertaken training in the last five years (Table 3.7). Nonetheless, nearly three quarters of respondents reported that the *amount* of in-service training made available to them was too little, with only a quarter reporting that it was "about right". Training generally comprised short courses of one to two days. Moreover, as we shall see in Chapter Four ('Barriers to participation'), there have been significant cutbacks to provision in recent years. In the course of the interviews, it emerged that the same courses were repeated many times and that new courses were often focused on the latest policy initiative, such as the new *Children first* guidelines. Not surprisingly, the content of in-house training varied considerably, depending on the work setting.

Courses and workshops

Apart from post-qualifying HE and in-service training, over two thirds (68%) of respondents reported that they had undertaken other professionally relevant short courses, workshops and similar events. The IASW was the main course provider/coordinator, though an additional 70 organisations were listed by respondents, including, for example, Barnardos, the Crisis Pregnancy Agency, the Council of Irish Adoption Agencies and the Irish Association for Palliative Care. Course content was similarly diverse, ranging from baby massage to working with older people. The *main* course content areas listed by participants were: attachment; bereavement; suicide prevention and awareness; supervision and practice teacher training; child protection; and mental health. Our findings suggest that employers play an important part in funding these courses, paying some or all of the fees (Table 3.8). Nonetheless, a substantial minority of respondents (33%) paid all fees; while 29% contributed to the fees. Some respondents elaborated on their answer, noting that employers paid for certain courses, but not others. Subsequent interviews suggested that employers were more likely to support courses that they saw as directly relevant to the work, though there were concerns that 'relevance' was being too narrowly defined.

Table 3.8: Payment of course fees

	Frequency	Per cent
Both myself and employer contributed	50	29
Employer paid all fees	65	38
I paid all fees	57	33
I received a grant/award	2	I

Notes: Based on 170 respondents: non-response (14); not applicable (98). Multiple response question; therefore, total may be greater than 100%.

Supervision, peer consultation and mentoring

As Table 3.7 indicates, the vast majority of respondents (86%) receive supervision, a slightly higher figure than that found in an earlier IASW survey (Peet and Jennings, 2010). Interestingly, most of those who did not receive supervision were senior, principal or head social workers. While some of these respondents could access 'informal supervision' if needed, supervision did not appear to represent a routine part of their working life (for a detailed discussion of supervision, see Chapter Five).

Nearly half of survey respondents were engaged in peer consultation, while just under a quarter acted as mentors or mentees (Table 3.7). The nature of these informal/in-house CPD formats was explored in the interviews and will be considered in more detail later.

Motivation for undertaking continuing professional development

As we saw in Chapter One, CPD is seen to have a number of functions, for example: preparing practitioners for changing roles and expectations; developing professional competence; and improving services to clients. In the course of our research, we asked social workers themselves why they decided to undertake CPD, and what they hoped to get from it. A mandatory system of CPD has not yet been introduced in Ireland and so all respondents would have participated on a voluntary basis (with a few exceptions where employees were required to attend specific training, for example, in health and safety).

As Table 3.9 shows, the majority of those who enrolled on a post-qualifying HE course did so because it was relevant to their current area of work (56%), or to help them respond to new challenges (47%). There was also evidence that respondents undertook courses because they found them interesting and fulfilling: 53% said that they were motivated by an interest in the course, while 36% wanted a new challenge. Career progression or career change appeared to feature in comparatively few cases: 13% of respondents said that they were motivated by hopes of a promotion and only 10% saw it as a means of moving into a different area of social work. Among the 'other' motivations listed in Table 3.9 was return to work and a desire to increase academic profile. This was a multiple response question, with many respondents indicating more than one reason for undertaking post-qualifying HE.

Table 3.9: Motivation for undertaking CPD

	Frequency	Per cent
Course was relevant to my current area of work	63	56
I was interested in the course	60	53
To help me respond to new challenges	53	47
I wanted a new challenge	41	36
To increase my chance of promotion	15	13
To move into a different area of social work	11	10
Other	16	14

Notes: Based on 113 respondents: non-response (3); not applicable (166). Multiple response question; therefore, total may be greater than 100%.

Social workers' motivation for undertaking CPD (both formal and informal) was explored in greater detail through the interviews and focus group. One of the major themes to emerge from these discussions concerned the changing nature of the social work role. Respondents noted that policy, theory, research and ideas about practice were constantly evolving, and they sought to keep abreast of these developments by undertaking courses and other forms of CPD. The following are some of their comments:

> "I suppose commitment to the profession. Needing to – I know it's a bit of a cliché – but to be as good as you can be. And to do that, you have to recognise that things don't stand still, and that it's a constantly evolving profession, both in theory and in practice. And really if you are to have any professional self-respect, you have to keep abreast and keep up with research and practice, and changes in practice." (Focus group respondent 1)

> "Yes, because if you don't, you may end up doing things that may have been the norm in 1974 but they have long

since been proven not to work or not to be very reliable or whatever. If you are not going to courses, or reading or discussing with colleagues, you are just going to do the same thing." (Focus group respondent 2)

"I see it as important because I'm five or six years out [of college] and things are already changing. So I can only imagine people who are out even longer than me. I suppose it's about keeping your toe in the water, not getting dried up and forgetting what's going on out there." (Social worker)

"In social work, I think you are never finished learning, because of the fact that we work with society and things are constantly changing. So I think that there is the need to do CPD." (Social worker)

For some respondents, undertaking CPD was a means of addressing a specific training need resulting from a job change or changes within their existing role. One social worker, for example, told us that she had a varied caseload where a "glut of bereavement cases" could be followed by several months of relationship counselling. In order to meet the needs of these client groups, she had undertaken courses in different aspects of social work. In two other instances, respondents had undertaken post-qualifying HE courses because they had been promoted to management level but felt that they did not have some of the skills necessary for their new role. Interestingly, this training was undertaken *after* they became managers rather than before.

Aside from the need to respond to changing roles and expectations, respondents saw CPD as an opportunity to reflect on their own practice, something that was often absent from their day-to-day working lives. They spoke, for example, of being able to "critically analyse" their work and consider "why you do things in a certain way", of "opening oneself to the possibility of reviewing one's practice" and "maintaining a degree of reflective practice". In addition, *delivering* CPD events could be an opportunity for reflection because of the "questions that are thrown your way" by participants. Moreover, respondents saw learning as an ongoing process that continued throughout their careers: they did not feel that they "knew it all" or were "experts" simply because they had qualified and practised in social work. Consequently, there was a commitment to lifelong learning, as some of the following comments illustrate:

"There is no point where you can say 'Yes, I am a fully developed social worker', there's always something else you can go on to, wanting to find out what there is to find out.... When you are in a profession, there should be a drive, a sort of self-actualisation thing." (Focus group participant 2)

"Sometimes you go to a conference and you hear someone really interesting, who really knows what they are talking about. And if you meet them later in smaller groups, they will always have questions to ask. They always want to find out more, they won't see themselves as this person who knows everything, they understand that they are always learning. Most people know you are always learning. And that's the thing about CPD." (Focus group participant 1)

"I'd hope to say that I'd get some extra knowledge and understanding of what I'm doing [from CPD], and why I'm doing what I'm doing. And, again, I'd go back to say I'm not an expert ... I'd hope to say I took up social work for lifelong learning." (Social worker, child protection)

"I suppose I don't see learning as ever stopping, I see it as a lifelong process.... So whether I was in a different job, it wouldn't matter, I would still want to learn so that's really my motivation, so it's not for, it's not necessarily for promotion or for advancement, although obviously at some stage that would be great, but it's not about that. It's about bettering myself [so that] I can provide a better service." (Social worker, child protection)

This desire to provide "a better service" was reiterated by most other interview/focus group participants. They spoke, for example, of wanting to be "better at my job ultimately", to be "as good as you can be" and to become "a better social worker". Interestingly, none of the interview/focus group participants said that they undertook CPD in order to gain a promotion or pay increase. However, this may be due, in part at least, to the lack of incentives and rewards for CPD, a topic that we will return to in Chapter Four on the barriers to participation.

Outcomes of continuing professional development

When asked if undertaking post-qualifying, in-service or other professional courses had helped them in their work, the response from IASW members was overwhelmingly positive (see Table 3.10). In each case, the vast majority of survey respondents indicated that their training had been either helpful or very helpful, with 'other professional courses' receiving the highest rating (98%), followed by HE (91%) and in-service training (86%).

Table 3.10: Views on courses undertaken

	Very helpful	Helpful	Little/no impact	Unhelpful	Very unhelpful
HE	54%	37%	8%	0%	<1%
In-service training	27%	59%	13%	1%	0%
Other professionally relevant courses/ workshops	63%	35%	<1%	0%	<1%

In an open-ended question, respondents were asked to comment on their answer. With regards to *HE*, course participants said that they had gained a deeper understanding of complex issues, and a means of reflecting anew on their work. The following were typical comments:

> "The orientation of the training increased my understanding of process and systemic approaches, which has really helped me to be more aware of my own as well as clients' issues and reduces the likelihood of getting stuck in the work." (Social worker)

> "Undertaking research provided me with a deeper understanding of the complex challenges which social workers face in managing the range of competing demands arising from the needs of parents, their children, their agency and the courts." (Social worker)

A related point was that post-qualifying HE had enhanced their knowledge of different areas of social work. This was particularly important for those who felt out of touch with current research and policy. One respondent noted, for example, that her course had provided an "opportunity to access recent research and ideas and reflect on practice", while for another, "it has brought me up to speed with current theories on bereavement". Respondents also commented on the skills that they had acquired through training – for example, in counselling and mediation – and the relevance of the course to their work. The benefits derived from HE – whether in terms of greater understanding, new knowledge or skill sets – led in turn to a greater sense of confidence. In addition, HE could be personally fulfilling and intellectually stimulating, as one social worker pointed out, "[it] helps in keeping my brain cells alive".

One of the main benefits of *in-service training*, as reported by IASW members, is that it is often very practical and directly relevant to their work. There was a sense, in some of the replies, that the training was designed by agencies (and selected by participants) with very specific tasks or roles in mind, as the following examples illustrate:

> "The training is put together by the practitioners as it relates to the needs identified by the practitioners. I think this is the way forward as there is no point having in-service trainings for topics that are not of the highest importance, as practitioners need to balance their training times appropriately with cost, training days available and workload."

> "I undertook targeted and specific training (eg one-day workshops) that would directly impact on my day-to-day work – it had to be relevant."

Other perceived benefits of undertaking in-service training included: the opportunity to network and share ideas with colleagues; access to information on current issues, policies and legislation; and a chance to reflect and recharge. As one respondent summed up: "training helps staff to take time out, reflect, get energised and network – social workers need to do this more!". Similar issues were raised with regard to other short courses and workshops, such as those provided by the IASW: respondents commented on their relevance, opportunities for networking and access to new knowledge and ways of understanding their work.

While the majority of comments on different courses were positive, there were also a number of criticisms, primarily in relation to in-service training. One of the main concerns raised by participants was that opportunities for in-service training were inadequate and had declined further in recent years as a result of the recession. Others focused on the quality of the courses themselves, describing them as too basic or too generic. In some instances, this was because social workers were working with other professionals (eg in hospitals) and a 'one-size-fits-all' approach was taken to training. The following were some of their comments:

> "I work in a psychiatric hospital, so the training is very helpful, but it's geared towards medical professionals rather than social work. It would be a lot more helpful if at least some of it was aimed at social work."

> "[We are provided with] general training around health and safety matters. Social-work-specific training is not provided and has to be sourced outside the HSE and paid for by the worker."

About a fifth of respondents to this question commented on the inconsistent quality or relevance of in-service training, which, as one social worker noted, could vary from "excellent" to "useless". In some instances, the same courses were repeated without being updated, and no new courses were offered. Moreover, social workers were not always able to put into practice what they had learned through in-service training.

Informal and in-house continuing professional development

Our focus so far has been on the more formal types of CPD: post-qualifying, in-service training and short courses/workshops provided by a range of organisations. The survey revealed that social workers also participate in peer consultation (see Table 3.7). The format and outcomes of informal and in-house CPD activities were explored though the interviews and focus group, with particular reference to peer groups and practice teaching.

More than half of the interview/focus group participants were involved in *peer review* or *peer consultation groups*, making this the most common type of informal CPD. Although there were some variations, these groups appear to have two main purposes. First, they provide an opportunity for practitioners to review particular cases and discuss issues arising from their work. Second, peer groups offer a support mechanism through which participants can voice their concerns and 'let off steam'. Peer support was seen to be particularly important where practitioners worked in stressful situations, did not have access to regular supervision or did not feel that supervision met their needs. One child protection worker summed up the main elements of her monthly peer consultation meeting in the following terms:

> "Well, we all sit around in a circle. Each person talks about how they are, how they are feeling. One person usually brings in a case to discuss, if they are having any issues with that case and want to discuss it with the rest of us. And we give them feedback. Then, at the end, we go around the circle again and each person just briefly says something positive. The idea is that we don't end on a negative note [laughs]. It's very informal. Managers don't go to these meetings."

In most cases, peer groups are made up of practitioners who work in the same team or organisation, and they are usually based in the same location. However, social workers who work on their own (eg as is the case in councils) have to look outside their immediate surroundings in order to find peers. In these instances, peer groups can be a means of keeping up to date with developments within the profession, addressing issues of common concern and offsetting the sense of isolation that some 'lone' social workers experience in their role. Similarly, two senior managers who received no professional supervision told us that they joined outside peer groups in order to access the kind of support and learning opportunities that were not provided in the workplace.

Overall, interview/focus group participants reported that being part of a peer group was hugely beneficial because of the support and the exchange of ideas that it promoted. Only one social worker hinted at the tensions that could arise within these groups, noting the importance of trust and the potential for 'disaster':

> "Peer review is where you take maybe one little aspect of a case and look at it in great detail, deconstruct it. Maybe the person presenting it will put out one or two questions, you know, what could have been done differently (that's the usual one) and how it was done. And the group works on it. Now it takes an awful lot of trust, that's the only thing. Because if you are not sure about the piece of work you are presenting, or you are not sure of how well you did it, it takes a lot of trust to expose yourself to the group. It can work out really well or be disastrous. You have to have a cohesive team to do it properly."

Acting as a *practice teacher*[8] for social work students was identified as another significant element of in-house CPD by interview/focus group participants. In this role, practitioners were given the impetus to re-examine and reflect on their own practice, key elements of CPD. As one hospital social worker pointed out:

> "I would see [being a practice teacher] as part of my own personal professional development.... Because it really challenges you. And you really have to think about your practice. And you have to think about why you do certain things in your work, that you take for granted. You become more conscious of what you are doing because you have to convey that to a student, and they have to absorb it into their learning. It's been an excellent experience for me. Obviously hard work and it takes a lot of time, but it's really worthwhile. It's a huge area of CPD for me."

Similarly, focus group participants noted that students "are great for the emperor's-new-clothes-type questions – they ask 'Why?' [and] you actually have to find an answer". Another child protection worker added that having a student on site prompted her to read the latest publications relevant to her field, saying that it was "a bit like preparing for an interview". What was interesting in all of these replies is that CPD was perceived as something that should ideally 'challenge' practitioners; and they saw themselves as being in *partnership* with their students, rather than as being the 'experts'.

Impact of continuing professional development on practice

As we saw earlier, IASW members were generally quite positive about the different courses and informal CPD activities that they had undertaken. In the course of the interviews and focus group, we looked in more detail at how participation in CPD had actually impacted *on practice*. In a few instances, respondents could point to particular courses that had had a direct impact on some aspect of their work. One social worker told us, for example, that she had attended a training course on child investigative interviews that raised issues around how to interview boys as opposed to girls, noting that "it was a very specific, targeted piece of work that changed my way of interviewing boys". A child care manager described how the financial management and systems modules of her MSc in Health Services Management helped her "to shape what I put onto the agenda at various meetings and what I brought to the attention of my line manager at the time", concluding that attending a management course "does make you think differently, no doubt about it". In another example, a child protection worker explained how attendance on a number of courses had made her more aware of service users' perspectives and this in turn changed the way in which she interacted with them.

The responses from most participants suggested that the impact of CPD on their practice was usually quite gradual. For example, one child protection worker felt that while her practice had been informed by the various courses that she had attended over the years, there was no "light-bulb moment" that profoundly changed her thinking or work. Similarly, another participant said that she would introduce changes to practice in "subtle ways" rather than adopting new ideas wholesale. At the same time, certain CPD events could have a long-term impact on practice. A senior social worker recalled that "for me, a big change factor would have been a mediation course I did way back at the beginning of my career and I still find I'm putting things into practice from it from time to time".

A few participants also acknowledged that while they were enthusiastic about certain courses that they had taken, this was not necessarily translated into practice because "other things take over":

> "I think sometimes I'll come away from a course and feel really energised, and think 'Yeah, I can do that' and be really attuned to those particular issues. But then maybe other things take over, but I think it's always there in the back of your mind [what you learned from the course]. And then sometimes, when you are busy maybe, you go back to old ways of doing things. But I've started much more now – I'm eight years' qualified – I've started to refer to resources, dipped into things that I wouldn't have done before, like handouts and stuff that you get. I've dipped into things when I'm wondering 'What will I do with this family?'. I definitely think that CPD has changed my practice and improved my practice. I hope it has anyway."

As these comments suggest, it is difficult to assess the *impact* of CPD on practice: enthusiasm for a course alone will not change practice, but, at the same time, practitioners may return to certain ideas or resources at a future date.

Future continuing professional development

In the final section, we will report of what types of CPD social workers want and the form it should take, and address the difficult question of who should pay for CPD.

Course content

IASW members were asked in the online survey to indicate the areas in which they would like to undertake CPD; their responses are set out in Table 3.11. Child protection was the most popular choice (44%), followed by research and evidence-based practice (43%), family therapy (42%), mental health (41%) and staff supervision (40%). There was also a clear interest in the legal aspects of their role, with 39% opting for legal issues/concern and 39% selecting family law. Rehabilitation, working with offenders and juvenile justice were the three least popular choices – this may have been a reflection of the under-representation of the probation service in our sample.

Preferred form of continuing professional development

Survey respondents were also asked how they would prefer to undertake CPD (see Table 3.12). The findings indicate a willingness to undertake CPD in different forms, though the majority preferred relatively short-term undertakings, including short courses/workshops (91%), followed by conferences, seminars and professional presentations (78%). Nonetheless, HE courses also featured strongly, with 58% expressing an interest. These are (arguably) the more conventional learning formats, based on a teacher–student relationship, whereas less familiar formats (such as work-based research) featured less strongly.

Course delivery

While just over half of survey respondents prefer courses to be delivered face to face, there was also support for blended courses that combine online and face-to-face interaction (see Table 3.13). Very few wanted courses to be delivered exclusively online.

Table 3.11: Continuing professional development needs

	Frequency	Per cent
Child protection	117	44
Research and evidence-based practice	114	43
Family therapy	113	42
Mental health	110	41
Staff supervision	106	40
Family law	104	39
Legal issues/concerns	104	39
Addiction/substance abuse	93	35
Stress management	84	32
General counselling	84	32
Relationship counselling	82	31
Domestic violence	76	29
Psychotherapy	74	28
Disability services	69	26
Adolescent services	69	26
Management and administration	69	26
Sexual offenders	68	26
New technology	52	20
Sexual counselling and education	52	20
Adoption and fostering	48	18
Care for older persons	46	17
Health counselling – general	46	17
Palliative care	45	17
Community development	42	16
Rehabilitation	39	15
Working with offenders	39	15
Juvenile justice	28	11
Other	19	7

Notes: Based on 267 respondents: non-response (15). Multiple response question; therefore, total may be greater than 100%.

Table 3.12: Preferred form of continuing professional development

	Frequency	*Per cent*
Short courses/workshops	241	91
Conferences, seminars and professional presentations	207	78
Certified higher education course (eg postgraduate diploma)	154	58
Self-directed learning (eg reading books, articles, etc)	135	51
Supervision	114	43
Peer support group	115	43
Work-based research projects	88	33
Contributing to professional knowledge (eg writing articles, conducting workshops)	87	33
Mentoring	71	27
Other	7	3

Note: Based on 266 responses: non-response (16).

Table 3.13: Course delivery

	Face-to-face	*Online*	*Blended*	*No preference*	*Number of responses*
HE courses	54%	2%	39%	5%	257
Other professionally relevant courses	53%	2%	40%	5%	241

Who should pay for continuing professional development?

When asked who should pay for CPD, 33% of survey respondents said that it should be the employer, 3% said that it should be the participant themselves, but the largest group (59%) indicated that costs should be shared between the employer and participant. Some elaborated on their answer, explaining that payment of fees depended on the type of CPD and whether it was directly related to work:

> "Depending on the course, I think the person themselves should pay some expenses if it's a big course that will be useful to the person in other workplaces in the future. For smaller courses more specific to the particular workplace at that point in time, I think the employer should pay the whole cost."

> "If it is something an employer would like me to do, they should pay the cost. If it is something I am personally interested in, then I would pay the cost."

> "Depending on the expense, if the CPD is a considerable amount of expense and specialised, I think a contribution from the participant should be expected. Training specific to on-the-job issues, such as risk management, communication, current issues etc, should be paid by the employer."

Others pointed out that responsibility for payment would depend on how much training the social worker wanted to undertake, how long they had worked for the organisation and how long they planned to stay. For example, one respondent suggested that if the employer paid all training costs, the social worker should agree to remain with the employer for a specific period of time. There was also recognition that in the current financial climate it would be difficult for employers to shoulder the full cost, with one respondent suggesting that CORU should fund some courses "if we are to have to pay them such huge fees". Another social worker noted that while in principle she thought that the employer should pay, in practice, this was no longer possible:

> "I really feel that the employer is responsible for paying for CPD activities, but I understand that they do not have the budget for it and that is why I have always paid for my own if my salary allows it. I have had to turn down the opportunity of attending due to not having enough money."

The question of who should fund CPD will assume added significance over the next few years as CPD becomes a mandatory requirement for the renewal of registration with the Social Work Registration Board.

Conclusion

Our research with members of the IASW suggests that a wide range of CPD activities – both formal and informal – are undertaken by Irish social workers. In-service training appears to be almost universally available, though concerns were expressed about the variability in quality of these courses. A surprisingly high proportion of respondents (41%) had completed, or were currently undertaking, post-qualification HE courses. The IASW plays a significant role in providing short courses and workshops, as do 70 other organisations in the voluntary, statutory and private sectors. Informal and in-house CPD generally took the form of peer review/consultation groups, journal clubs, supervision and practice teaching. The motivations for undertaking CPD reported in the research were similar to those indentified in the international literature (see Chapter One). Social workers regarded it as a means of keeping abreast of changes within the profession, preparing for a new role and reflecting on their own practice. CPD, in its various forms, was also seen as a means of supporting the practitioner by providing opportunities for networking and peer consultation.

Some of the research findings raised issues about the nature of the social work profession in Ireland. As noted earlier, the focus on counselling and therapy courses may be indicative of a rather individualistic approach to practice (as noted by Skehill, 1999). Most interview participants saw counselling skills as important as they often worked with people who had experienced adversity in their lives. At the same time, a few participants pointed out that social work practice was moving away from therapeutic approaches and becoming more bureaucratic and concerned with *organising* services for clients. Clearly, it is not possible to make generalisations based on a small interview sample, but this is an issue that warrants further research. The nature and development of the social work profession in other countries, particularly the UK, has been the subject of heated debate, as outlined in Chapter Two. Given the introduction of regulation and the policy changes of recent years, a similar debate within Irish social work would be timely.

Overall, the social workers who participated in this research were committed to ongoing learning, in one form or other. At the same time, they identified a number of barriers to participation, most notably, the lack of funding for external courses, workload and time constraints, the location of courses, and limited course choice. These issues are explored in Chapter Four.

Notes

[1] CORU is a multi-profession regulatory body that was set up under the Health and Social Care Professionals Act 2005. It is an umbrella body, made up of the Health and Social Care Professionals Council and 12 registration boards, one for each of the professions named in the Act, including social work. The word CORU is not an abbreviation, it 'originates from an Irish word, 'cóir' meaning fair, just and proper' (CORU, 2013).

[2] IASW members who were students or retired were not included in the survey as a significant number of questions would not have applied to them.

[3] A workforce survey carried out by the National Social Work Qualifications Board (NSWQB, 2006: 22) reported that the number of male social workers employed in 2005 was 388 (16.8% of the workforce) compared with 1,928 (83.2%) female social workers.

[4] Again, this is broadly in line with the NSWQB (2006: 23–4) workforce survey, which reported that the largest proportion of practitioners (837; 36.2%) were in the 26–35 age bracket. This was followed by the 36–45 (595; 25.8%) and 45–55 (572; 24.8%) age groups. However, while those in the 56–64 age range make up only 6.8% of the workforce in 2005, they made up 15.6% of our sample.

[5] The 2005 NSWQB survey also found that the majority of social work posts were full-time and permanent, although over 17% of posts were filled by non-permanent contracts (NSWQB, 2006: 2).

[6] There are 14 Institutes of Technology in Ireland providing HE.

[7] A further 16% of respondents did not specify their course level.

[8] Student social workers on professional programmes are assigned to work with social work practitioners, who (in this capacity) are referred to as practice teachers. The role of the practice teacher is to provide practice-based learning opportunities for the student within his/her agency.

FOUR

Barriers to participation

Over the last decade, continuing professional development (CPD) has come to be seen as an essential part of the professional life of social workers. Regulatory bodies have made it a condition for maintaining registration while professional associations routinely promote it among their members. Policymakers claim that CPD has the potential to increase rates of recruitment and retention, boost the flagging morale of the workforce, and improve services to clients. To meet the challenges of contemporary social work, practitioners are expected to constantly upskill. However, despite the current enthusiasm for CPD, international reports suggest that practitioners continue to face significant barriers to participation. In this chapter, we will consider the existing literature, and present the findings of our own research with Irish social workers. The research, as already noted in Chapter Three, was based on an online survey of members of the Irish Association of Social Workers (IASW), followed by a focus group and interviews with 20 practitioners. Our findings suggest that it has become more difficult for practitioners to access CPD over the last few years. Ironically, a reduction in employer support for CPD has coincided with the setting up of the regulatory body, CORU,[1] which is currently putting in place a system of regulation whereby social workers will be required to undertake CPD in order to maintain their registration.

Barriers to participation: previous research

A major component of CPD in the UK has been the post-qualifying (PQ) awards (see Higham, 2009). However, take-up of PQ courses in England has been lower than expected while the drop-out rate is surprisingly high: in some cases, up to 33% of entrants (General Social Care Council, 2010: 8). The Social Work Task Force (SWTF, 2010: 119) reported that the numbers going on courses leading to PQ awards have been affected by workload pressures and difficulties around arranging staff cover. Those attending training knew that they would be putting additional pressures on colleagues. Moreover, social workers felt conflicted between their responsibility to undertake CPD and their more immediate responsibility to their clients. Difficulties in freeing social workers to attend courses were seen to be symptomatic of much wider failures in the system:

> Social work lacks shared understanding of the overall direction, shape and content of its programme of professional development. The current position is a recipe for inconsistency, confusion and poor practice. It is bad for retaining people in social work and for the status of the profession. We need more employing organisations ready to support ongoing training and learning (as well as initial training), in support of a profession with a much clearer sense of what career long development should mean. (SWTF, 2009: 38)

Barriers to participation and learning are also raised in Lord Laming's (2009: 54) review of the child protection system in England. Like the SWTF, Laming notes that there have been shortfalls in CPD and PQ training for social workers, together with reticence from employers to release and sponsor staff to take up such opportunities. Moreover, there is no clear link between CPD and career progression and this impacts upon staff morale and their motivation to remain in post and develop their careers. As a first step, Laming recommends that the relevant government department introduce a 'practice-focused children's social work postgraduate qualification' to be funded centrally and with protected study time made available.

Doel et al (2008) indentify the factors that both support and hinder PQ study, based on a survey and focus groups with past and current candidates for PQ awards in England. Lack of time was the most frequently mentioned hindrance, followed by organisational issues/workload pressures and personal commitments. Many candidates reported that a lack of awareness of the PQ world was a hindrance, especially for those working in non-social work settings. For some respondents, the structure and content of the PQ programme was also seen as problematic. Those who felt that course content was a hindering factor unanimously cited a lack of relevance to day-to-day work as the primary concern. Other factors that hinder post-qualifying study included: lack of support and quality of the mentor; lack of motivation; poor information about courses; uninspiring course content and difficulties accessing resources such as library materials (Doel et al, 2008: 562). In some cases, there was also a belief that it was more difficult for people who had not had recent experience of social work education, 'not just because it was difficult "to get back on the bike" but because the bike itself had changed fundamentally' (Doel et al, 2008: 562).

The difficulties that some social workers experience on returning to education, and their antipathy towards certain aspects of the PQ awards, have been explored through a series of case studies of particular courses. Keville (2002) argues that the high drop-out rate from Part 1 of the PQ award in social work (PQ1) is partly due to a lack of confidence in study skills. Her research on a PQ1 programme provided through the South and West London and Surrey (SAWLAS) partnership suggests that social workers who had not studied for a number of years found it hard to identify the theories, research and values underpinning their work, even though they had kept up to date with the legal and policy context of their work. They were also less likely to be familiar with the reflective and competence-based approaches to learning in PQ programmes, which may not have been taught when they qualified. Keville (2002: 36) concludes that 'without a firm foundation in approaches to learning, what might have begun as lack of confidence in study skills had for some students led to a high level of anxiety, which prevented them completing the PQ1'.

Students' attitudes and anxieties were also explored in an ethnographic study carried out by Kroll (2004) with a group of social workers enrolled on a PQ childcare course. She found that those who had elected to come on the course were positive and optimistic, though apprehensive about the amount of work that would be required. However, others on the course 'had clearly been pressurised into coming and were generally more wary, defensive and occasionally hostile' (Kroll, 2004: 656). In addition, the reflective, holistic approach used in the course could be quite challenging for some participants because it encouraged them to re-examine their practice and their own feelings; it was also quite different to the competence-led approach that is a feature of much social work education and practice:

> We knew that, by giving participants thinking space around their practice, this may force them to confront some of the powerful mixture of feelings evoked by their work and threaten some of their well organised defences against anxiety.... In addition our process-focused, holistic approach might challenge a number of cultural norms within work settings. These include an emphasis on 'doing' rather than 'being', encouraged by the competence-led approach which now characterises social work education. (Kroll, 2004: 657)

Kroll's study suggests that there may be significant 'barriers to learning', particularly if social workers feel that they have been pressurised into undertaking a course and have not been provided with sufficient organisational support in terms of study leave, staff cover and resources. Moreover, the objectives of PQ study may be at odds with social work practice:

> What is revealed is a fundamental tension ... between on the one hand, the employers' desire for staff to develop their practice and, on the other, fear of the impact of new ways of thinking on compliance, outcomes and targets. (Kroll, 2004: 654)

A further tension arises, according to Postle et al (2002), when generic approaches to social work education appear to be irrelevant in the face of increasingly specialised and fragmented social work practice. This can lead to impatience and dissatisfaction with what participants perceive as irrelevant knowledge, leading to their disengagement from the learning process. The balance of generic versus specialist course provision is difficult to achieve and depends, the authors argue, on the quality of dialogue between staff delivering the course and course candidates (Postle et al, 2002: 161).

While the focus of the research discussed so far has been on the PQ awards, other studies have considered CPD more generally, often reaching similar conclusions regarding the barriers to participation. In the discussion paper *Continuing professional development for the social services workforce in Scotland* (Skinner, 2005: 12), Skinner raises a number of concerns in relation to access. She notes that the cost of staff release for training is a significant factor in a service where staff who are not present 'on the shop floor' must be replaced, and there is an emerging difficulty in finding the staff with whom to replace those away on training. There were variations in levels of access to CPD, Skinner notes, not only from one organisation to another, but also from one staff group to another in the same organisation. In addition, there are some differences in the funding of CPD, as private social services organisations are not funded for their development activities in the way that voluntary and statutory organisations are.

Research undertaken in other countries reports similar barriers to participation. A study commissioned by the Victoria branch of the Australian Association of Social Workers (AASW) found that the main barriers to attending continuing professional education (CPE) programmes were cost, lack of time and the physical distance to travel to these events (Boulet et al, 2007; Vurtel, 2008). Some respondents also reported that the courses on offer were not relevant to their work or to their specific field of interest. The reasons for the perceived lack of relevance varied, reflecting the conflicting needs or perspectives of the wide range of members. While some social workers reported that they were not long out of university and so did not feel the need for further education; others, who were very experienced and near the end of their careers, found CPE too basic. In addition, CPE programmes were seen as repetitive, with not enough new content being provided. A lack of incentives was another potential barrier: CPE was perceived to be largely irrelevant to career development. Research with AASW members in the Northern Territory again highlighted the difficulties experienced by those working in remote areas in accessing CPE and quality professional supervision (West et al, 2009).

Barriers to participation in other professions

Similar barriers to participation in CPD have been identified through research in the nursing and teaching professions. In Ireland, a survey conducted by the National Council for the Professional Development of Nursing and Midwifery (2004: 34) found the following 'inhibitors' to CPD: family/home commitments; financial constraints; availability of appropriate education; accessibility of and ability to attend further education; and lack of organisational support. Provision of access to and uptake of CPD activities by respondents located in rural areas of Ireland was reported to be significantly lower than that of staff working in towns or cities. In addition, respondents noted that there was little time to participate in or instigate formal ward-based learning due to the pace of clinical life, high staff turnover and poor skill mix. Other problems such as professional jealousy and bullying were described in interviews. In some instances, there was a degree of hostility towards individuals who had chosen to undertake further academic study:

> ward staff felt threatened by new knowledge and would resist any attempt to explore new practices or 'buy in' to any change in practice which might be instigated by a fellow colleague who had undertaken a degree or higher education. (National Council for the Professional Development of Nursing and Midwifery, 2004: 26)

Similarly, a study on continuing education for nurses employed by the Western Health Board (McCarthy and Evans, 2003) found that the majority of participants had experienced difficulties in applying new skills or changes to their work environment following the completion of their courses. Resistance to change by staff, managers and medical staff was the most common barrier reported in the research, followed by lack of resources. In a small number of cases, professional resentment and a lack of interest from colleagues was also noted.

Hustler et al (2003: 146–7) considered the factors that facilitate and inhibit participation as part of a wider study of teachers' perceptions of CPD in England. Interestingly, most teachers felt that senior management and school policy were the most likely to *facilitate* access to CPD (although this notion of 'facilitate' can be variously interpreted), while financial cost and workload were the most likely causes of non-participation. However, the authors also note that there are strong indications that some teachers themselves were reluctant to leave their classrooms, either because they felt that supply staff were not of a high enough quality, or because they simply felt that their own presence in the classroom was more important. Similar findings emerged in other studies regarding how personal circumstances, distance and timing made it difficult for many teachers to undertake CPD.

Barriers to participation in social work continuing professional development in Ireland

As part of a wider study of CPD among Irish social workers (outlined in Chapter Three), we sought to identify the barriers to participation that practitioners faced. The research was based on an online survey of members of the IASW. At our request, the association emailed 750 of its members to inform them of the research and to invite them to complete the questionnaire, which could be accessed through a web link. In total, 282 questionnaires were completed during June/July 2011, a response rate of 38%. In addition, semi-structured interviews were held with 16 IASW members, while a further four members participated in a focus group. Further details on the methodology and the research participants are outlined in Chapter Three.

Survey findings

The majority of respondents to the survey (83%) reported having experienced barriers to participation in CPD. Lack of time and the cost of courses were the two main issues identified (see Table 4.1). In addition, nearly half (47%) of respondents reported that a lack of management support or recognition was either a major or significant barrier, though a sizeable minority (29%) said that it was not a barrier. Personal and family commitments were seen to be a major or significant barrier in 27% of cases, and a minor barrier in a further 31%. Interestingly, the percentage who said that their commitments were a major/significant barrier was slightly higher for men than for women (26% compared with 32%, respectively). In terms of age range, those in the 36–45 category were the most likely to see personal and family commitments as a major/significant barrier (51%). The issue of personal and family commitments is, of course, linked to difficulties in getting leave from work: course attendance may have to be taken out of annual leave and study undertaken in one's own spare time. This could be off-putting, particularly for those with families, as one respondent pointed out:

> "In the past, the HSE [Health Service Executive] gave you the time to attend conferences – this is becoming an issue on some teams and as I have a young family, I am reluctant to give up my own time for conferences etc."

As Table 4.1 indicates, the timing and location of courses was also a major or significant barrier to participation according to approximately one third of respondents. Several noted that courses of specific interest to them were held in Dublin, making it difficult for them to attend. On a more positive note, most respondents reported that 'a lack of support from co-workers' was not a barrier. In addition, a lack of interesting or relevant courses was not, in most cases, seen as a significant problem.

Interviews and focus group

The barriers to participation were explored in more detail through the interviews and focus group. The main themes emerging from these discussions are outlined in the following.

Funding for courses

One of the main barriers, mentioned by almost all interview and focus group participants, was the lack of funding to undertake training. Some social workers reported that there was now no funding available to pay for their attendance at external courses; others had access to very limited training budgets, which generally covered short training events of up to one or two days. In the current climate of austerity, various arrangements were devised in order to meet course costs, for example,

Table 4.1: Barriers to participation

	Major barrier	Significant barrier	Minor barrier	Not a barrier	Number of responses to this question
Cost of programmes/ courses	37%	42%	14%	7%	255
Lack of time	33%	38%	18%	11%	257
Insufficient management recognition/support for CPD	15%	32%	23%	29%	248
Not available in a convenient location	13%	20%	29%	39%	246
Not available at a convenient time	11%	21%	31%	37%	248
Lack of incentives to undertake CPD	11%	21%	31%	38%	234
Lack of recognition for career development	11%	20%	21%	48%	240
Personal and/or family obligations	11%	16%	31%	42%	252
No courses available relevant to my work	7%	16%	26%	51%	245
No courses available in which I am interested	2%	12%	20%	66%	245
Lack of support from co-workers	1%	7%	20%	72%	237

the employer pays for the course fee but the attendee pays for travel and subsistence (or vice versa), or the course fee is shared between them. In one case, social workers were required to make their application for funding *after* attending an event, with no guarantee of how much (if anything) they would receive back from the employer. Difficulties also arose when several members of the same team requested support for a particular conference or course but funding was only available for one or two people to attend. In these situations, a decision was sometimes reached by means of a random selection, or by negotiation between the staff and management. Overall, the arrangements for providing funding for social workers to attend external courses appeared to be ad hoc and the amount of funding was extremely limited. Several participants compared this with the comparatively generous funding of previous years (before the recession), when some or all fees for PQ education were paid for by the employer.

With the cutbacks in funding for CPD, social workers now had to pay course fees themselves. However, this was an expense that they were finding increasingly difficult to afford in the face of wage cuts, the introduction of registration fees and personal circumstances (eg a young family). Consequently, social workers are becoming more selective about the courses that they attend, often choosing those that are more affordable or of particular relevance to their practice. As one social worker pointed out:

> "Years ago, you could go and do [a course], and it wasn't a big deal if it wasn't overly relevant because there were elements that would be transferable. Whereas now, you need to think long and hard about if I'm going to give up my time, if I'm going to give up my finances, how is it going to affect my work here, or benefit it or whatever?"

Workload and time constraints

Difficulty in getting time off work to attend courses was seen as another major obstacle to participation. Heavy workloads and staff shortages mean that it is increasingly difficult to arrange for staff cover; those attending courses are generally expected to make up the time when they return. Whereas some participants had been able to undertake diploma or certificate courses in the past, they were now lucky if they got time off to attend courses of more than one day. As one participant told us:

> "You can apply, but it is difficult. You have to justify why do I need this training, and does this training benefit the organisation. It can put me off. You really have to fight your corner. I have to think beforehand of all the points I will make if I want to attend a training course. You might be able to get a half a day, if it's something like a seminar. Or maybe a day. But anything more than a day, it's really hard to get."

A team leader, who had worked in child protection in the HSE, painted an even bleaker picture of workload pressures within the sector, and the implications for professional development:

> "The main barrier when I worked at the HSE was the workload. Since I've left, which is about a year ago, I've seen

> the workloads of my previous colleagues increase massively. And workloads were too high before I left. So I think that when people are working under that pressure constantly, with such massive responsibility, it [CPD] is bound to get lost. At the end of the day, the safety and protection of the child is going to be more important than your CPD. And your name is on a file if something happens to that child. And very few people would feel that the HSE would stand by them if something was to happen."

As this quotation suggests, social workers (and management) sometimes see themselves as being presented with rather stark choices, in this instance, between "the safety and protection of the child" and time off to undertake CPD. Interestingly, when talking about the process of applying for time off for CPD, social workers often described it in terms of a conflict: "it's nearly a *battle* to get the time off"; "we were *fighting* to do stuff"; "you really have to *fight* your corner"; "it was a constant *battle*"; "you will have to *argue* for it"; and so on. Not surprisingly, the difficulties in getting time off work can lead to tensions between staff and management. Indeed, one respondent claimed that she no longer asks for time off because she knows that her request will be turned down and she will be aggrieved at the refusal.

Heavy workloads may also inhibit the type of reflective 'on-the-job' learning advocated by the Munro review of child protection in England (Munro, 2011), discussed in Chapter Two. A few interviewees noted that attending courses provided them with the time and space to reflect on their practice – something that was almost completely absent from their day-to-day work. As one team leader told us:

> "When I worked in [name of organisation], I didn't have time to do case notes for months and months…. So then to actually try to learn something new, and look at your practice, and reflect on what you are doing, it's just not there, you know."

Whether or not learning in the workplace was also inhibited by the type of 'compliance' culture identified by the Munro review (see Chapter Two) was a question beyond the scope of the current study. It certainly warrants further investigation in the future.

Management support

Lack of management support, as previous research has shown, is a significant barrier to participation. Our research suggests that there can be considerable variations, both within and between organisations. While some managers were supportive of CPD, others were not. There appeared to be little sense of a shared vision for CPD, leading to inconsistencies across different services. Clearly, much depended on the resources (in terms funding and staff) that were available to managers, but the manager's own views on the value of CPD also played a role, as one newly qualified social worker explained:

> "Part of it comes down to your team leader or your boss or your superior in your organisation. I suppose in my first proper social work job, that was an issue. [CPD] was not seen as being needed at all. I think officially I was allowed, I think, maybe two or three days in the whole year to do training and training was very much you go on a day course and that's it. So it was a constant battle to try and, I suppose, reframe my boss's mind about what CPD was, because she didn't appear to understand what it was, so that was really frustrating. That was a huge barrier in my first year. But my last two bosses have been very supportive and understanding of what professional development is and understand that it comes in many different guises and forms, and that if I'm happy in my work, I will do my work well and I'll have more investment in it ... I think very much in the initial stages, for a new social worker anyway, it's very much your team leader, your boss, how they see social work, and how they see it can define how easy or hard it is to engage in professional development."

In some instances, social workers felt that while their immediate managers were supportive of CPD, they were constrained by organisational policy and financial cutbacks. So, while a team leader might be able to sanction the occasional training or study day (often on an 'informal' basis) for staff, it was generally not within their power to provide more comprehensive support, either in terms of funding or time off. Certainly, the managers whom we interviewed saw themselves in this light – as providing as much support for their staff to go on training as they could, but under tight budgetary and workload restrictions.

The lack of organisational support for CPD was seen as short-sighted and ultimately damaging to the profession. However, a few respondents had mixed feelings: while they valued CPD, they believed that scarce resources should be channelled towards service users. As one child protection social worker explained:

> "If we look for additional training, [the funding for that] has to come out of the budget for this department. And then it's looked at as 'Is it a half-day's training for a social worker or is it an assessment for a child?'. And you are balancing that then. Is it a parenting capacity assessment, is it play therapy or is it a half-day training for the staff? And what could you say to the parent 'We're having a half-day training so your child will have to wait for play therapy'? Parents wouldn't be too happy and I think we wouldn't be too happy either. So again it's that balance and trying to agree where the priorities are."

Similarly, another respondent – who worked with families – pointed out that:

> "To be fair to the HSE management, they are not that concerned about me wanting to go on a course when there are children on a waiting list, queuing to get into services. So I can kind of understand where they are coming from, but that doesn't leave you much in the way of options if you want to go and do something."

A few participants commented that their managers will only provide funding and time off for courses that are seen to be directly relevant to their current work. These social workers had to justify how the training would benefit their practice and (in some instances) their team. However, this raised questions as to what constitutes 'relevant' training, with differences of opinion emerging between staff and management. Again, much depended on the individual manager. One acting unit manager, for example, told us that he would actively "encourage staff to go on training that isn't necessarily related only to the work we do [child sexual abuse assessment] so that they don't feel that they're getting pigeon-holed into one area". Similarly, another participant questioned whether a narrow focus on relevance could limit the scope of social work education and practice.

Location of courses

The location of courses was identified as a significant barrier to participation for about half of the interview/focus group participants, most of whom lived in the south of the country (Kerry, Cork, Waterford). Many of the courses in which they were interested were being held in Dublin city, a journey of between three to five hours. There was a degree of frustration at what was perceived as the Dublin-centric focus of social work education, as one child protection worker made clear:

> "The difficulty for me is that an awful lot of training is Dublin-based. Stuff that you think you could learn something from, or that sounds really interesting, or you're working with a particular case and you might like more information about it. But a lot of that training is Dublin-based, which makes it very inaccessible.... Cost and location are the two big things. [When a course is announced,] people are always saying 'Where is it?'. And it will be Dublin. And everyone will say 'Oh no, not Dublin again'."

The IASW came in for a degree of criticism in this regard. While the training events provided by the association were seen as interesting and affordable, they were frequently held in Dublin, making it difficult for those in other counties to attend. Several respondents were aggrieved that their professional association, to which they pay an annual fee, focuses so much of its energies on one geographic area, particularly at a time when members are struggling to get time off work to attend courses. In response to this situation, some IASW members in the regions have set up subgroups that meet regularly and provide courses locally.

Course provision and content

One of the issues raised in the interviews was that there are not enough courses being run for social workers, either by higher education institutions or employers. For social workers who had trained or worked overseas, this was seen as a major weakness within the profession in Ireland. One participant, for example, pointed out that there is a "complete dearth of education at the post-qualifying level", and that social workers may have to undertake courses that are not the most appropriate to their needs because of "the complete lack of alternatives".

She went on to argue that the universities "really need to step up in terms of the courses they offer" and also to provide more affordable options. Another participant noted that there were regional variations in the provision of HSE in-service training – not all areas had training units. The lack of courses was seen to be particularly problematic given the imminent introduction of a CPD framework by CORU, under which all social workers will be required to undertake CPD in order to maintain their registration.

Other problems identified in the interviews and focus group related to course content. While participants were generally satisfied with the higher education courses they had taken, they were critical of certain aspects of in-service training, particularly that provided by the HSE. Courses were described as being too basic or generic, consisting of introductions or overviews of particular topics, which did not lead to more advanced levels. In some cases, the training was designed for a number of different professions and so might have little or no relevance to social work. For example, one participant told us:

> "I work in the HSE and there's nothing appropriate to social workers as far as I can see. I mean, where I am, it would be first aid, and it would be medical things. Some of the [training] that's put on is through the nursing department, so I can go to it but it's not really appropriate to me … it's very clinically led as opposed to socially led."

In addition, the programme of events was repetitive – the same courses were provided each year, with little or no new material. When new training was provided, it was generally concerned with the latest policy initiative, such as the new *Children first* guidelines. Participants in the focus group also felt that the HSE courses were not sufficiently rigorous; they did not involve assessment or provide accredited awards. The only requirement was that participants attend:

> "That's where I have an issue with the HSE [courses]. You can go and collect CPD points, but like – what did I learn? You've got this certificate that shows you physically turned up; I sat in a seat for the day; I didn't hear anything maybe; but I sat in a seat for seven and a half hours. And they gave me a certificate at the end for CPD. In terms of the integrity of the training, the integrity of yourself, that's not benefiting anyone. It's like jobs for the boys in CPD. But it's not doing the profession any good. It's a tick-box

procedure from what I can see. And I question the relevance and the value of it, in that sense."

Lack of incentives

The interviews suggest that there are very few incentives, in terms of pay or career progression, for social workers to undertake CPD. Social workers do not generally receive a salary increase if they undertake additional training, as is the case in some other professions, including teaching. This is seen as particularly onerous, given the cost (in time and money) of undertaking PQ study:

> "Another thing is that you might give up time and money, and maybe get another qualification, but there is no financial recognition from within the HSE. If you look at teaching, if you get a certain degree or attain certain skills, there is a reward for it. But here, you can go on and do a Masters or a PhD or whatever but there won't be any tangible recognition of it."

In addition, there did not appear to be any clear connection between CPD and promotion. One child protection social worker, for example, told us that her colleague had undertaken several PQ courses but that this was not in any way acknowledged or rewarded by management. On the other hand, another participant pointed out that her manager had been promoted to that position without ever having undertaken management training. It would appear that promotion is not dependent on additional qualifications. Overall, respondents felt that the link between career progression and CPD was at best tenuous, and that there were no real incentives for them to undertake CPD. Indeed, one child protection worker wryly noted that in her organisation, gaining additional qualifications would probably be frowned upon as it would necessitate time off from work.

The social workers whom we interviewed did not necessarily see this lack of incentives as being a barrier to participation – they were all highly motivated and committed to professional development already. However, it could be argued that the lack of incentives is symptomatic of the undervaluing of CPD within the social work profession.

Lack of motivation

A few participants pointed out that not *all* social workers are committed to CPD. In some instances, social workers may regard their qualifying course as the end point of their education, and are consequently reluctant to undertake further training. One childcare manager, for example, commented that "some people just plodded along and did their own thing, and maybe some of them could have done with a bit of retraining". With the introduction of a regulatory system, however, all social workers will be required to undertake CPD in order to maintain their registration.

Lone practitioners

Most of those whom we interviewed worked either for the HSE or in hospitals, and they were often part of teams. A few others worked as lone practitioners for organisations that employed comparatively few social workers, for example, county councils. While the obstacles to participation encountered by these staff were much the same as those in the HSE, there were a number of additional challenges. Because so few social workers were employed by these organisations, in-house training was not tailored to their needs. One participant pointed out that there was little point in her attending in-service training because it was not relevant to social work. Her only option was to attend external courses, but she had difficulty in getting funding and time off work, particularly as there was no one to provide cover for her while she was away. From accounts provided by three interviewees, there appeared to be little or no culture of CPD within the organisations for which they worked. They suggested that social workers employed by the HSE were in a stronger position because there was at least an *expectation* that staff in the health service undertake CPD, however limited that might be in practice. As one participant pointed out:

> "It depends on the organisation that you are in. I suppose my organisation isn't the best for that, their sense of priority for [CPD] would be basically non-existent.... Whereas when I was working in a hospital, you had set training dates, there was a set budget, and it was just accepted that as a social worker you should be engaging in training and continuing professional development. Whereas the attitude in this organisation is: 'Just go and do your work and leave us alone'. That's pretty much it. With the setting up of

CORU, we, as social workers, could now say that we have registration and we have to do this training. But I think that if they [CORU] make it really strict, the organisation will just see us as more trouble than we are worth and get rid of the social workers from the organisation. In an organisation like this, we have a function and purpose, but really, do they care if we are there or not? It's debatable."

In addition, social workers who work on their own have limited access to informal CPD, such as journal clubs or peer support groups, and they can feel very isolated in their role. Indeed, in some cases, they do not have access to regular supervision because there is no one on site to provide it (see Chapter Five).

Continuing professional development in the context of regulation

With the setting up of the regulatory body, CORU, it is envisaged that social workers will be required to undertake CPD in order to maintain their registration. Interview participants were asked for their views on this development, and how they thought it would impact on the status and provision of CPD within the social work profession. The response was largely positive. Participants believed that the new regulations would lead to a greater recognition of the value of CPD; it was also felt that managers would have to be more supportive of staff development now that it had been sanctioned by the regulatory body. As one participant pointed out:

"There will be an onus on us to do these things, that maybe have just been viewed as a luxury before, whereas now we have to do this, its part of our professional registration, so I think it will work in our favour."

At the same time, respondents were anxious that employers might not be willing to provide the necessary time and funding needed for training, they might not see this as being their responsibility. Alternatively, social workers may be expected to accumulate the necessary points through in-service training, which, as we saw earlier, not all social workers found useful. The end result may be that registrants undertake courses not because they view them as beneficial to their work or professional development, but because they have to accumulate a certain number of hours of CPD. As one team leader pointed out: "people are just going to be doing training for the sake of it and not necessarily gaining or learning anything from it". She went on to describe the reaction of her colleagues to the introduction of registration for social workers:

> "I think people were a bit panicked. I think staff on the ground were panicked about how are we going to get all these CPD [points]; and how's that going to be managed in the HSE; and are we all going to be sent on training [courses] that aren't worthwhile."

Although the framework for CPD has not yet been announced, it is interesting to note that, in the majority of cases, respondents were pessimistic about how their organisations would respond to the new requirements. There was a sense that while the CPD framework was a good idea *in theory*, the reality could be quite different because the structural barriers to participation had not been addressed.

Overcoming barriers to participation

Social workers were asked how they addressed the barriers to participation described earlier and whether they had found alternative means of accessing CPD. Some had opted for online or correspondence courses, which could be undertaken at a time and place convenient to them. In addition, it was now possible to view conferences online. However, distance learning was not suitable for everyone: one respondent told us, for example, that she lacked the self-discipline to undertake self-directed online courses. In some organisations, social workers who attend courses are expected to give a presentation on the course so that their colleagues can benefit from their attendance. Social workers were also involved in informal, peer-centred forms of CPD, such as journal clubs or peer support groups (see Chapter Three). These in-house initiatives have the advantage of being free of charge and do not require travel. Moreover, as one participant pointed out, a wide range of topics can be explored through a journal club, while peer groups provided mutual support.

Social workers are clearly finding different ways of pursuing CPD within their organisations. However, with the setting up of CORU, it was felt that a more systematic approach was needed, including ring-fenced funding for training. Several respondents suggested that discussions should be held between the main stakeholders at the national level in order to put in place a system that would support social workers to meet the new requirements. One childcare manager, for example, commented that these issues need to be addressed on a national basis; otherwise, CPD provision and uptake will become chaotic and inconsistent. Access to CPD should not be at the discretion of individual managers, with social workers having to negotiate time off on an individual basis:

> "I think it would be chaotic if it happened like that, there would be regional and local variations. This has to be looked at at a national, systemic level, otherwise you will have individuals who don't have the information, individuals who will block other people from doing stuff, there has to be a mandate, there has to be a national discussion. CORU should ask for meetings at that level – with CORU, with the National Children and Families Office, with the minister's office – and have a mandate about what the minimum baseline is going to be. Otherwise, it will be just chaotic, as we know, chaotic. And people lose out."

Conclusion

In line with previous studies on CPD, our research suggests that heavy workloads, time constraints and a lack of funding are the main barriers to participation. While these may be perennial problems, it is clear that support for CPD from employers has declined significantly over the last few years with the onset of recession and the imposition of major funding cutbacks to health and social services. Social workers who had been able to undertake PQ academic courses in previous years were now struggling to attend courses of more than two days' duration. Ironically, this has coincided with the setting up of a system of regulation whereby social workers will be required to undertake CPD in order to maintain their registration.

The reduction in employer support for CPD – particularly at the higher education level – is likely to have significant implications in terms of course provision. In Ireland, there are relatively few postgraduate higher education courses that are relevant to social work, and fewer still that are specifically designed for social workers (see Leinster, 2009). This situation is unlikely to change significantly unless practitioners are supported and encouraged to undertake PQ education. Without sufficient student numbers, it will be difficult for schools of social work to provide the wide variety of options social workers want. There may also be repercussions in terms of the long-term development of the social work profession in Ireland. On the basis of our interviews, it seems unlikely that public-sector employers would support practitioners to undertake doctoral-level studies. And yet, as Beddoe (2006: 105) has pointed out in the New Zealand context, without this kind of support, social work will remain a poorly resourced profession in terms of growing our own knowledge base.

The stipulation that CPD will be a requirement for continued registration was largely welcomed by interview and focus group participants on the grounds that it would raise the profile of CDP within the profession and (hopefully) secure greater employer support. At the same time, there were concerns that employers might regard the new requirement as the responsibility of the practitioner, or that if support is provided, it will be in the form of in-service training days. While participants found some aspects of in-service training to be helpful (see Chapter Three), they also identified a number of limitations, including the generic and repetitive nature of some of the programmes on offer. Unless the structural barriers to participation are acknowledged and addressed, opportunities for undertaking CPD in social work will remain limited under the new regulatory system.

Note

[1] As noted in Chapters Two, and Three CORU is a regulatory body that has responsibility for 12 professions, including social work. It is an umbrella body, made up of the Health and Social Care Professionals Council and 12 registration boards, one for each of the relevant professions. The word CORU is not an abbreviation, it 'originates from an Irish word, "cóir" meaning fair, just and proper' (CORU, 2013).

FIVE

Supervision

Supervision is important for social work; however, controversy often surrounds its provision. Furthermore, its function, form and content can vary between countries, contexts of practice and organisations. It is generally regarded as essential to achieving an effective social work service and is considered the most common form of continuing professional development (CPD). As previously acknowledged, supervision takes on many forms and it is experienced by many as a context where professionals meet together to examine the evidence and professional judgements of practice. It plays a pivotal role in the development and enhancement of professional practice. It can involve the provision of regenerative opportunities to enhance practice, improve performance and mediate tensions arising between competing values and sometimes contrasting cultures of practice.

In this chapter, we will consider the issues that are currently shaping supervisory practice, including an increased concern for accountability and 'risk management'. Survey data will also be used to map current supervisory practice, referencing issues of availability, frequency, content and more general issues related to practitioners' experience of supervision (for details of methodology and participants, see Chapter Three). The chapter will link the findings of our research to the findings of public inquiry reports into failures in supervision and it will deliberate on the important issues raised for supervision.

Context of supervision

A review of the literature and the results of our survey identify supervision as a complex and multifaceted activity that involves to varying degrees the examination of both process and outcome aspects of practice. Significant variables influencing the construction and delivery of supervision are located at the interface between the supervisor, supervisee and organisational culture. Frequently, it is in the context of supervision that all kinds of pressures, both internal (personal) and external (organisational, professional, service user and societal), arise. In recent years, social workers along with other professionals have been the subject of public critique, leading to what has been described as a '*crisis of trust*' in professionals. Concern about public safety and a fear of public criticism – particularly in the light of several high-profile child abuse cases – has resulted in an increased focus being placed on issues of accountability and the proper management of cases in both social work practice and supervision. According to some commentators, these developments have resulted in approaches to supervision, particularly in child protection practice, becoming overly concerned with and focused on issues related to performance measurement, case management, resource allocation and the control of risk, with a consequential lowering of emphasis on the more educational and formative elements of supervision (Hawkins and Shohet, 2000; Morrison, 2001).

Social work has grown as a profession throughout the world in the last 15–20 years and it has recently been established as a registered profession in Ireland and in the UK. Undoubtedly, supervision is recognised as an essential component in the provision of quality services. Referring specifically to the importance of supervision in social work, the Office of the Minister for Children and Youth Affairs (OMCYA, 2009: 42) in Ireland stated that 'Supervision is an essential and lifelong component of professional social work. For the protection of the public and promotion of quality service, social workers require access to formal supervision that is regular, consistent and of a high quality'. Similarly, in 2005, the Irish National Social Work Qualifications Board stated that 'Supervision is an essential and lifelong component of professional social work' (cited in Burns, 2012: 222). Moving beyond Ireland, the importance of supervision in the context of changing cultures of professional practice is further emphasised by researchers like Langer (1989), who believes that the more managed approach to social work practice popularised in recent times has served to reduce practitioners' cognitive ability on the job, thus encouraging them to resort to more automated and formulaic-type actions that can lead to what she calls 'mindlessness'. For Langer, mindlessness is the opposite of critical reflection, it entails a routine reliance on ideas and perceptions formed from habitual actions, and she contends that it is likely to encourage behaviour that is rigid and rule-governed. Conversely, behaviour that is based on mindful engagement is represented by Langer as more systematic and rule-guided. Mindfulness, Langer contends, is dependent on the availability of conditions that are essential to its practice, that is, space, time and opportunity to reflect on the process as well as content of one's work.

The work of Nakkula and Ravitch (1998) supports Langer's call for a professional practice that is more engaged and thoughtful and not overly reliant on the application of rules and regulations. They suggest that it is the provision of opportunities for the explicit articulation of ordinary, everyday acts in one's practice that allows one to become aware of the pervasiveness of habitual processes involved in professional practice. These habitual processes support mindlessness and can result in professional practice that is uncritical and, in some instances, downright dangerous, as evidenced in the reports on child protection practice by Laming (2009) and Munro (2011). Our survey results support the views expressed by Langer (1989), Nakkula and Ravitch (1998), and other commentators that supervision should help to encourage critical reflection, challenge mindless practice and support a more active and mindful engagement by practitioners in the processes of decision-making.

The importance of providing quality supervision in child protection practice has been emphasised in Ireland in the Roscommon Report (Gibbons, 2010) and in the UK by Laming (2003, 2009) and Munro (2011). Supervision is represented as important by the Office of the Minister for Children and Youth Affairs, who state that 'social workers require ongoing training, support and supervision to deliver safe and good quality service' (OMCYA, 2009: 42). However, Burns (2012), in a study carried out with child protection social workers in Ireland, found the Health Service Executive (HSE) deficient in attending to its supervision responsibilities, as laid down by national and agency policy. Social workers in our survey clearly stated the importance of supervision in terms of its contribution to their ongoing professional development and to the promotion of good-quality practice, and this was communicated clearly in the survey and in interviews. However, the survey also highlighted deficits in the quality and availability of supervision and draws attention to the need for supervision to be ongoing throughout social workers' very busy working lives.

While a variety of views, expectations, models and methods of professional supervision abound, the views of our research participants, when considered alongside related research, provide us with an important reference to progress our understanding of practitioners' experiences of and need for supervision. Furthermore, the results of our survey provide us with important information that will help us to reconfigure social work supervision and its role, purpose and function in the context of the challenges posed for social work in the 21st century. Although our survey demonstrates that the majority of respondents receive supervision in their workplaces, it also reveals contradictions, tensions and dilemmas associated with issues of supervisor availability, training and the overall quality of supervision practices. Unquestionably, participants' views and experiences of supervision are varied and quite mixed; nevertheless, our research demonstrates the impact of changing cultures and contexts of contemporary social work on supervision practice, an impact that has resulted in what many participants referred to as an increased focus in supervision on resource management, economies of scale and performance indicators.

Social work supervision: challenges and opportunities

Many writers have written about the wider social and economic changes that have impacted on social work necessitating practitioner engagement with activities that promote and facilitate ongoing and continuous professional development. Payne (2002, 2005b) concludes that considering the increased uncertainty and complexity associated with outcomes in social work practice, social work organisations are becoming increasingly bureaucratic, with a consequential growth in practice procedures and protocols developed in an effort to enhance and systematise practice. Writers have commented on the unwanted effects of these developments, where an undue focus is placed on performance management and measurement rather than on the exercise of professional judgement (Fook, 2002; Payne, 2002; Thompson, 2005, 2006; Davy and Beddoe, 2010).

Sue White (2011) is critical of developments in social work where management and economic principles are prioritised over issues of quality provision and service delivery. She has highlighted the dangers of adopting a more bureaucratic approach to social work, which she views as downplaying the type of work that has 'uncertainty' and 'ambiguity' at its core:

> The raft of [UK] government reforms, particularly the implementation of various e-enabled assessment instruments, pushes social workers towards precipitous categorisations and action. Institutional categories are pistons inside a swift disposal device. Varieties of moral judgement and the limber knowledge disseminated in handbooks provide the lubrication for the machine's efficient execution. (White, 2011: 183)

White (2011) reflects on the consequences for social workers of changes in cultures and contexts of practice. She elaborates on the resultant work pressures experienced by UK social workers in relation to the burden placed on them by ever-increasing caseloads and the requirements on them to respond efficiently to more complex practice situations:

The bald fact is that many social workers in statutory settings do not have the time to notice uncertainty in their work. They may repent at leisure after they have acted, or when mistakes become retrospectively obvious, but they go about their business nevertheless and are forced to do so by the organisational systems that are in place. (White, 2011: 183)

Supervision practice takes place in statutory settings that are busy and stressful, similar to those described by White (2011). Certainly, the working environment and cultures of practice have a direct influence on the structure, form and content of supervision practice. In a climate of practice where a more managed approach to service delivery is valued and supported, many writers have commented on the dangers of promoting supervision policies and practices that are overly concerned with adherence to rules, roles and protocols, as Payne (1994, cited in Davy and Beddoe, 2010: 81) reflects: 'the unthinking adherence to politically and bureaucratically defined roles'. Conversely, we believe that supervision must promote critical awareness and support ongoing reflection by practitioners in and on their practice so as to develop and sustain a vibrant profession of engaged, thinking professionals. Karvinen-Niinikoske (2004: 30) likewise recognises the challenges faced by social workers in attempting to respond meaningfully to changing contexts and constructions of social work. She advocates a type of supervision that supports a more dialogical and reflective encounter between the supervisor and supervisee:

Professional supervision in the changing and contingent context of professional and expert action can be seen as a way of orientation and gaining deeper understanding of our agency. It is a process of scrutinizing and reconstructing professional orientation. This orientation is constructed in the dialogue of our experiences and the meaning perspectives we hold. (Karvinen-Niinikoske, 2004: 30)

Karvinen-Niinikoske (2004: 32) emphasises the role of supervision in encouraging and supporting the reflective engagement of practitioners, where meanings and understandings may be critically examined and reconfigured:

In order to develop professional expertise in social work, supervision should help social workers to reflect and reconstruct their meaning perspectives, working orientation

and 'self-understanding' of social work. The core of meaning
perspectives lies in understanding the object of social work,
which is the everyday life and action of people and all its
complexities. (Karvinen-Niinikoske, 2004: 32)

As the literature and the results of our survey attest, social work practice
is represented and experienced as a complex, diverse and variable
activity. Davy and Beddoe (2010: 104–5) highlight the challenges posed
for social workers in the 21st century. They identify the conditions
necessary to ensure the provision of good-quality professional social
work services. They draw attention to the professional requirements of
social workers to facilitate an appropriate response in difficult situations
and circumstances. They conclude:

> Professional practice in the current practice climate of the
> 21st century is experienced as uncertain, ever changing
> and anxiety laden. To survive the practitioner requires a
> strong professional self and an ability to critically analyse
> and assess themselves in a range of diverse situations. The
> old 'truths' of practice no longer apply and professionals are
> being called upon to make rapid decisions and take action
> in ever-changing professional landscapes.

Accepting that social work, as described earlier, is a context-bound
activity requiring of practitioners the development and creation of
new and different knowledge and the application of a variety of
methods of intervention, practitioners of necessity need to be both
creative and responsive to the diverse challenges that practice presents.
Today, more than ever before, social workers are required to draw on
all their knowledge, skills and experience to respond reflexively to
many unforeseen and unpredictable events. In some instances, they
may be required to be creative and to develop new knowledge in and
for practice (Schön, 1987). Furthermore, supervisors are frequently
called upon to act as mediators and arbitrators when attempting to
reconcile the interplay between the conflicting needs and requirements
of professionals, employers and employing organisations. Furthermore,
Rath (2010), writing on teacher education, observes that a key challenge
presented for supervisors lies in their openness to valuing innovative
cognitive processes in practice and in their ability to support and mentor
practitioners to achieve greater '*agency*' over their work.

In support of Rath's (2010) call for teachers to work towards
developing greater '*agency*' over their constructions of professional

practice, writers in social work have promoted reflective supervision as a way forward in terms of cultivating practitioner engagement and promoting more innovative and creative professional practices. Karvinen–Niinikoske (2004: 38) argues that:

> Supervision may become a forum for engaging practitioners in systematic inquiry into experiences gained in professional practice. It can be seen as a way of orientation and gaining deeper understanding of our agency.... Supervision as a forum for reflection allows social workers to reflect their experiences and emotions, and through critical reflection to understand them in the wider context of work and thus to look for alternative methods of reaction, action and agency.

As previously stated, we recognise that supervision takes many forms, and balancing its main educative, supportive and management functions is not always easy or possible. Interestingly, it has emerged in our research that practitioners can at various times in their careers have a need for greater emphasis to be placed on one aspect of supervision more than others, for example, a social worker early in their career may require more administrative and case management-type supervision to equip them with the knowledge to undertake various roles and responsibilities. Our survey serves to reinforce the view that supervision practices are not influenced solely by individual and professional issues. Unquestionably, social, political, economic and organisational cultures are variables that shape the form, content and frequency of supervision.

Public inquiries: revitalising interest in social work supervision

As recent public inquiry reports demonstrate (Laming, 2009; Gibbons, 2010; Munro, 2011), social workers along with other professionals have become the subject of extraordinary public commentary and critique. Increased demands placed on services have resulted from rising public awareness of professionals and heightened expectations. A climate of increased public scrutiny has resulted in demands for greater transparency and accountability in practice. Consequentially, public service reforms have embraced principles of efficiency, value for money and professional accountability. According to Beck (1992), writing on the '*risk society*', the shift in the way we think about risk from the more traditional view that regarded risk as a predetermined uncontrolled act of God, to a more modern view that people can control and manage risk, has resulted in significant problems for all professionals, including social workers. Beck (1992, 1999) argues that changing ideologies have created even greater problems for professionals whose work is centrally involved with issues of risk and uncertainty. He links the growth in more defensive, risk-averse practice to changes in how we engage with constructions of risk. Cree and Wallace (2005: 115), picking up on the themes of risk and uncertainty, refer to the dangerousness of life in the 21st century and to its influence on social work:

> Just as we are confronted by risks at every corner, so we have come to expect that we should be protected from risk as never before. Within the field of social services there is an increased expectation that risk should be controlled so that vulnerable children and adults are protected. When social work or health agencies fail in this endeavour, the public outcry is characterised by hurt and anger. The underlying message is clear: We trusted you, and you let us down.

Accepting that social workers work in domains of increased risk and cultures of practice where there is a noticeable loss of trust in professionals, as evidenced in an ever-increasing number of public inquiries, particularly in the area of child protection, what are the challenges posed for social work? In the context of public service delivery, the challenges are represented by an increased preoccupation with public accountability, performance management and a desire on the part of organisations and governments to avoid risk. Many writers in social work believe the challenges posed by changing contexts and constructions of practice have resulted in a revitalisation of interest in supervision (Davy and Beddoe, 2010).

Thompson (2005) reflects further on the wider structural and cultural agendas that impinge on the work of social workers. As social work takes place in an organisational context, he reflects that 'the complexities of organisational life are likely to impinge a great deal on day to day practice' (Thompson, 2005: 63). Consequentially, an organisation's perception of risk and its response to it will have an influence on the construction of supervision and its delivery. Management's heightened anxiety with risk and a concern to minimise it can result, according to Cree and Wallace (2005), in an overconcentration on risk management and control. This, they believe, will inevitably result in the application of unnecessary restrictions on practitioners and in the subsequent curtailment of creativity and practice initiative – 'a real possibility in social work, as workers become afraid to show creativity and initiative, and become procedure-driven and overly concerned with self-regulation' (Cree and Wallace, 2005: 125).

Public inquiries have clearly highlighted the stressful nature of social work and they have resulted in a call for a root-and-branch review and revision of supervision practices in statutory agencies. Lord Laming (2009: 4) reflects:

> Frontline staff in each of the key services have a demanding task. Their work requires not only knowledge and skill but also determination, courage, and an ability to cope with sometimes intense conflict. This must be recognised in their training, case-loads, supervision and conditions of service and their managers must recognise that anxiety undermines good practice. Staff supervision and the assurance of good practice must become elementary requirements in each service. More should be done to ensure the well-being and confidence of the staff who undertake such an important task on behalf of us all.

While acknowledging future supervision needs, the Laming Report (2009: 31) also draws attention to the results of surveys that highlight deficits in the quality of supervision on offer that significantly impact of the provision of quality services:

> However, surveys continue to show that too many social workers do not get access to this type of supervision. As a result, they feel that their original skills are stagnating and they are not acquiring new ones. They become reluctant to think critically or creatively about the judgments, they need to make and fall back on a more mechanistic approach to their work. They can begin to question their own effectiveness and experience 'burn out' through a combination of heavy workloads and low support.

Furthermore, the Laming Report (2009: 10) proposes that more and better-quality professional and post-qualifying educational and training opportunities be made available to ensure that social workers are appropriately skilled to respond to the many challenges and complexities of child protection work:

> There are training and workforce issues to be resolved, and data systems that need to be improved to support

professionals better, but ultimately the safety of a child depends on staff having the time, knowledge and skill to understand the child or young person and their family circumstances.

The reform ambitions articulated in the UK Social Work Task Force report (SWTF, 2009: 6) incorporate the views of many of the interviewees in our survey when they recommend the development of new standards for supervision that are binding on employers: 'the importance of regular, good quality supervision, improved working conditions – with employers signing up to new standards for the support and supervision of their frontline workforce that make good practice possible'. Referring to variations in the quality of supervision on offer at all professional levels, this report recognises the pivotal role of supervisors in the supervision process. It points to the need for the provision of more and better opportunities for managers to train as supervisors and, in addition, for the provision of space and time in the working day to participate in such training.

Similarly, Munro (2011: 115) draws attention to the poor quality of supervision on offer to child protection workers in the UK, with its overemphasis on case management and performance functions to the neglect of its more supportive, developmental and educational functions. She also points to the need for the provision of more and better opportunities for supervision:

> A common experience amongst social workers is that the few supervision opportunities are dominated by a managerial need to focus on performance, for example, throughput, case closure, adhering to timescales and completion of written records. This leaves little time for thoughtful consideration of what is happening in the lives of children and their families.

The Munro (2011) report locates reflective engagement at the heart of professional development and good professional supervision. The provision of supervision, where conversation and mutual dialogue can take place, is identified as crucial. Munro (2011) underscores the contribution that the educative and supportive functions of supervision can make to developing critically engaged, analytic practitioners:

> Intuitive and analytic reasoning skills are developed in different ways, so child protection services need to

recognise the differing requirements if they are to help practitioners move from being novices to being experts on both dimensions. Analytic skills can be enhanced by formal teaching and reading. Intuitive skills are essentially derived from experience. Experience on its own, however, is not enough. It needs to be allied to reflection – time and attention given to mulling over the experience and learning from it. This is often best achieved in conversation with others, in supervision, for example, or in discussions with colleagues. (Munro, 2011: 122)

In Ireland, the *Children first* report (Department of Children and Youth Affairs, 2011) reflects the findings of UK reports, notably Laming (2009), the Social Work Task Force (SWTF, 2009) and Munro (2011). It similarly emphasises the importance of providing adequate and regular supervision to front-line workers and points to the need for the development of national policies that support the development of good supervision practices. The experiences of social workers interviewed lend their support to such a development.

What represents good-quality supervision?

Many writers have endeavoured to open up to inquiry the complex multilayered aspects of the supervisory process and to construct a framework that attempts to incorporate some of the levels and layers of complexity contained therein (Hawkins and Kadushin, 1992; Page and Wosket, 1994; Hawkins and Shohet, 2000, 2006; Morrison, 2001; Davy and Beddoe, 2010). Morrison (2001), writing on supervision in social care and social work, recognises the strains placed on practitioners in relation to the pace and pressure of change in all contexts of social work and social care. According to Morrison (2001: 1), supervision should provide the context and opportunity to examine the many challenges and difficulties of practice:

> Supervision is the helper's most important relationship. It is an integral part of the service delivery and intervention system for the users of social services.... It is also the fundamental performance management tool – the meeting point between professional and managerial systems and the bridge between the employee and their agency.

Morrison locates front-line managers in health, community, social services and justice settings as key to ensuring that practice standards are maintained at a high standard and that professional staff are given the appropriate support to ensure consistency in the delivery of best-quality practice. Furthermore, he asserts that supervision must not only take account of the roles, responsibilities and tasks associated with the work, but also acknowledge the complex and emotionally demanding nature of the profession: 'put starkly, it is not the existence of supervision per se that makes a difference; what is necessary is good supervision' (Morrison, 2001: 2). We believe that good supervision policies and practices are vital to developing a more coherent response to the criticisms highlighted in our survey and in recent public inquiries undertaken in Ireland and in the UK. However, Morrison (2001: 3), while acknowledging the current resource and fiscal challenges facing social work, warns that the role of supervision is being relegated to a position of lesser importance within organisations:

> the experience of organisations and staff is one of being stretched to the limits, by unprecedented levels of demand, rising public expectations, efficiency savings, relentless change and crisis in staff recruitment and retention. The paradox is that at the very time when supervision has never been more important to the process of change, it may also be one if its first casualties.

As we have already acknowledged, supervision has many components, not least of which is its importance in relation to the management and administration of services and professional personnel. Jones (2004) writes about the important role that supervision plays in mediating between conflicting organisational and personal concerns, 'embodying both professional and organisational concerns, supervision existed at the interface, sufficient to satisfy organisational requirements while retaining licences for the exercise and moderation of professional judgement' (Jones, 2004: 12). Differences in emphases, as represented in the various models and methods of supervision, have resulted in much debate and some controversy in determining best practice. However, writers like Jones (2004) and Morrison (2001) contend that supervision plays a vital role in mediating the conflicts that emerge between organisational goals, professional practices and good emotional support of professionals.

In a defining text, *Supervision in social work* (Kadushin, 1992), Kadushin clearly outlined the three primary functions of supervision, that is, administrative, supportive and educational. These functions have become generally recognised as the mainstay of good supervision practice. The '*administrative*' function refers to the practitioners' and supervisors' accountability to the policies, protocols, ethics and standards prescribed by organisations, legislation and regulatory bodies. The '*educative*' function refers to professional skill development and the resourcing of practitioners. The '*supportive*' function refers to the emotional support received in the relationship between the supervisor and supervisee (Davy and Beddoe, 2010: 25). Morrison (2001) builds a model of supervision that includes management, development and support functions, similar to those functions described by Kadushin (1992). However, Morrison (2001) also includes an important additional mediation function that relates to the negotiation of tensions that can arise in relation to competing interests. He concludes that organisational resource issues may claim precedence over professional concerns and that organisational mandate may pose ethical challenges for professionals, sometimes resulting in tensions and conflicts that are difficult to resolve within the supervision relationship, hence the importance of its '*mediation*' function. Furthermore, as supervision in social work is set to serve several masters and purposes all at once, that is, education, support, management and mediation, Morrison (2001) acknowledges that the supervisor's role must be to hold the various functions of supervision in tension with the achievement of stated outcomes. Commenting further on the mediating function of supervision, Coulshed and Mullender (2001: 163) conclude that it is a remarkable achievement of the social work profession that it has succeeded in combining several different competing requirements in one process:

> Because it is the norm in social work to hold these functions in a fruitful tension, the biggest shift for the newly promoted manager in field work or group care is in having to face in two directions at once – both towards the staff they are supervising to meet their support and development needs and to help them exercise judgment in their assessments and interventions, and towards their own managers, so as to meet the needs of the organization in getting the work done appropriately and managing the human resource.

Writing on contemporary social work practice, Healy (2000) also acknowledges the many competing challenges posed for practitioners as they struggle in a variety of contexts to make decisions in cases where ambiguity, conflicting interests and incompatible expectations are commonplace, and where professional judgements and decisions are frequently contested. As previously stated, in this contested professional domain, many writers claim that managerialism has come to dominate supervision practice without due regard for the needs of practitioners. Consequently, according to Thompson (2005), issues related to performance measurement and performance management have, in many instances, replaced the more educative and reflective functions of supervision. Our survey supports the belief that supervision is key to engaging social workers in the difficult exercise of addressing and redressing the many stresses and tensions contained in the work. Supervision has always been regarded as fundamental to the development and maintenance of good professional standards and conduct of behaviour in social work. Today, more than ever before, the significance of supervision needs to be restated and its importance re-established in organisational and professional policies and practice. Morrison (2001) lends his support to this view and clearly advocates the development of policies and practice protocols linked to supervision, thereby ensuring consistency and quality of standards in the delivery of supervision across diverse practice contexts. Such policies, he maintains, are essential for supervisors, whose personal and professional authority needs to be linked to an organisational mandate that assures transparency and accountability for all concerned: the organisation, service users, the public, supervisors and supervisees. He further argues for the monitoring of supervision practices and for the application of quality assurance criteria. Morrison (2001: 45) concludes that 'supervision practice is rarely monitored or audited in terms of either frequency or quality'. He supports the view that supervision needs to be clearly embedded in organisational policy and he asserts that for supervision to be effective, it should be located at the heart of all performance management processes and systems.

We support the argument that supervision should be about promoting learning and achieving improved outcomes for everyone involved. While we acknowledge that the provision of opportunities to engage in supervision is key, we also know from our research that cultures of supervision also need to be advanced by managers and supervisors in organisations. Supervision provides a necessary space where workers and supervisors together attempt to identify and reconcile the blocks to good practice in the actions of the professional or in the cultures and practices of organisations. It is generally agreed by social workers in our survey and by writers in the area (Morrison, 2001; Davy and Beddoe, 2010) that a coherent and uniform approach to supervision is required, necessitating clearly articulated supervision policies and protocols that carry rights and responsibilities for all concerned. As supervision is located at the interface of training and practice, achieving a balance between personal and organisational concerns poses challenges for all involved with its construction and delivery. It is generally accepted that when personal reflection and professional development are absent from supervision, critical reflection and the opportunity it can afford workers to consider the wider political and organisational context in which their practice is located and preformed can be lost (Phillipson, 2002). As social work is becoming even more context-bound, much of professional practice involves inventing and reconfiguring new approaches to practice. We believe that supervision can provide a training opportunity and a space where professionals are facilitated to engage in thoughtful, deliberate inquiry and assisted to reconfigure their practice in association with changing understandings and constructs of practice. As previously stated, social work can be highly emotional and involve a high level of emotional investment on the part of the practitioner. Many writers on supervision believe that when emotional issues arise in work that are not adequately addressed in supervision, there can be a considerable impact on the practitioner and on practice outcomes (Morrison, 2001; Hawkins and Shohet, 2000). Hawkins and Shohet (2000) clearly highlight the adverse effects on social workers' health and effectiveness of unspoken and unresolved emotional issues arising from the work.

In Ireland, the social work profession is expanding as a result of extensive legislation (eg the Children Act 2001). As we have previously acknowledged, the escalating stresses involved in child protection work, as represented in recent UK reports (Social Work Reform Board, 2010; SWTF, 2010), coupled with developing managerialism in statutory social service agencies, pose challenges at many different levels for the profession. As researchers and educators, it is imperative that we find ways to harness the interests and energies of professionals so as to engage them in good-quality supervision and to provide them with opportunities for relevant and constructive CPD and post-qualifying education, where the big concerns and challenges arising in practice may be examined, discussed and suitably addressed.

Experiences of supervision

The data from our survey and interviews provide a good account of participants' experiences of supervision across a wide variety of social work practice contexts, both statutory and voluntary. While some reference has been made to the views expressed by participants earlier in his chapter, this section provides a more complete summary of the findings of the survey and it also includes some additional data collected in interviews.

A high level of commitment to the process of supervision and a valuing of its contribution in terms of developing high-quality practice and helping to sustain a more engaged practitioner workforce surfaced throughout our research. As one social worker reflected at interview: "Supervision is about support, it's also about accountability, and it's also about the professional aspect of the job as well. It's vital."

A relatively inexperienced social worker in our survey emphasised the importance of case management-type supervision for early-career social workers. Reflecting on supervision, she identifies the type of supervision that she receives as almost exclusively fitting into a case management style. Ideally, she felt that supervision should include elements of case management, emotional support and education. However, she believed that when time did not allow for the provision of all three functions, the focus should be on case management. Conversely, when interviewed, a more experienced social worker placed a higher value on the developmental and educative functions of supervision:

> "[Supervision] has helped me to look into the future, you know, what I want to achieve professionally. If there are areas where I am not feeling really competent yet, the supervisor is helping me to find resources, like articles to read and other information."

A social worker working as a sole practitioner reflected on the challenges she faces in attempting to make sense of the work in a local authority setting. She highlighted her lack of confidence in undertaking responsibilities associated with the work, resulting in feelings of professional isolation. She identified the absence of support and supervision on the job, necessitating the seeking out of private supervision outside of the workplace to sustain her in the work:

> "It is challenging and the biggest challenge is that I feel insecure about what I'm doing, I don't know if I am doing it right. I do talk to outside social workers and I receive one-to-one outside supervision. But it is a very lonely place to be."

Our research also uncovered participants' negative experiences of supervision. Two social workers interviewed highlighted deficits in their experiences of supervision that reflect adversely on the content, quality and style of supervision offered to them:

> "Well it's like this, if it's just going to be about case management, it's not going to develop you as a professional."

> "But if it's just about deadlines – 'Have you got that report done, grand, thanks' – if it's just case management ... I think you end up just losing motivation."

Another interviewee acknowledged the undue attention given to case management in supervision: "Yes ... but in general it tends to be case management when you get it. And even then, it's going to be cases that are screaming, rather than your whole portfolio."

Although it is acknowledged as an important part of continuous professional development, the practice of professional supervision in social work is very differently experienced by participants in our survey. A social worker interviewed as part of our study referred to her experience of supervision as ad hoc and inconsistent: "But it doesn't happen that often.... You might put supervision in the diary but if anything else came up, supervision would be out the window."

Respondents were presented with a series of statements on supervision with which they could agree or disagree. As Table 5.1 indicates, the majority of respondents (89%) felt that supervision had helped them in their work and 73% said that it contributed to their professional development. However, only 22% strongly agreed that they had received emotional and personal support, with 67% strongly agreeing that supervision is centred on case management. Furthermore, only 19% strongly agreed that they had learned a great deal through supervision. A mere 20% strongly agreed that they were satisfied with supervision, while a further 40% agreed that they were satisfied with supervision. There is an overall sense from the survey that social workers' satisfaction with supervision was qualified. The interviews and focus group data support this conclusion. It is notable that a sizeable minority (25%) said that they were *not* satisfied with supervision; over half of these respondents had earlier indicated that they received too little supervision. Manifestly, supervision is a problematic issue in social work practice, which is evident from our research and is further supported in public inquiry reports.

While our survey and interviews reflect a variety and diversity of experiences, supervision was generally recognised as important and its association with the provision of quality services was acknowledged.

Table 5.1: Experiences of supervision

	Strongly agree	Agree	Neither agree nor disagree	Disagree	Strongly disagree	Number of responses
Supervision has contributed to my professional development	34%	39%	15%	10%	2%	220
Supervision has helped me in my work	44%	45%	6%	4%	<1%	222
I receive emotional and personal support through supervision	22%	30%	20%	17%	10%	218
Supervision is centred on case management	34%	33%	19%	13%	2%	220
I have learned a great deal through supervision	19%	41%	26%	9%	5%	212
Overall, I am satisfied with my supervisory experience	20%	40%	15%	18%	7%	218

Linking supervision to continuing professional development

In Ireland, the setting up of the Social Work Registration Board under the Health and Social Care Professionals Act 2005 has had and will continue to have a significant influence on the development of social work. Registered social workers are now required to undertake CPD in order to maintain their registration, and thereby their right to practise. As stated previously, while CPD in one form or another appears to be well-established within the social work profession, the introduction of registration is nonetheless highly significant in locating CPD at the heart of professional and educational debate and practice.

When undertaking this survey, supervision emerged for participants as an important consideration in CPD and it was identified as a significant aspect of ongoing professional development. As one social worker reflected: "I'd see supervision as pivotal to CPD in the sense that, for you to develop your own professional self, you are going to need to look at how you carry out your work."

An experienced social worker reflected further on the value of supervision and its importance in terms of ongoing professional development and CPD:

> "That [supervision] has been incredibly helpful. It has kind of helped me to ... because I have so many roles where I work, it has helped me to keep everything on track. And it has helped me to look at things maybe a little differently than I would have. And it has helped me to access all the knowledge and information that I already had, but didn't know I had.

Conversely, commenting on the supervision she received on the job, a social worker interviewed pointed to its limitations in terms of CPD development and drew attention to an overemphasis on case management:

> "I do [receive supervision on the job]. But I wouldn't consider that as really upskilling me professionally. We just look at issues around my caseload, issues in the organisation, issues around the roster [laughs]. That's basically it. It's issues to do with the running of the place where I work. It's practical things."

While CPD participation appears to be accepted as important to and well-established within the social work profession, locating supervision at the heart of professional and educational debate and practice is vital to ensuring a professional practice that is ethically sound and reflexive and responsive to diversity in all its forms.

Cultures and contexts of supervision

Interviewees commented that supervision primarily focused on service delivery and practice interventions. Reconciling the varying and frequently conflicting tensions that arise within and between the various domains of practice was considered an important focus for supervision. One social worker interviewed reflected on the importance of developing a strong culture of supervision, linking it to the provision of high-quality service delivery. The same interviewee also highlighted the deficits associated with her experience of supervision:

> "But that culture of supervision isn't as strong as it should
> be within social work. Yes, it does affect me because there
> are times when I will get stuck in a situation. I have my
> peers I can talk to but it's still not the same in terms of my
> development. You know, as a social worker, you never stop
> developing. And you are always going to get stuck in things.
> So it's difficult."

A local authority social worker who had returned to Ireland having
worked in social work in the UK professed her absolute surprise at
the absence of supervision in her workplace and the lack of emphasis
placed on the importance of supervision in terms of ensuring the
provision of a good-quality service to service users: "I'm completely
baffled … you know it's part of the culture shock of returning to
Ireland … absolutely incredulous that they don't provide supervision.
But that culture of supervision isn't as strong as it should be within
social work." After returning to Ireland having worked as a social work
manager in the UK for many years, an interviewee advocated for the
provision of more and better opportunities for supervision at senior
levels in social work in Ireland: "I've only ever had supervision in the
UK, right up along as a manager and a team manager. So supervision
is quite embedded in my head." At interview, the same senior social
worker demonstrated her absolute commitment to providing good-
quality structures and processes of supervision for her team members:

> "With my staff, I've put in place a strict supervision system.
> Everyone is supervised and they have to have supervision.…
> We have a group that reviewed supervision policy last year
> … we have revised supervision policy, making it a bit more
> alive for some people. There were some people for whom
> supervision had gone stale."

Her commitment to supporting ongoing training initiatives among her
team is supported in her release of a staff member to do a part-time
one-year course in supervision: "One of the supervisors here [on the
team] is doing a course on supervision in UCC [University College
Cork]. I think supervision is one of the fundamental pillars of social
work."

In our survey, most respondents (86%) stated that they receive some
form of supervision, of the remaining 14%, they said that while they
did not receive supervision, they could, in some cases, access 'informal
supervision' if needed. A social worker working in the HSE stated

that "we have informal supervision.... We work in pairs here, one interviewer and one observer. There's a lot of intense work done around that." However, for some interviewees, regular, formal in-house supervision did not seem to represent a routine part of their working life:

> "I asked my manager if she would pay for me to have supervision, because I need to have professional supervision and she said 'No'. I haven't given up.... I've been asked to develop a policy and I've been promoting awareness about child protection. I'm the designated person and I will need to be supervised. I'm going to approach them from that angle, that I will need funding for supervision. You know, in terms of safety around children, I need to have supervision."

The majority of respondents (79%) reported that the organisation for which they work has a policy in place for supervision. However, 16.5% said that their employer did not have a policy, while a further 4% did not know what policies, if any, prevailed. Not surprisingly, it was primarily senior social workers in our research who stated that they did not receive supervision.

As one experienced social worker reflected:

> "I personally, as I have said, would like to have more supervision, and supervision which was more supportive and educational. But this organisation really isn't into that, and there is no one to push, no one to fight for that. It would be easier if you worked for an organisation like the HSE. They are more accountable."

Another social worker interviewed also highlighted the organisation's responsibility and senior management's role in relation to making appropriate provision for supervision: "When I was at the HSE, there were attempts to do something like that [group supervision] but it was very difficult, because of time." While recognising the increased emphasis in Ireland in recent years on management in the public service, an experienced social worker who had returned to Ireland having worked in the UK for some time commented at interview on the differences that she experienced between social work practice in the UK and in Ireland:

> "the bureaucracy here is nothing like in the UK. In the UK, there are a lot more forms, a lot more targets, and standards, social work is a lot more managed in the UK than it is here…. There is less to manage [in Ireland] because we don't have the services. It's a very difficult one to weigh up. What was happening with social work [in the UK] was that increasingly you were assessing the person and putting in services to meet those needs. You weren't necessarily working through longer issues, you weren't working through more complex relationship issues with the person you were meeting. Or you weren't doing a lot of the grief work that needs to be done. There were all sorts of things that weren't being done because of the need to provide services."

As can be seen from her comments, she experienced social work in Ireland as being more concerned with traditional professional concerns like providing support, building relationships and assisting service users to make decisions. The focus of practice in Ireland, she maintained, is on more qualitative-type concerns. Conversely, she found that in the UK, the practice focus was more on the delivery of quantitative-type services. Understandably, the challenges posed for calculating effectiveness using bureaucratic performance measurement techniques are obviously greater when referring to a more qualitative-type practice than more quantitative service delivery functions. Elaborating further on this matter, the same social worker concludes:

> "One of the debates we were always having was 'OK, we can count how much home care they are getting and all sorts of other things that touch their lives. But how do we count the sort of relationship-building that happens with the social worker that enables that person [the service user] to make decisions about their lives, or their families or themselves'. There is no tangible way of counting that. It was that whole argument of the qualitative versus the quantitative … and it wouldn't have been supported by senior management."

While cultures and contexts of social work practice are generally regarded as having changed across different jurisdictions, it would appear from our survey that a commensurate response in supervision policies and practices is required.

Frequency and quality of supervision

Social workers interviewed as part of our survey commented critically on issues related to the frequency and quality of supervision on offer. They drew attention to the challenges faced by supervisees and supervisors. When referring to the challenges for supervisors, issues related to scarce resources, lack of time and work pressures were identified. As one social worker reflected:

> "most of my supervision was around case management. That would have been due to caseload and time pressures, and pressures on the supervisor. Obviously, team leaders are under a lot of pressure to be available to the rest of the team. If they had the time and space to do it [provide for other aspects of supervision], I think they would have. The will was there but not the time."

Nearly half of the 228 survey respondents who stated that they were receiving supervision do so on a monthly basis (see Figure 5.1). Just over one fifth (21.6%) have supervision every six weeks. For 10% of respondents, supervision is a more frequent occurrence, which is undertaken weekly, fortnightly or every three weeks. However, 14% of respondents said that they met with their supervisors only every two, three or four months. Of the 5% who ticked 'other', most said that they received supervision on an ad hoc basis, depending on workloads and the availability of the supervisor.

A respondent referred to the sporadic nature of supervision: "sometimes once a month, then after a while none, then once a month again". Seniority may also be a factor, as one social worker noted: "I am senior so it is not often and an informal five or 10 minutes". Another experienced social worker interviewed commented on the lack of consistency of supervision and she highlighted variables related to personality and work pressure that influenced supervision practice: "But it doesn't happen that often. Or it varies. I think that things were better with my previous supervisor.... During 2011, I think I had three supervision sessions in total."

Another interviewee commented on the total absence of supervision on the job: "It's years since I've had supervision; this job, there's no supervision." In order to respond to this situation, the social worker commented that she and a number of colleagues came together to provide peer supervision to each other:

Figure 5.1: Frequency of supervision

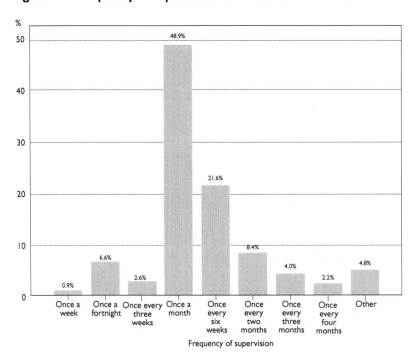

"Just on a side issue, you know I have colleagues in other counties who are in the same situation so we have sort of, I suppose, we have a very informal peer supervision … which is basically a complaints mechanism … that's awful."

Lack of availability and lack of consistency in relation to supervision were the main challenges facing social workers in our study: "I organised that [supervision] myself because I felt that I did not get enough supervision as it was. It was extremely inconsistent. The longest period I was without in-house supervision was a year."

Despite issues of irregularity and infrequency of supervision arising from our survey and discussed in interviews, the majority of respondents (72%) indicated that the amount of supervision they received was 'about right', but for a further 26%, it was 'too little'. Only 1% of respondents said that the level of supervision they received was 'too much': these respondents had supervision either on a monthly basis or every three weeks.

Further analysis suggested that those who received supervision every one to three weeks or once a month appear to be the most satisfied with their level of supervision (see Table 5.2). This is followed by those

Table 5.2: Frequency of supervision and satisfaction with level of supervision

	Between one and three weeks	Once a month	Once every six weeks	Between two and four months	Other
Too little	9% (2)	12% (13)	31% (15)	70% (23)	64% (7)
About right	87% (20)	86 % (96)	69% (34)	30% (10)	36% (4)
Too much	4% (1)	2% (2)	0	0	0
Total	**100 (23)**	**100 (111)**	**100 (49)**	**100 (33)**	**100 (11)**

Note: N = 227.

who have supervision every six weeks; although, as Table 5.2 indicates, even within this category, 31% reported that it was too little. Not surprisingly, those who received supervision once every two, three or four months, or on an 'other' (usually ad hoc) basis, were more likely to find this insufficient.

Respondents were presented with a series of statements on supervision with which they could agree or disagree. The majority of respondents felt that supervision had helped them in their work (89%) and contributed to their professional development (73%). Nonetheless, only 60% of respondents said that they were satisfied with their overall supervisory experience. A sizeable minority (25%) said that they were *not* satisfied.

Elaborating on the reasons for her dissatisfaction with the supervision she received, an interviewee referred to its focus on crises and to the absence of constructive feedback and acknowledgement for the good work done:

> "In the case of supervision – even though I had good supervisors – it was generally crisis-driven, or it was about what's happening in the cases as opposed to actually looking at your practice, or actually sitting down with people and saying, 'Well these are the things you are really good on and these are the things you need to improve'."

A senior social work manager highlighted the absence of supervision at management level. She attributed this to the lack of relevant professional qualifications among managers and an apparent disregard for the importance of supervision:

"My last formal supervision was eight years ago. They just don't give it for heads of service, or for service managers. What has happened in the past is that most managers of principal social workers or service managers are from non-professional backgrounds themselves. They are general managers; they tend to be ex-administrators/managers. So they don't see a need for it [supervision]; maybe they are not able to do it either. So when it gets to head of service level, most people do not have professional supervision."

Compensating for a lack of supervision, the same social work manager pointed to how she attempted to address the situation by looking for outside interdisciplinary supervision/support: "I was involved in a group for a couple of years for professional role consultancy. We didn't call it supervision. Say a school principal, or a senior speech and language therapist ... we did that outside of work." A senior social worker working in an agency where there are few social workers and fewer managers pointed to the difficulties associated with senior staff receiving supervision 'in-house' because of the absence of senior staff in the agency: "it's difficult for heads to get supervision anyway. Because there are so few people in senior positions in social work, so few senior positions where I'm at. So where are you going to get it from anyway?"

Forms of supervision

Supervision is, in most cases (75%), offered on an individual one-to-one basis. Only 15% reported that they received a combination of individual and group supervision, while less than 3% received group supervision only (see Table 5.3). Interestingly, when asked in a follow-up question which form of supervision they would *prefer* to have, the majority (44%) opted for a combination of individual and group supervision, followed by individual one-to-one (44%) and group supervision (3%).

The majority (85%) of respondents – including some of those who did not have supervision on a routine basis – reported that they could get access to informal supervision if needed. A small proportion of respondents also received additional private professional supervision, while nearly a quarter were involved in mentoring (acting either as a mentor or a mentee). In addition, 48% said that they engaged in professional peer consultation.

Highlighting the importance of and the challenges associated with developing good peer supervision, an interviewee pointed to the need

Table 5.3: Forms of supervision

	Frequency	Per cent
Individual	170	75
Group	6	3
Individual and group	35	15
Other	16	7
Total	227	100

Notes: Based on 227 responses: non-response (1); not applicable to a further 54 respondents who did not receive supervision or are unemployed.

for trust-building and for the development of a cohesive team structure that supports participants:

> "Peer review is where you take maybe one little aspect of a case and look at it in great detail, deconstruct it.... Now, it takes an awful lot of trust, that's the only thing. Because if you are not sure about the piece of work you are presenting, or you are not sure of how well you did it, it takes a lot of trust to expose yourself to the group. It can work out really well or be disastrous. You have to have a cohesive team to do it properly."

Asked about supervision practices for senior members of staff, a senior social worker referred to the importance of both individual line management supervision and peer supervision:

> "It's internal [supervision] – it's internal by my line manager, who comes and we review what's – so it's maybe every six weeks, and it's, reviews what's going on in the unit, any particularly difficult cases, court cases, and then the management of staffing, office needs, things like that. I suppose the other form of supervision that I would think that I get most, obviously, would be, we have our weekly team meetings, which is like our group supervision process, and where people can talk about difficulties that are coming up in cases, difficulties that are coming up for them ... I would see that as a space within which I can talk about what's going on, you know or how a case is particularly difficult within our multi-d [multidisciplinary] team and as kind of peer support and peer supervision."

Elaborating on the value of regular peer supervision, a social worker remarked: "on a case basis, [peer supervision] can sometimes be more meaningful than the other form of supervision". While there were varying opinions proffered in relation to the form that supervision ought to take, it was generally agreed that supervision is important.

Supervision training

One third of respondents said that they supervise staff in their current post, and the majority (68%) of these had undertaken CPD programmes to prepare them for their role. However, a sizeable minority (32%) of those who supervise staff had *not* received training in this area. As Table 5.4 indicates, most supervisors (88%) would like to undertake CPD in supervision. Although many had already received training in the area, there was clearly a desire for further provision.

Table 5.4: Continuing professional development in staff supervision

	Yes	No	Number of responses
Supervise staff in current post	33% (86)	67% (175)	261
Have undertaken CPD in staff supervision	68% (58)	32% (27)	85*
Would like to undertake CPD in staff supervision	88% (74)	12 (10)	84*

Note: * This question was addressed to supervisors; therefore, the number of responses is much lower here.

Our survey highlights the importance of and need for the provision of training opportunities for supervisors. A senior social worker with supervision responsibilities commented:

> "A course that would even give you the practicalities of it [supervision], because in essence I think a lot of people who supervise are almost thrown into it. Like, I haven't had proper training going into it, I'm learning from what I took from my past supervisors and from what I want myself. And from talking with the girls and asking them what they want."

The responsibility for supervision and for the provision of ongoing training opportunities for workers is firmly located at the employers' feet by a number of social workers in our survey. As one social worker reflected at interview:

> "But I do think that there needs to be more onus on the employer to have a responsibility in it. At the moment, I don't know an awful lot about it, but from what I've read, it's very much the responsibility of the employee – that's not going to work. The employer has to have a responsibility, like they do in New Zealand. Because, at the end of the day, they have the responsibility of releasing you, they have the responsibility of ensuring that you can get to training, and to ensure that supervision is actually looking at not just case management, but that it's actually looking at practice. And if that's not part of their responsibility, it's not going to happen. If it's not both parties' [employer's and employee's] responsibility, I don't see how it can work.... If the employer doesn't have a responsibility, it places the employee in a very difficult position."

The supervisor's responsibility to construct a safe space where quality supervision can take place with trained supervisors was regarded as very important by a social worker, who was herself a supervisor of staff:

> "I'm thinking something, even looking at the practicalities of it, or something [supervision] that presents research around what works and what doesn't work. Like, I find when I go to supervision, I'd like to get the sense that whoever is supervising me is 100% there. I don't like phones being present. I don't like being in a room where there is too much traffic going outside, all those kind of things."

The same interviewee pointed to the dearth of appropriate training opportunities for social work supervisors with responsibility in this area to better inform them of the value of supervision and of the practicalities of it.

Elaborating further on the absence of training opportunities for supervisors, another senior social worker commented:

> "Since I took up the post, I was able to do a course, a five-day course, in the Tony Morrison's model of supervision, that was broken down over three sessions, but I was

supervising people from 2005. It took me until 2010 to be able to get on the course."

Highlighting the need for specialised training in supervision, an interviewee pointed out that while she was an experienced practitioner, this did not necessarily translate into her being a good supervisor:

"I mean I could say 'Oh, I have been a social worker for 16 years and I know it all', but that wouldn't make me a good supervisor and I wouldn't want to be a supervisor unless I had some academic qualification to say that I know what I'm doing and that I could do it."

Lack of availability of dedicated supervision training programmes was highlighted as a problem by a number of interviewees. A senior social worker remarked: "I've requested it [supervision training] and I know my manager is looking into it at the moment to try and source some for me. Primarily, it's sourcing it, really. It's getting someplace that I can do it."

Content of supervision

Clinical work and administration/case management are the areas that feature most frequently in supervision. However, the majority of respondents also reported that supervision, to some extent, provides emotional/personal support, educational opportunities and professional development (see Table 5.5). But it is clear that a much lower priority is placed on the latter issues in supervision. This reinforces the concern that supervision is led by a managerial agenda, with the personal needs of the supervisee being relegated to subordinate status. The need for supervision to extend beyond case management was reiterated by one interviewee: "I have a manager who manages me. But I don't receive social work supervision."

The emotional and supportive function of supervision was acknowledged as important by another social worker in our survey; however, she professed to being obliged to seek this in private supervision, sourced outside of the organisation and personally financed:

"My last supervisor didn't really focus on emotional support; my current supervisor probably does more of that. She will ask how you are, 'How are things going?', and that sort of thing. The main problem is that we just don't meet that

Table 5.5: Content of supervision

	Always	Very often	Regularly	Occasionally	Never	Number of responses
Clinical work	61%	12%	14%	7%	6%	218
Administrative matters/case management	51%	18%	18%	10%	3%	219
Support (emotional/ personal)	24%	11%	23%	28%	14%	221
Education	8%	10%	17%	51%	14%	210
Professional development	9%	8%	20%	44%	19%	211
Career development	6%	5%	9%	38%	43%	197

often. I've started to see a supervisor outside the organisation – a psychotherapist not a social worker. But it's 60 euro a session so I haven't gone a lot."

Another interviewee also points to the need for structure, challenge and direction in supervision. The importance of supporting supervisees to engage in critical reflection and the benefits of receiving outside support are also highlighted:

"I would like supervision that would help me to 'box off' my role because my role is constantly changing according to the clients' needs. And it is the demand of the organisation as well. So I would need a supervision that would help to guide me through that. And a supervision that would help me be reflective about changes in society. We do have case meetings in-house about our cases each week. But I don't tend to discuss much about my cases at these meetings. But I think I need someone from outside to look at my cases also; otherwise, you get a kind of tunnel vision. I would like a form of supervision that would challenge me professionally."

Recent developments related to registration requirements of social workers in Ireland have resulted in a fresh impetus to seek supervision and to use registration requirements to lobby within organisations for the provision of increased resources. One interviewee asserted: "we are using that [the CORU requirements] as a way to negotiate with HR [Human Resources] and hospital management to say we need someone in situ to offer us regular supervision as part of our professional registration." A recently graduated social worker who placed a high value on supervision expressed her clear dissatisfaction with her current supervision. She believed that supervision should include elements of both affirmation and challenge. Practitioners need, she believed, to be helped to think critically about their practice, thus supporting their ongoing professional development:

> "I'd like to be challenged. I'd like someone to say 'What you did there, is there any other way you could have done that?', or 'Have you ever thought about this or that? I'd suggest maybe you go and have a look at this.' There was none of that kind of thing. It was all, like, 'You're doing a great job', and I wanted more. I wanted to get better at what I was doing. So I would have liked to have been challenged more."

In the absence of sufficient in-house supports, seeking help from outside the agency in situations of challenge/difficulty did not seem to pose a problem for one interviewee, who spoke about searching for and finding supervision support when issues related to challenging practice and/or policy concerns arose:

> "If there were particular issues … if you were overwhelmed by a particular piece of work that was going on and you weren't receiving professional supervision, or any type of non-management supervision, in work, a number of us went and sought, kind of, support and guidance and consultancy outside of work."

When asked about the focus and content of their supervision, one interviewee expressed the following views: "It would certainly be the first two – the support and the case management. But the education doesn't really [have a specific slot]."

One senior social worker clearly elaborated on his understanding of what good supervision should be about, connecting with the importance of reflective engagement and demonstrating a good knowledge of all the functions of good supervision:

"You need to have somewhere to go, maybe not as often as what your staff would get. But certainly about three or four times a year you should be able to go somewhere and have some type of structure you could go to discuss critical issues of concern, critical issues of importance, and also just to feel supported or to reflect upon things. It's vital, absolutely vital.... Absolutely, I think it's hugely important."

Supervision in social work sets out to serve a number of different purposes: education, professional development, management and support. Our interviewees report receiving supervision that involves maybe one or other of the four main functions, but seldom succeed in achieving all four functions.

Conclusion

An organisation's staff is its major resource not just because of the intrinsic worth of its social workers, but also because their work publicly 'showcases' the organisation. The provision of good-quality supervision and opportunities for CPD is regarded as central to ensuring that the workforce is appropriately prepared to respond to the challenges of uncertain and changing social and economic times. Responding to the expressed needs of practitioners in terms of CPD and supervision is vital to ensuring that the highest standards of service delivery and professional practice are maintained. In supervision, reconciling the tensions that surface in our survey and in the literature between personal and professional agendas and management and organisational issues is difficult. Traditionally, supervision has provided a context where these tensions can be encountered and mediated.

The findings of our survey and interviews reveal that the concept of supervision has a contested meaning. The experiences of our research participants demonstrate that practices of supervision are varied and erratic. We have found in our research that supervision policies and practices are largely determined by a number of variables. The variables identified include organisational cultures, managers' attitudes and social workers' own commitment to engaging with the process. There are clear differences between the supervision experiences of social workers in Ireland and in the UK. Many of the interviewees' accounts of their experiences of supervision reflect the challenges and tensions that exist in seeking out a form of supervision that is appropriate and responsive to their professional needs.

More positive developments in supervision relate to reflective practice, which relies on practitioners being afforded opportunities in supervision and CPD to stand back and question their approach to their work. Why should organisations promote reflective supervision among professionals? Because the profession is defensively positioned – having to continually explain its decisions – it is necessary to have professionals who have a clear sense of purpose and a strong sense of agency in what they do. The audit language of performance indicators has been criticised in terms of progressing a more formulaic approach to practice, thereby reducing and discouraging independent critical thinking among social workers, particularly in the public sector (Munro, 2011). As we have seen in previous chapters, social workers work in a much-contested environment of practice. Respondents in our survey speak of a professional work environment that can be both stimulating and professionally isolating. We believe that the provision of regular, good-quality professional supervision by trained supervisors and the making available of opportunities for CPD is vital. We believe that practitioners need to be able to articulate clearly and publicly how they work to achieve change at many different levels, and, in addition, they must be willing and able to demonstrate how accountability is represented in their work practices, if they are going to build professional and public confidence. Supervision practice that attends to management, educational and supportive functions, that promotes the reflective engagement of practitioners, and that is delivered in a wider organisational culture that endorses learning and ongoing professional development, we believe, points a way forward for social work that is progressive and responsive to the many practice challenges that have been highlighted in our research and commented upon throughout this book. We support the contention that supervision as a learning experience is closely linked to reflection. We will now turn to consideration of the relationship between learning and reflection in Chapter Six.

SIX

Learning and reflection

Earlier chapters elucidated the complexity of the fluctuating social, political and economic cultures in which current social work practice is embedded. This chapter will examine how reflective engagement as a learning paradigm promotes and supports social work practitioners by offering them a lifelong tool and a technology that will govern an effective response to clients over time. Both the literature and empirical studies carried out in the School of Applied Social Studies in University College Cork (UCC) support this stance (Halton et al, 2007; Dempsey et al, 2008; Murphy et al, 2008, 2010). In particular, this chapter will outline the nature of reflective inquiry and review how it forms and re-forms social workers in relation to continuing professional development (CPD). The roots of reflective inquiry are in educational theory (Dewey, 1933; Schön, 1983; Freire, 1996 [1972]). Its primary tool, the portfolio, is best described as a developmental and formative assessment tool (Lyons, 1998), which can be used at all stages of social work training and in ongoing professional development. As a result, it has the potential for generative and creative learning in the social work context. It can help social workers to reclaim the moral and ethical stance of the profession, and promote a sense of agency among professionals (Fook, 2002; Rath, 2010) through the formation and articulation of professional judgement. We believe that a more informed and proactive professional judgement fortifies the practitioner to face the challenges of the fluctuating cultures and contexts of contemporary postmodern practice (Fook et al, 2000). This chapter will consider the contribution that reflective inquiry can make in terms of helping social workers to respond with thoughtful and intentional deliberation to the many uncertain conditions and contexts of practice. It will also explore the potential of reflective learning in terms of supporting and facilitating practitioners' ongoing professional development and what Ferguson (2001: 45) has called 'the re-negotiation of their professional identities'.

Complexity and professional judgement

As the complexity of the social work role has grown, so too have the requirements of social workers, whose work is situated within changing and competing social and political contexts and where presenting problems reflect human intricacy and unpredictability. Social work is an inherently practical and contextual activity that involves making professional judgements about people, service users who do not follow the immutable laws of physics or chemistry. Vulnerable people turn to social workers for help to navigate their way through a period of personal, social, emotional, economic and/or cultural instability. Indeed, this very instability is recognised implicitly in the discourses of managerialism and risk management that dominate social work practice (Payne, 2002, 2005b).

Professional judgement involves making decisions about complex and often competing agendas associated with safety, risk, need and availability of resources. Social workers lead a precarious existence as they try to balance compliance with the rules of their organisation, the values of their profession and the variability of human nature. Social work is not an orderly, predictable activity; conversely, it is a human service profession, where workers are frequently challenged to respond with creativity and reflexivity in situations where risk, threat and uncertainty prevail (Fook, 2011). Social worker practitioners need a strong sense of agency in their work to counteract the insecurity and instability that can lead to a sense of hopelessness that postmodern thinking can engender in client and practitioner relationships. If professionals are to respond appropriately in practice, they will require opportunities and processes to systematically inquire into their practice so that they can evaluate, review and further develop their skills and capacities. These systems and processes of inquiry need to be embedded in organisational cultures, practice and protocols (Baldwin, 2004), and supervision can provide a fundamental context where this process is assisted and supported. We believe that it is too important an issue to be left to the discretion of the practitioners to develop these skills alone and independently from their employing agencies.

In addition, many social workers operate within bureaucratic structures, organisations that in seeking to regularise practice to achieve greater efficiency and consistency, develop a range of practice protocols and procedures. These implicitly inform practitioners' judgements and can seem at times not to be in the clients' best interests or supportive of the practitioners' own professional and/or moral and ethical codes of behaviour. The resulting perplexity and cognitive dissonance requires them to engage in systematic inquiry in order to resolve the doubts and complexities that arise in the work (Dewey, 1933). If systematic inquiry is not promoted and engaged with, practitioners will not be in a position to examine and build upon the evidence and feedback received from the outcomes of their interventions in the lives of vulnerable human beings, a fundamental aspect of all CPD.

Dewey's (1933) theory, with its emphasis on how people think, forms the foundation of reflective inquiry. Schön's (1983, 1987) theory further develops core ideas from the work of Dewey. He supports practitioner reflection 'in' and 'on' action and he encourages practitioners to engage in reflective inquiry on their everyday interventions in practice. Freire (1996 [1972]), a keen advocate of educational reform, promoted the liberating and transformative potential of reflective inquiry at an individual and a societal level. Overall, the work of these important researchers, philosophers and educators form the bedrock of reflective practice and of the development of professional portfolios as agents and at the service of agents of transformational change.

Contextualising social work

Social work services are located within a wider network of diverse organisations and systems. On a macro-level, political, social and economic agendas govern the structure of the organisation and the development of legislation and policy reform. On a micro-level, organisations' policies and procedures influence the attitudes of social workers, shaping the form that their professional practice will take. Our research demonstrates that social workers are experiencing a number of work pressures associated with working in a rapidly changing social and political landscape in organisational contexts where fiscal concerns dominate (Murphy et al, 2008, 2010).

A postmodernist world view poses many contextual, epistemological and ideological challenges for public service organisations and professionals employed within these structures. A lot has been written about the influence of globalisation and the rise of postmodernism and their contribution to the development of complex, uncertain and changing contexts for social work practice (see, eg, Pease and Fook, 1999; Healy, 2000, 2005, 2012; Fook, 2002, 2004, 2011; Dominelli, 2004; Thompson, 2005; Cree, 2009, 2011). Unquestionably, globalisation has brought with it more pluralistic societies; it presents a formidable challenge to the institutions of the state, including social work, and to the modernist agenda on which the welfare state was founded. Postmodernity flourished in the context of a mounting disillusionment with the epistemological premise of modernity and from a developing cynicism with the institutions of the state (Parton and O'Byrne, 2000). Social work theorists in the postmodern tradition speak of the world as an ambiguous, uncertain and constantly changing context, which demands a flexible, reflective and reflexive workforce capable of responding in the immediacy of a variety of practice contexts (see, eg, Gould and Taylor, 1996; Pease and Fook, 1999; Healy, 2000, 2005; Parton and O'Byrne, 2000; Gould and Baldwin, 2004). The literature on globalisation stands alongside discourses of risk and risk management, economic rationality, bureaucratisation, and managerialism in social work (see Chapter Seven).

The issue of risk is located at the core of postmodern concerns (Beck, 1992). More recently, the literature has drawn our attention to how the management of uncertainty and risk has increasingly become the responsibility of social workers, on whom responsibility for the assessment, supervision and regulation of risk behaviour usually falls (Fook, 1999, 2002, 2011; Parton and O'Byrne, 2000). While, traditionally, professionals in the public sector operated with a degree of professional freedom and discretion, they also had considerable autonomy in the day-to-day management of their work. Conversely, in today's climate of increasing public accountability, issues related to economies of scale take precedence, leading to increased monitoring of professional activity. Consequently, bureaucratic structures and practice protocols have been developed in an attempt to standardise and regulate professional practice, thus resulting in what many writers regard as a reduction in the discretionary powers of professionals (Healy, 2005; Thompson, 2005; Parton, 2011).

These changes can be linked to a growing public demand for the exercise of greater managerial control over the activities of professionals. The increasing emphasis on 'managerial power' as part of a wider process of de-professionalisation has been criticised by professional practitioners and researchers alike. According to Thompson (2005), this movement attempted to reduce the autonomy of social workers. Certainly, management and accountability have become integral features of reform of the welfare state. Value for money and effectiveness of services have become synonymous with service provision. In this milieu, managers become the arbitrators and decision-makers on the services they provide and their recipients. Frequently, it is market demands that direct such decision-making, where managers are responsible for achieving greater efficiency and effectiveness of service delivery (Healy, 2005; Fook, 2011).

Healy (2005) further observes that economic rationale is fast becoming the most important feature of public service provision and markets are regarded as the best means of coordinating human activities. Healy concludes that in the last decade, the marketisation of the public service, driven by economic principles of consumerism, has led to the advancement of more managed services and to the rising popularity of a managerial culture within public service organisations (Healy, 2005). On the other hand, social workers, while working as public servants, are required to balance the contradictory and changing needs of the market-driven policies of the state, its workers, service users and their professional values. Pressures arise for social workers from often contradictory organisational requirements that dictate policies and procedures and their own desire to retain some autonomy and professional discretion in their direct work (Healy, 2000, 2005; Halton, 2010). Taken together, these factors can work as a constraining force, placing limits around practitioners' work practices and often causing confusion, frustration and disillusionment in their daily work. Understandably, reconciling and mediating across the many competing social, economic and political interests is a stressful and demanding task ascribed to social workers across community and institutional contexts. The fallout from these situations for practitioners is represented in the narratives of social workers' experiences, as described in our survey and also supported in the literature (Fook, 2002; Gould and Baldwin, 2004). Indeed, this book attempts to address the contemporary concerns of social workers as they seek answers to the practice challenges revealed in these studies.

Undoubtedly, social workers are charged with the difficult task of responding to people experiencing all kinds of distress. We believe that the new managerialism in statutory social work agencies only adds to and does not alleviate the stress. Our survey demonstrates that a working culture that supports economic principles of value for money, coupled with a scarcity of resources for the provision of supportive services, leaves social workers frustrated and stressed as they struggle to deal with professional demands that are excessive. Furthermore, social workers also have to work within changing constructs and epistemologies of practice that cause additional stresses (Healy, 2005). Ife (1997), writing about the stress involved in the work, coupled with a new managerialism in statutory social service agencies, pointed out that in Australia, 'social work has ceased to be professionally rewarding and has become a simple matter of survival. Many social workers report increasing levels of stress, burnout is not uncommon and morale in many social agencies seems to be extremely low' (Ife, 1997: 2).

Dominelli (1996) draws attention to the effects that an overemphasis on economies of scale and competitiveness has on the delivery of human services, leading, she believes, to a diminution in the valuing of professionals and professional knowledge, some of the results, she concludes, of globalisation. Unsurprisingly, it is within this complex milieu of increasing complexity and diversity that 'evidence-based practice' has gained increasing popularity across the professions. The requirement of workers to apply measurement instruments in diverse practice domains presents additional conceptual and epistemological challenges for social workers and is symptomatic of the quest of public service organisations to achieve certainty within practice contexts that are uncertain and constantly changing. It is, however, simply one response to reinstating the validity of professional judgement. Later, we will argue for an alternate response, CPD. We can see that social workers are situated within two oppositional epistemological references: a modernist reference that values expert knowledge and expertise that is supported by agency policies; and, conversely, a more constructivist approach to knowledge that takes into account changing cultures and contexts of practice, valuing practitioner experience and practice wisdom. In practice, social workers are vested with mediating between these two opposing epistemological paradigms, and, as our research will demonstrate, it is not easy terrain for practitioners to navigate and negotiate.

Fook (2002, 2011), writing on social work practice, comments on the deficits of adopting a more traditional approach to knowledge and expertise. She presents a fundamentally different approach to knowledge construction for social work practice and proffers the view that knowledge is contextual and culturally bound and is therefore necessarily uncertain. This perspective represents a profoundly different epistemological approach to knowledge and knowing than that proposed by a more modernist approach that supports an expert view of knowledge, that is, what is known and scientifically proven. Fook, writing on the challenges faced by social workers working within the prevailing uncertainties of professional practice, states that it is within this construct of social work as a contextual and culturally bound professional activity that issues of 'uncertainty' and 'risk' are experienced and best understood. Fook (2002: 31) concludes that 'This uncertainty means that the ability of professionals to practise effectively on the basis of tried and tested knowledge is undermined considerably'. Fook further considers that for social workers to work effectively within the context of global, cultural, economic and political diversity and change, legitimate knowledge alone is insufficient to respond to practitioner need. She advocates the development of better systems and practices for generating and processing knowledge, which have at their core a fundamental acceptance and acknowledgement of the uncertainties embedded in the work. Accepting the uncertainties associated with social work is fundamental and, according to Fook

(2011), a necessary requirement of all practitioners, organisations and managers. Furthermore, according to Fook (2011), if we are to work towards reducing/limiting the uncertainties associated with practice, which is also an important consideration, and try to manage the risks associated with the work, we must have a clear understanding of the concept and endeavour to embrace it as a reality of practice.

In her more recent work, Fook (2011) acknowledges the paradox of the paradigm of uncertainty: the certainty of uncertainty embedded in all human and social experiences and the challenges this poses for human service professionals – 'the paradox of professional practice is the certainty of uncertainty, and the corresponding need to provide certainty with uncertainty' (Fook, 2011: 31). While recognising the practice challenges posed for practitioners in attempting to reconcile competing tensions in the work, she invites professionals to seek out ways of engaging in both responsible and responsive practice. Specifically, Fook (2002: 34) notes: 'What professionals need therefore in the current environment is a legitimate form of knowledge, and legitimate forms of generating knowledge, which allow for effective and responsive practice in changing, complex and uncertain environments.' Fook (2011: 31) further argues that this requires of social workers a better understanding of the 'contextuality' of practice learning and knowledge and 'a reframing of uncertainty as positive opportunity'. 'Contextuality', for Fook, requires an understanding of the whole context and its influence on actions. She emphasises the need for social workers 'to think and act beyond individual situations and to transfer knowledge across situations' (Fook, 2011: 32). Fook (2011: 33) concludes:

> the new professional requires not only a contextual ability to make and remake appropriate knowledge but also an ability to ground this knowledge in specific contexts and to transcend those contexts through maintaining broader values. Professionals use values to provide continuity and certainty and as a guide for remaking contextual knowledge and practice.

Fook's work poses real challenges for the current construction of statutory social work. The tenets of her contextual representation of practice are contra-cultural and their implications in terms of practice development are challenging for all concerned. Rath (2010), writing on educational practice, finds favour with Fook (2002). Both imply that knowledge is not a 'given', a stand-alone revealed to all in raw data and numbers; rather, it is made and remade through the active and intentional agent, the practitioner whose values and judgement interface with evidence to construct practice. In her work, Fook (2002, 2011) acknowledges the variability of practice; thus, she presents an explicit challenge to social work managers and employing agencies to commit themselves to developing structures of support that are responsive to practice situations and to the consequential needs of front-line professionals. For Fook, promoting professional confidence in turbulent times is a primary endeavour and reflective practice is represented as a way forward.

Public inquiries into social work: the challenges posed for the profession

How has this concept of '*uncertainty*' influenced the construction of social work and its representation in recently published public inquiry reports? Munro (2011) highlighted the shortcomings of an over-bureaucratised child protection service, which limits professional judgement by a too close adherence to rules. The concomitant loss is a less child-centred service and the absence of relationship-building and trust:

> The demands of bureaucracy have reduced their capacity to work directly with children, young people and families. Services have become so standardised that they do not provide the required range of responses to the variety of need that is presented. (Munro, 2011: 6–7)

Munro poses a challenge to social workers and their managers to reclaim their professional expertise and not to shy away from the exercise of professional judgement:

> This review recommends a radical reduction in the amount of central prescription to help professionals move from a compliance culture to a learning culture, where they have more freedom to use their expertise in assessing need and providing the right help. (Munro, 2011: 6–7)

While the development of practice procedures and protocols were originally intended to improve the quality and consistency of practice delivery, contrarily, Munro's research reveals that they have resulted in an over-regulation of social work and the promotion of more procedural-led practice. She claims that the centrality of relationship-building with families and children has been undervalued in a system that has become overshadowed by bureaucratic rules and protocols:

> Complying with prescription and keeping records to demonstrate compliance has become too dominant. The centrality of forming relationships with children and families to understand and help them has become obscured. The review is making recommendations to enable social workers to exercise more professional judgment but is also concerned to improve their expertise. (Munro, 2011: 7–8)

Munro further acknowledges the practice challenges that a movement away from a prevailing culture of compliance will pose for practitioners and social work managers. However, she emphasises the necessity for social workers to embrace the uncertainty contained in the work and the responsibility of organisations to support practitioners to exercise greater professional judgement in practice situations where uncertainty and risk prevail:

> A move from a compliance to a learning culture will require those working in child protection to be given more scope to exercise professional judgment in deciding how best to help children and their families. It will require more determined and robust management at the front line to support the development of professional confidence. (Munro, 2011: 5)

While Munro's research was situated in the UK, the challenges posed for social workers and managers in child protection services have resonance in Ireland and internationally. In addition, an earlier report by Laming (2009), which was commissioned in the wake of the death of 'Baby P', highlighted the many challenges faced by child protection workers in the exercise of their roles and responsibilities. Moreover, in Ireland, the Roscommon Child Care Case Report (Gibbons, 2010) made the case for a full review and revision of child protection services. The intensification of media interest in all matters related to child protection and welfare has resulted in a proliferation of public inquiries that involve the interrogation of professionals and their work practices. Undoubtedly, social workers feel under threat when situated within a prevailing public climate of distrust, working in organisational contexts where systems of accountability have been developed in response to the forces of managerialism, and practising daily in a professional context that is ridden with risk and uncertainty.

The reports of Munro (2011), Laming (2009), the Social Work Task Force (SWTF, 2009) and Roscommon (Gibbons, 2010), and other high-profile investigations, have placed a premium on issues of accountability and case management within social work practice. In addition, they have strengthened the argument in favour of the provision of ongoing opportunities for practitioners to engage in post-qualifying social work education and training programmes to assist them to respond in a more informed and responsive way in situations of risk and uncertainty. In support of CPD, Munro highlights the need for social workers to be continually engaged in knowledge and skill development over the course of their careers:

> Building on the work of the Social Work Task Force (SWTF) and the Social Work Reform Board (SWRB), this review makes the case for radically improving the knowledge and skills of social workers from initial training through to continuing professional development. (Munro, 2011: 7–8)

Overall, the dominant message being delivered in recent reports and inquiries is that social workers need to be vigilant in seeking out opportunities to upskill and to engage in CPD. In addition, organisations need to provide structures and frameworks of support that assist practitioners to engage in these activities.

Morrison (2001), writing on professional supervision, asserts that social workers need to be challenged on their assumptions, questioned on their decisions and supported to inquire into their understanding of information received. He asserts that they need not only the time to carry out the work, but also the opportunity afforded them to engage in a systematic examination of their decision-making and interventions. Banks (2006), too, warns that in the current climate, where fiscal rectitude dictates, professionals must be careful to adhere to the ethics and values of the profession in all matters pertaining to the delivery of service. Reflective practice in social work, specifically the work of Fook (2002, 2011), provides a practice paradigm that may help to address many of the concerns represented in public inquiry reports. Fook's approach to practice inquiry invites social workers to investigate the intuitive understandings and meanings that help inform their interventions. She concludes that social workers need to reflect critically on all aspects of their learning and they must endeavour to reclaim the moral and ethical stance of their profession, which is continually challenged by fluctuating cultures and contexts of practice (Fook et al, 2000; Fook, 2011).

Connecting reflective inquiry to social work education and continuing professional development

Throughout this book, we have been reflecting on a profession that has been directly influenced by fluctuating organisational and political contexts and altering practice cultures. It is worth noting that changes have been made to accreditation in the social work profession alongside, if not as a result of, societal changes. Over the last decade, CPD and upgrading of skills after graduation has come to be seen as an important part of the professional life of social workers worldwide. Increasingly, registration bodies have made CPD a condition for maintaining professional registration and, in addition, professional associations consistently promote it among their members. It is understandable that there will be a need on the part of social workers to constantly upskill if they are to competently respond to the challenges of contemporary social work practice. This is partly due to the fact that social work qualifying courses are often generic in nature; they do not necessarily equip graduates with all the skills they will need throughout their careers to respond appropriately in a wide variety of practice contexts and eventualities. Our survey results and follow-up interviews demonstrate respondents' commitment to seeking out opportunities to engage in CPD; however, the survey also points to worrying barriers and impediments to their engagement that reflect poorly on managers and organisations.

At a time when epistemologies of practice are changing, social workers must be prepared and able to respond effectively in demanding and stressful practice situations. This perspective presents as non-negotiable. Official reports, including Laming (2009), the Social Work Task Force (SWTF, 2009) and Munro (2011), support the view that we should examine possible ways of supporting social workers to critically respond to the demands of the work. Contemporary social work practice demands that social workers become active agents in the construction of practice knowledge and skilled in the transferability of that knowledge beyond individual practice situations and contexts. Developing the skills of a proactive and responsive service delivery that takes account of issues of agency responsibility and public accountability is fundamental to the development of a strong professional voice and also to the regeneration of the profession. We believe that CPD must be firmly located within organisational cultures and practices to ensure that professionals are provided with the necessary time, space and opportunities to participate fully.

Our survey indicates that practitioners' views are consistent with the recommendations outlined in other research. An experienced local authority social worker interviewed as part of our research linked reflection with CPD; she pointed out the important opportunities to reflect, to take some time out and to reflect on her work that are provided by participation at CPD courses:

> "It was the opportunity to discuss and learn from peers ... and a time for reflection, and a time to question, and a time to consider how it affects your practice, and what you could change, so that kind of time and space is important."

In addition, an experienced mental health worker at interview acknowledged the importance of reflection and CPD in ensuring that professionals' work practices are as good as can be. He stated that he was searching for knowledge to assist the work and not just receiving evidence, that is, knowledge as static and immutable:

> "Needing to be – I know it's a bit of a cliché – but to be as good as you can be. And to do that, you have to recognise that things don't stand still, and that it's a constantly evolving profession ... I suppose constant self-questioning and looking for knowledge."

Accepting the merits of reflective practice in social work, we begin to conceptualise the reflective process and our understanding of it. In examining the concept of reflection, Dewey's (1933) seminal text, *How we think: a restatement of the relation of reflective thinking to the educative process*, continues to wield considerable influence in the context of professional education, with contemporary writers continually referencing the work (see, eg, Schön, 1983, 1987, 1991; Boud et al, 1985; Gould and Taylor, 1996; Lyons, 1998, 2010; Rath, 2000, 2010; Shulman, 2005; Loughran, 2006). For Dewey, an educationalist and philosopher, the challenge of learning is about learning to think, the process of thinking, not just the content:

> it is evident that education is ... vitally concerned with cultivating the attitude of reflective thinking, preserving it where it exists, and changing looser methods of thought into

> stricter ones wherever possible ... we state emphatically that, upon its intellectual side education consists in the formation of wide awake, careful, thorough habits of thinking. (Dewey, 1933: 78)

His identification of reflection as the central process through which learning from experience takes place is central to the formation of professional judgement. His definition of reflective thinking is widely accepted as:

> the kind of thinking that consists in turning a subject over in the mind and giving it serious and consecutive consideration.... The active, persistent and careful consideration of any belief or supposed form of knowledge in the light of the grounds that support it and the further conclusions to which it tends constitutes reflective thought. (Dewey, 1933: 9)

Reflective thinking, as so described, clearly places a premium on the development of and building upon evidence. Reflective thinking is knowledge-generating and requires the justification of thinking in the light of evidence. Furthermore, the acquisition of knowledge in and of itself was not sufficient for Dewey, attitudes of mind need to prevail for reflection to occur. Dewey believed that reflective thought requires motivation and responsibility on the part of the learner, a curiosity with and a commitment to systematic inquiry. He refers to three attitudes of mind that are essential preconditions for reflective inquiry: 'open-mindedness', 'wholeheartedness' and 'responsibility'. These characteristics are central to reflective engagement as they foreground learning processes and learner engagement rather than concentrating exclusively on the acquisition of skills and competencies.

His work will resonate with any practitioner who has experienced the tentative nature of truth in the client–practitioner relationship. Uncertainty is a forerunner to and the driving force for learning and reflection, which is our starting point too. He states that precursors to reflection involve a state of doubt, hesitation, perplexity, mental difficulty and an act of searching, hunting and inquiring to find material that will resolve the doubt and dispose of the perplexity: 'We are doubtful because the situation is inherently doubtful. Inquiry begins with the inherently doubtful – with confusing, obscure or conflictual situation' (Dewey, 1933: 121). This approach to learning challenges learners to engage in a process of mutual sharing and questioning in search of new meanings and understandings. The task of those dedicated to the promotion and development of reflective practice is 'to cultivate the attitudes that are favourable to the best methods of inquiry and testing' (Dewey, 1933: 260).

Having established the validity of uncertainty as a starting point in reflective thinking and a prerequisite for training professional judgement, it is time to look at the work of another scholar, Donald Schön. He adds the dimension of intuition and 'thinking in action'. Schön, a philosopher and educator, was deeply influenced by the work of Dewey. In a definitive text, *The reflective practitioner: how professionals think in action* (Schön, 1983), he concentrates attention on representing the professional's process of reflection, that is, knowing in action, as an intuitive act. He suggested that professionals know more than they can articulate. He attributes this to the higher value placed on scientific/ technical knowledge in dominant educational and organisational cultures and discourses, thus making it difficult for professionals to represent their work in these terms.

Schön, in the same vein, challenged the more traditional, technical rationality view of knowledge and concentrated his research efforts on investigating professionals' *'knowing in action'* (Schön, 1983, 1987, 1991). Schön's work involved the systematic investigation of the process of professionals' knowing as it pertained to the performance of their work. He prized professional knowing and his research focused on bridging the gap between the academic rigour of education for the professions and the complexity and indeterminacy of the problems that faced these professionals in their everyday work. Schön's (1983: 42) description of this tension as the gap between 'the *"high"* ground of academic rigour and the *"swampy lowlands"* of practice' is familiar to educators in social work and other human service professionals.

Schön, in committing himself to excavating the terrain of the 'swampy lowlands', needed to develop a systematic and pervasive methodology to support the process. An important feature of the type of reflective engagement advocated by Schön is the discouragement of practitioners from retreating into the more routine responses and procedures that are primarily designed to control and manage unpredictability – as Fook (2011: 33) asserts, attempting to make the uncertain, certain.

Schön's work is also important because he extended his investigations beyond the practitioner into reflective inquiry in organisations. Schön, in association with Argyris (Argyris and Schön, 1978, 1996), extended reflective inquiry into organisational learning, examining the influence of organisational cultures and contexts on changing constructions of professional practice. As statutory social work settings tend to rely on procedural and policy protocols that attempt to minimise risk and uncertainty, Ruch (2005: 22) points to the challenges posed by such an approach: 'In such organisational contexts, professional manifestations of social constructivist and hermeneutic epistemological perspectives, relationship based practice, reflective practice tolerance of ambiguity, uncertainty and risk –are viewed with scepticism'.

Writing about the challenges posed by a more reflective approach to practice within procedurally driven organisations, Argyris and Schön (1978, 1996) assert that an organisation that copes well with change is best described as a 'learning organisation'. They maintain that such organisations are constantly challenging themselves, redefining their mission in relation to new information. Their work highlights the responsibilities of employing organisations and line mangers, suggesting that effective management of organisational change and transition cannot rest with individuals; it is predicated on the presence of communication systems and processes where space and time are centrally located to assist and support the change process. Thompson (2006) also supports the development of cultures in organisations where learning is valued and change is embraced.

Freire, in *Pedagogy of the oppressed* (Freire, 1996 [1972]), extended the work of Dewey and presented a more critical and radical theory of education than either Dewey (1933) or Schön (1983, 1987). He advocated mutual learning and he introduced the notion of co-construction of knowledge between a teacher and a student. The transformational power of knowledge was key. His work informs the construct of agency that is also central to Rath's (2000, 2010) work. Together, teacher and student engage in a learning activity, the raising of consciousness through a process that he called 'conscientisation'. Freire's work challenges the banking concept of education in which the student becomes objectified:

> the scope of action allowed the students extends only as far as receiving, filing, and storing the deposits. They do it is true, have the opportunity to become collectors or cataloguers of the things they store. But in the last analysis, it is men themselves who are filed away through the lack of creativity, transformation, and knowledge in this (at best) misguided system. For apart from inquiry, apart from the praxis, men cannot be truly human. Knowledge emerges only through invention and re-invention, through the restless, impatient, continuing, hopeful inquiry men pursue

in the world, with the world, and with each other. (Freire,
1996 [1972]: 46)

Freire's work is deeply political as he investigated the embedded
knowledge situated in political, social and cultural contexts. He insisted
that the oppressed, in whatever guise, must engage in reflective inquiry
on their concrete situations. Furthermore, he concluded that reflection
must always lead to action. Freire concentrated on representing the
transformative potential of his ideas in terms of education. He believed
that in education, learners must experience 'reality' not as a private
limiting construct, but as a much wider situation and force that they
can potentially transform. They must come to perceive reality as 'a
process, undergoing constant transformation' (Freire, 1996 [1972]: 48).
His views on education were highly politicised and quite radical for
the time. His educational philosophy represented students and teachers
as co-constructors of knowledge:

Teachers and students (leadership and people), co intent on
reality, are both Subjects, not only in the task of unveiling
that reality, and thereby coming to know it critically, but
in the task of re-creating that knowledge. As they attain
this knowledge of reality through common reflection and
action, they discover themselves as its permanent re-creators.
(Freire, 1996 [1972]: 44)

Freire believed that education was critical to achieving transformation
across all social, cultural and political divides. His work extended the
meaning of reflection into public dialogue and ultimately to praxis.
In support of Freire's ideas, the authors suggest that in social work
education, there should also be a critical component to reflectivity.
This alerts students to the potential in their practice for addressing
the many tensions – personal, political and professional – contained in
the work. Reconciling the tensions that arise at the interface between
personal and professional attitudes and values on issues of social
justice, whether arising on grounds of gender, race, class, age, disability,
religious persuasion or sexual orientation, can be difficult. The two
objectives – reflectivity and a critical perspective – we believe are highly
compatible, in that they both place an emphasis on change and prize
social work values of empowerment, partnership and collaboration in
both social work education and practice. They also support Freire's
critical philosophy that links reflection to action: 'true reflection leads
to action. On the other hand, when the situation calls for action, that

action will constitute an authentic praxis only if its consequences become the object of critical reflection' (Freire, 1996 [1972]: 41).

The traditional view of knowledge that emphasises the primacy of reason over emotion and the acquisition of facts as the important outcome of learning is challenged by a reflective paradigm that places learning and the process of coming to knowledge centrally within the learning endeavour. We believe that if reflective engagement, as represented in the works of Dewey (1933), Schön (1983) and Freire (1996 [1972]), is to be promoted in social work, it will require the valuing of practitioner knowledge and practice wisdom, a recognition of its usefulness in the context of practice, and a shared commitment on the part of practitioners and organisations to engage in a shared dialogue to bring about change to systems and cultures of practice that support the process.

Reflection and social work

There has been a lot written about the reflective process in educational literature (eg Dewey, 1933; Freire, 1996 [1972]; Schön, 1983, 1987; Brookfield, 1995; Brockbank and McGill, 1998). More has been written in recent years in social work literature (Yelloly and Henkel, 1995; Gould and Taylor, 1996; Fook et al, 2000; Fook, 2002, 2011). Specific research into students of social work experiences of reflection has also been completed by Halton et al (2007), Halton and Lyons (2007), Dempsey et al (2001, 2008) and Murphy et al (2008).

The research demonstrates that reflective engagement provides a coherent organising schema for integrating knowledge, context-specific requirements and identity formation for social work students and practitioners. Many of the tools of reflection, that is, portfolio, learning journals and peer group support, promote and facilitate students and practitioners to develop new skills in a responsive way to changing circumstances. They ensure that practitioners will be open to ongoing paradigmatic transformation in the light of new knowledge or perspectives (Halton and Lyons, 2007; Dempsey et al, 2008). When working in the realm of uncertainty arising from the constantly changing complexity of social work practice, practitioners require an ability to make conscious choices about action. We believe that a reflective paradigm that encourages an experiential, interactive approach to learning involves the re-formulation of knowledge in the light of new perceptions, views knowledge as dynamic and changing, and requires of professionals their active engagement with the production and reproduction of knowledge for and in practice (Schön, 1983, 1987).

Paradigmatic shifts thereby go hand in hand with changes in action. In professional education, the portfolio, when used as a reflective learning tool, invites students to bring together the practical situations of practice with relevant theories and also facilitates them to identify the personal lens that they bring to both. This approach to learning distinguishes social work as a practical activity, engages the practitioner in a deeply personal way and generates knowledge and theoretical understanding of its own practice (Dempsey et al, 2001).

The work of Gould and Taylor has been important in promoting reflective engagement in social work education. They argue that there is 'considerable empirical evidence, based on research into a variety of occupations, suggesting that expertise does not derive from the application of rules or procedures applied deductively from positivist research' (Gould and Taylor, 1996: 1). Furthermore, they support the work of Schön in suggesting that educators must recognise that 'practice wisdom rests upon highly developed intuition which may be difficult to articulate but can be demonstrated through practice' (Gould and Taylor, 1996: 1). Winter et al (1999) support the view that reflective engagement in practice can provide a way of redressing the devaluation, deskilling and alienation now suffered in social work, resulting from a greater emphasis on fiscal and economic concerns:

> The reflective paradigm assembles its theoretical resources in order to defend professional values, creativity, and autonomy in a context where they are generally felt to be under attack from political and economic forces which threaten to transform the professional from an artist into an operative. (Winter et al, 1999: 193)

Moreover, Gould and Taylor (1996) advocate the promotion and support of reflective inquiry in social work and they offer a definition of reflective learning that takes into account the epistemological and moral challenges, cited previously, experienced by social workers in their everyday practice: 'Reflective learning offers an approach to education which operates through an understanding of professional knowledge as primarily developed through practice and the systematic analysis of experience' (Gould and Taylor, 1996: 1).

We believe that reflective engagement undertaken by professionals can help to redress many of the challenges represented in our surveys and interviews by diversifying contexts, activities and changes in social work. Importantly, it has the potential to permit practitioners to proactively shape the diversity of practice locations, activities and roles that they inhabit and to develop a real sense of agency in their work (Rath, 2000, 2010). As Thompson (2002: 222) notes:

> the reflective practitioner is a worker who is able to use experience and theoretical perspectives to guide and inform practice. Reflective practice involves being able to apply theory to practice, drawing on existing frameworks of ideas and knowledge so that you do not have to reinvent the wheel for each new situation as it arises but also being aware of 'ready made' solutions.

Thompson stresses how reflective inquiry encourages social workers to bring to their conscious awareness the conceptual frameworks that inform their practice, thereby promoting a real sense of responsibility to become active agents in the construction of practice. He concludes that 'If we do not recognise that frameworks of ideas and values are influencing how we act and interact, we are not in a position to question those ideas and ensure they are appropriate and constructive' (Thompson, 1995: 29). Knowledge for social work practice is a political and contextual activity constructed with reference to a number of related sources, research, personal and professional values and ethics, legislation, agency policies, and procedures. As Eraut (1994: 33) reflects, learning about practice takes place 'within the context of use', which involves a complex process of interpretation and modification of existing knowledge and paradigms in order to get to grips with the messy situations encountered in real life. Engaging in ongoing inquiry into one's practice is key to maintaining vibrant, responsible and responsive practitioners, and the provision of opportunities to engage in CPD is fundamental to this whole endeavour.

Reflective praxis: implications for organisations

The promotion of cultures and contexts of practice where reflection can develop and thrive is critical to its successful implementation. According to Argyris and Schön (1978, 1996), the provision of space and time permits workers' voices to be heard and their opinions to be considered in situations of change and transition; a necessary requirement, they allege, for the development of the learning organisation and for the successful promotion and implementation of change in organisational policy and practice. In support of Argyris and Schön (1978, 1996), Jennings and Kennedy (1996) state that if workers are to truly engage in reflection and CPD, a culture of inquiry must prevail within organisations, where structures are established to support and sustain it. Reflective engagement facilitates change and transition; however, it is crucial that the process is scaffolded and supported. The central position of managers in promoting the reflective endeavour is acknowledged, with some writers stating that those managers who are committed to furthering their own learning and CPD will be more open to the development of reflection throughout the organisation (Eraut, 2001; Thompson, 2006).

Embedding the reflective learning process within organisations will present a significant challenge as we struggle to manage organisational change and to provide good models of critically reflective practice. In placing a high value on the reflective learning process, it is necessary to demonstrate collaboration, partnership and empowerment in the way that we interact with each other. In work contexts that place a much higher value on outcomes, as opposed to process, reflective engagement can be viewed and experienced as countercultural. The process of critical reflection challenges the hegemony of a more positivist construction of knowledge in the fields of practice and research. It invites practitioners not only to examine their personal constructs of the world and the influence they have on shaping their approach to practice, but also to challenge the dominance of forms of professional practice that are outcome-driven and that value technical and theoretical knowledge above practice concerns and the development of 'practice wisdom' (Schön, 1987). As stated earlier, Freire (1996 [1972]) also sees reflection and reflective engagement as a necessary precursor to change and a driving force in achieving personal and political transformation.

Gould (2004) believes that individual learning alone is not a sufficient condition for organisational learning. He maintains that learning takes place across multiple levels within organisations and it necessarily involves the construction and reconstruction of individual and collective meanings and world views. He advocates the development of systems within organisations where reflective practitioners will be supported and thrive.

While much of the literature on reflective inquiry has concentrated attention on the internal and developmental process of reflection for reflective practice to develop and thrive in professional spheres, the organisations and agencies that employ these professionals need to be supportive of the process. The challenge for organisations is to recognise their shared responsibility to professionals in their employment to make available a range of opportunities for the promotion of reflective practice in supervision and through CPD. In this regard, the contribution that the portfolio can make to promoting and supporting practitioner reflective inquiry requires serious consideration.

Supporting reflective engagement: the portfolio

The portfolio as a tool for documenting the process and outcomes of one's work has been very well developed in relation to teacher education by researchers like Shulman (1994) and Lyons (1998, 2010).

Shulman describes a teaching portfolio as 'the structured documentary history of a (carefully selected) set of coached or mentored accomplishments substantiated by samples of students' work and fully realised only through reflective writing, deliberation and serious conversation' (cited in Lyons, 1998: 3). Reflection is the central learning paradigm on which the portfolio is constructed and it is represented through the portfolio process. According to Lyons (1998: 263):

> Reflection takes place over long periods of time in which connections, long strands of connections are made between one's values, purposes, and actions towards engaging students successfully in their own meaningful learning. Such understandings are constructed through conversations with colleagues, as all interrogate their practices, asking why they are engaged in them and with what effectiveness. These critical interrogations serve to foster awareness and knowledge of practice and of oneself as a teacher.

So described, the portfolio is a written record of the process and outcome of practice interventions that encourages writers to identify and interrogate their thoughts, feelings and actions. It is recognised as an important tool for supporting and scaffolding reflective learning in professional education (Lyons, 1998; Rath, 2000, 2010; Halton et al, 2007; Dempsey et al, 2008). Reflective practice, as documented through the portfolio process, sets out to systematically uncover the interpretive lens that practitioners bring to their work. The portfolio is vital to the development of a supportive structure, which can include reflective journal writing, reading, listening and sharing with peers and supervisors. The latter provide the mentors and 'critical friends' (Lyons, 1998) that are necessary to have reflective conversations.

The portfolio is a tool that supports reflective engagement and helps to make explicit the knowledge, values and assumptions that are implicit in their practice. Rath views reflective engagement as a habit of mind that needs to be supported and scaffolded in professional spheres: 'In order for this introspection to be useful as a professional tool, it must become a disciplinary habit of mind, attended to on an on-going basis, and linked to action in the professional context' (Rath, 2000: 155). This *'habit of mind'* is akin to Dewey's *'attitudes of mind'*; they are what the practitioner brings to the situation, the added ingredient that brings to the situation a sense of the individual as a meaning-maker, an agent of change. In addressing the issue of bridging the divide between theory and practice, Rath, writing on teacher education, links reflection to the development of a sense of agency among learners and practitioners. Agency is defined by Rath (2000: 154) as:

> the consciousness of oneself as an agent in the world, actively constructing meaning in one's engagement with reality. This sense of agency is central to taking responsibility for one's actions and for defining 'who we are, what we think and what we do' and is central to understanding active learning at all levels.

This sense of agency is essential for practitioners who are required to transfer knowledge, values and skills into the widely varying range of settings and situations in which they work. As noted previously, this call for the development of a sense of agency can be seen in public inquiry reports (Laming, 2009; SWTF, 2009; Gibbons, 2011; Munro, 2011).

While social work literature has focused significantly on the demonstration of core competencies that are applicable in, and transferable to, varying settings, it is the authors' contention, supported in research by Pease and Fook (1999), Fook (2002), Halton et al (2007), Dempsey et al (2008) and Murphy et al (2008, 2010), that the concept of reflection provides a more coherent organising schema for integrating knowledge, context-specific requirements and identity formation for social workers. Research demonstrates that reflective engagement facilitates practitioners to develop new skills or competencies in a responsive way to changing circumstances.

The authors believe that reflective engagement supports practitioners to proactively shape practice contexts, activities and roles, that is, to be active agents in the construction of practice (Rath, 2000, 2010). Social workers learn most of their day-to-day work skills 'on the job', and their transferability into new practice sites is dependent on the practitioner's awareness and use of professional judgement. These are important components of the sense of agency described by Rath (2000).

The use of the portfolio on professional social work programmes in UCC has been researched by Halton et al (2007), Dempsey et al (2008) and Murphy et al (2008), who found that the portfolio is a document that supports the documentation of students' learning and professional development over time. The portfolio is represented in the work of Lyons (1998) as both a formative and summative learning tool and it has been found on social work education programmes to help students scaffold the development of their thinking as practitioners (Halton et al, 2007; Dempsey et al, 2008; Murphy et al, 2008, 2010).

We believe that the portfolio encourages writers to deconstruct practice on an ongoing basis and, in the process, to excavate and publicly display their underlying beliefs, values and knowledge and to demonstrate how they influence decision-making. The research demonstrates that on the Master of Social Work programme, some students were more capable of engaging in this process than others. Furthermore, many students had some difficulty in writing the portfolio, thereby requiring several layers of support and mentoring from tutors and supervisors. However, as the portfolio represented a new way of documenting both the process and the outcome of their learning, this posed challenges for them and for tutors and supervisors (Halton et al, 2007; Dempsey et al, 2008; Murphy et al, 2008, 2010).

Research into the use of the portfolio on professional social work education programmes demonstrated that this approach to teaching and learning was countercultural within more traditional formal educational settings. In the portfolio, students were asked to focus on the process of their learning, when previously they were required to focus on content. They were required to represent the personal values, beliefs, ideas and judgements that underpinned their practice decisions rather than focusing primarily on representing the work of theoreticians and academics. Ultimately, they were being asked to risk writing about their mistakes as well as their achievements. The portfolio invited students to write about ongoing, developmental, unfinished accounts of their thoughts and actions, when their previous experience had been of writing summative, 'polished' pieces (Murphy et al, 2010: 185). Once again, the concept of risk arises for those involved with portfolio construction, assessment and evaluation, that is, to accept the uncertainties that are embedded in social work practice and to embrace the inevitability of risk associated with this uncertainty. The portfolio challenges a more traditional epistemological orientation, and, as such, tensions can arise between all involved with their construction and assessment.

Overall, the portfolio provides a developmental framework for the documentation by practitioners of practice. It is represented as a reflective tool that helps to bring together academic and field-based learning. Rath (2010: 509) asserts that 'the portfolio helps to bring the world of theory and practice together through the process of reflection and the enactment in practice'. Writing about her experiences of developing a reflective learning curriculum in teacher education and her use of the portfolio as a teaching and learning tool, Rath (2010: 509) found in her research with students that 'the experience of writing down ideas and documenting teaching practices allows him [the student] to capture insights that he can return to, critically examine, and reconsider.... Thus, the process of producing a text becomes a developmental, transformational process'.

Inevitably, the question of transparency of practice arises. This brings the domain of 'thinking in action' into the eye of the public and makes it available for public scrutiny. We recognise that there has to be a public face to social work practice as the public funds the work and understandably demands to see how their money is utilised. When the public are given access to information that allows them to see where and how their money is spent and the justification for its allocation and consumption, they are more likely to be supportive. The portfolio is an evidential document that makes available to the practitioner (author) and its readers the process, content and outcome of reflective inquiry in practice. Reflective engagement supports transparency; it requires practitioners to interrogate their interventions with actual cases in practice and to document this process through the portfolio, which provides a public space and vehicle for deliberate, intentional inquiry, as Rath (2010: 511) concludes:

> they [portfolios] take seriously the formation of professional identities that are committed to responsible, open, and adaptive practices in service of a more socially just world. Reflective engagement creates a 'public space' for deliberate and intentional inquiry on the complexity of teaching and learning acts and the social and power relations that can sponsor their transformation.

In supporting practices of transparency and public accountability, trust-building is important (Dempsey et al, 2008; Murphy et al, 2010). This means attempting to develop public learning forums where joint learning and development can occur between practitioners and employers. Freidus (2001), writing on teacher education, refers to this process as 'enculturation' into the discourse of reflective teaching/ learning. She suggests that facilitating students to become competent reflectors on their own practice requires a 'relentless pervasiveness' of opportunities for reflection throughout whole programmes. This poses a challenge for universities and for organisations. However, Murphy et al (2010) found that the reflective process, by fostering a deep understanding by students of particular subject areas, can help to unify staff to achieve the 'pervasiveness' discussed by Freidus (2001).

Research into the use of the portfolio process on graduate and postgraduate social work programmes at UCC (Halton, 2007; Murphy et al, 2010) demonstrates strong support for the reflective approach to teaching and learning adopted on these programmes, and also their use of the portfolio as a formative and summative assessment tool. The portfolio, learning journal and peer support were regarded as essential learning tools on the programmes, and respondents linked their use to improvements in work practices (Murphy et al, 2008; Halton, 2010). Students connected the portfolio to evidence-based practice. In research carried out by Halton (2011), social workers on a postgraduate programme in practice teaching and supervision noted at interview that the portfolio was 'A great experience – evidence based practice in formation'; and 'I enjoyed doing the portfolio and the concept of evidence of learning. I have kept the portfolio and occasionally use it.' It was also noted that 'the portfolio brought organisation and clarity to the new language used in practice.' Emphasising the benefits of the portfolio in terms of showcasing and ordering her work, another research participant remarked that: 'This [the portfolio] helped to keep my work in order as well as my thought process. It also helped to show other colleagues and peers how much work is completed while on the course' (Halton, 2011).

In the same study (Halton, 2011), participants acknowledged at interview the potential of the portfolio for promoting 'agency', a sense of responsibility for one's own learning and in terms of authoring one's work. One respondent observed: 'It [the portfolio] leaves more control and power with the student [writer]'. In addition, the portfolio as a tool to reflect, to evidence and to map the process and outcome of one's practice was highlighted: 'This to me was the overall reflective practice of all my assembled process of work. It evidenced my learning and even now when I take it out I can map the progress of my learning'. Also:

> The portfolio was a great tool for learning. I found it very useful to gather information relating to my learning. I have looked back at the quality of work covered in the portfolio

> and I am very impressed with myself – Assignments and
> other evidences of learning. The guidelines provided for
> writing the portfolio were particularly useful. I particularly
> like the reflection on learning incidences. (Halton, 2011)

We believe that the promotion of the portfolio as a tool to encourage
reflective engagement in terms of CPD and practitioner ongoing
professional development in social work agencies will require careful
planning and consideration. Research has demonstrated that reflective
portfolio processes are both stimulating and challenging for practitioners
on a post-qualifying programme (Halton et al, 2007; Murphy et al, 2008,
2010; Halton, 2011). Our research supports the integrative nature of
the portfolio-building process and its potential to provide a structure
whereby values, belief systems, knowledge, skills, theory and research-
based knowledge are interwoven with practice experiences as evidence
to support professional assessments and recommendations.

Relationships will change as a result of registration requirements and
the implementation of CPD. Change is inevitable and the consequences
for practice and for the profession must be acknowledged. The
challenges of change must be proactively prepared for and responded
to with thoughtful deliberation. Hence, the case has to be made for
skilled managers, well-trained supervisors and teachers to help lead and
steer the course of this change. As practice inquiry through the portfolio
becomes a normal, taken-for-granted part of a professional's everyday
working life, the belief is that practitioners will become more open
to reviewing their practice in dialogue with colleagues, service users
and supervisors. Instead of the pressure to conform to a stereotypical
template of the all-knowing, all-competent, untouchable professional,
it will become increasingly possible to find an authentic identity where
'mistakes' are seen as opportunities for learning and where risk and
uncertainty are recognised as a normal, if challenging, part of social
work practice and not something to be avoided.

The public portfolio-making process encourages and celebrates
differences in practitioners and their styles of practice. Herein lays the
potential for acceptance of greater individual variation in the client base
and among practitioners. It makes visible the reality that practitioners
have different styles, emphases, theoretical orientations, practice
competencies and preferences in terms of social work methods and
skills, without compromising a common commitment to professional
standards, client service, social inclusion and ethical practice. It provides
a real opportunity for practitioners to embrace the varying levels of
complexity and ambiguity associated with social work and to represent

the creativity and diversity of practice in different work contexts. By doing so, it offers a lifelong tool for recognising just how each practitioner's actions (or inactions) help to shape not just individual practice, but also the agencies and their functioning.

The portfolio documents both the process and outcome of a practitioner's interventions, and their engagement in reflective practice represents an important CPD tool because of its 'public' nature. As an artefact that would be available to organisations and registration authorities, it would not simply be something that is 'private' and 'personal'. Using the portfolio to document practice and CPD would help to facilitate the making public of the processes and outcomes of practitioner interventions, thereby making them open to examination and scrutiny and available for feedback from peers, the institution and the public. We propose that use of the portfolio can help to make practice 'safer', not because of and through 'defensive' practice, but through systematic examination and evaluation that is thoughtful, reflective and responsive to the many questions emerging in practice and not merely focused on the perpetuation and salvation of the institution.

Conclusion

The literature on reflective practice, as documented through the portfolio process and supported and mentored in supervision, can, we believe, help to prevent professional atrophy. Both pose challenges at a personal level in a lifetime career, as well as at an institutional level. We know that over-compliance can also lead to atrophy. Furthermore, we know that many institutions close up and become defensive when faced with impending change. Moreover, practitioners have also learned from personal experience to regard compliance as the highest virtue. However, research on reflective practice views compliance as anathema to real learning and to ongoing professional development. Researchers like Dewey (1933), Freire (1972) and Schön (1983, 1987) provide learning theories that help to structure and support reflective engagement. The portfolio provides the tool for the documentation of the processes and outcomes of reflection. Social work as a profession needs practitioners who will be open to being proactive in pursuing change on all levels: individual, social, organisational and political. It also needs organisations and employers that will develop systems, practices and cultures where practitioners are supported to seriously engage in reflective inquiry.

Meeting change with what Dewey would call attitudes of mind – '*open mindedness*', '*wholeheartedness*' and '*responsibility*' – and with what Freire terms '*transformative ideals*' is imperative if social work is to respond reflexively to the many social, political, economic, professional and practice challenges documented throughout this text. Unless practitioners are encouraged and supported within the professional bodies and in their employing organisations to engage in reflective practice, we argue that social work practice will continue to be defined in terms of supporting the status quo, and defensive practice will continue. We have seen an incremental loss of trust by the public in institutions of the state. We believe that this loss of trust will continue and will be exacerbated if those institutions and public servants cease to be critically reflective, and continue to defend themselves. The challenge now posed for organisations of the state is to seriously engage in what Freire (1996 [1972]) refers to as a praxis that is performed in public and that has transformation at its heart.

How can social work maximise its potential to advocate on behalf of the marginalised and less well off in our community, as well as respond to the demands for evidence of performance and productivity? Social workers can become submerged by organisational cultures that demand greater accountability and compliance, which any professional will experience as oppression. We believe that compliance subjugates professional judgement and elevates the knowledge of the institution and its rules. Paulo Freire's work poses many ethical and moral challenges for the social work profession and for social workers because it links compliance and oppression. Freire highlights the importance of raising consciousness, which in and of itself is radical and ultimately a radical act if carried through to completion. Following through on professional judgement and taking an ethical and moral stance as opposed to 'doing what one is told' has the potential to transform social work practice.

Why should organisations and the registration authorities embrace the portfolio as a professional development tool? Because agencies, professionals and professional bodies are defensively positioned, they are in danger of being defined in that regard rather than as being a service for the public. Naturally, this could result in a further shrinkage of public funding support and further diminution of services at a public level. The only way social work has of sustaining itself through these turbulent professional times is through promoting and supporting processes where professional judgement is valued, a professional judgement that has safety inbuilt through systems, processes and tools that are open to public scrutiny, that is, the portfolio. The portfolio is recognised as a tool that promotes professional development across the professions (Lyons, 1998; Murphy et al, 2008; Rath, 2010). It supports the documentation of developmental processes in educational programmes at both graduate and postgraduate levels. Extending its use into CPD would seem to respond to the requirements of social workers, as recommended in public inquiries, to engage in reflective practice and to clearly and publicly articulate evidence of their practice interventions and outcomes. We argue that the portfolio supports the documentation of practitioners' ongoing professional learning and development in practice; a growth that cannot be measured in numbers, which is the scientific way of measuring change, but is measured by changed behaviour, adaptive behaviours and, ultimately, practices that demonstrate responsiveness and reflectivity in practice. Rath (2010: 512), writing on teacher education, suggests that the portfolio offers a structured approach to practising reflection that helps to structure the process of *'learning from experience'*. Rath's work in the field of teacher education has much to offer social work and other human service professions as they try to grapple with issues of uncertainty and changing epistemologies of practice. While social workers do not legislate for a particular social order, we believe that engaging in the process of reflective inquiry can help them to recognise the possibilities for transformation that are situated in their practice. Social workers can take their counsel from the words of Rath (2010), a teacher educator who wrote about the transformative and generative possibilities of reflective inquiry in the classroom. Rath (2010: 512) identifies the task of teachers in the classroom as:

> to transform learning cultures into environments where complex practice can occur and where learners can synthesize and integrate many different and opposing viewpoints and perspectives ... reflective engagement becomes a generative cultural tool for both teacher educators and teachers to reframe teaching as inquiry and as a practice of engagement with complexity.

Teachers and social workers are practitioners working within cultures of practice and organisations experiencing similar social and political challenges. Change is being advocated at every level within these systems and organisations. Undoubtedly, social workers, like teachers, are required to be efficient and effective within challenging institutional environments and practice contexts. Our research clearly demonstrates that institutional constraints can limit opportunities for reflection on practice and for practitioners' engagement with CPD. We believe that reflective inquiry, scaffolded by the portfolio process, offers new possibilities for lifelong learning, CPD and professional development in social work practice and proffers the same transformative potential and generative possibilities for social workers as for teachers. There are larger structural issues confronting social work that are situated at the interface between thought and action. These issues demand critical reflection if the social work profession is to remain faithful to its historic mission to the poor and oppressed. We now turn to an analysis of these policy and epistemological issues in Chapters Seven and Eight.

SEVEN

Thinking and acting

The classic period of the 'modern' state in the West was in the decades between 1945 and 1980. It was not a utopia by any means, but it did have certain key characteristics: a faith in the power of government to create better societies, a consequent prestige for the idea of public services as an admirable ethic, a commitment to the belief that societies should become more equal over time, and an optimistic view of human nature in which altruism, trust, self-sacrifice and mutual benefit were given at least as big a place as the potential for violence, hatred and self-destructive selfishness....

Beginning with a specific strain in mathematical economics in the United States, the idea took hold that human beings are actually isolated, coldly rational creatures who are programmed to seek only their own advantage. These instincts and desires could best be served and kept in equilibrium by understanding people as both competitors and consumers. They get resources by ruthlessly competing with each other and they express their individuality by using those resources to make consumer choices. Everything else – altruism, 'the public interest', 'public services' – is an illusion. Those who believe in such notions are either idiots or – in this mentality, more admirably – hypocrites, using rhetoric to mask their real pursuit of their own personal advantage. (O'Toole, 2012: 40)

This dark vision of the contemporary world, presented by writer and commentator Fintan O'Toole, captures the challenges that confront social work in an era we call 'postmodernity'. A societal rupture has taken place that is changing the context of social work. Viviene Cree (2011: 5) has observed: 'it is not certain what the future will hold for the profession of social work, but given the course of social work's history and its recent experience, it seems likely that more organisational and institutional upheaval lies ahead'. Continuing professional development (CPD) will play an important part in the future of social work by providing a forum where the profession can reflect upon the policy and practice challenges it faces and consider its responses in terms of a social work mission suited to postmodernity. In Chapter Three, we reported that our survey found only 2% of CPD course choices were focused on empowerment and social justice; albeit that some managers and practitioners expressed concern about an imbalance in provision in favour of therapeutic and counselling courses. As already noted in Chapter Three, one social worker observed: "it is the exact opposite of what social work purports to be about". In this chapter, we seek to address these issues of what CPD should be about by mapping the contours of contemporary social work and analysing debates about: critical theory and social work; the 'Big Society'; marketisation and managerialism; trust and risk; and possibilities for change. These debates, we argue, need to be incorporated into the social work educational curriculum that analyses the relationship between thinking and action. The questions they raise are not easy to answer. They could lead to analytic despair. We contend that the challenges for social work, posed by contemporary reality, are challenges for social work education. These challenges, in our view, ought to be addressed in the CPD curricula because they shape epistemology. We suggest a Freirean approach as a critical epistemology that rejects intellectual pessimism and envisages a critical theory of action. Freire (1996 [1972]: 62) asserts that education must be shaped by creativity and participation in a problem-solving process that critically engages with reality:

> The students – no longer docile listeners – are now critical co-investigators in dialogue with the teacher. The teacher presents the material to the students for their consideration, and re-considers her earlier considerations as the students express their own. The role of the problem-posing educator is to create, together with the students, the conditions under which knowledge at the level of the *doxa* is superseded by true knowledge, at the level of the *logos*.
>
> Whereas banking education anesthetizes and inhibits creative power, problem-posing education involves a constant unveiling of reality. The former attempts to maintain the *submersion* of consciousness; the latter strives for the *emergence* of consciousness and *critical intervention* in reality.
>
> Students, as they are increasingly posed with problems relating to themselves in the world and with the world, will feel increasingly challenged and obliged to respond

to that challenge. Because they apprehend the challenge as interrelated to other problems within a total context, not as a theoretical question, the resulting comprehension tends to be increasingly critical and thus constantly less alienated. Their response to the challenge evokes new challenges, followed by new understandings; and gradually the students come to regard themselves as committed.

Education as the practice of freedom – as opposed to education as the practice of domination – denies that man is abstract, isolated, independent, and unattached to the world; it also denies that the world exists as a reality apart from people. Authentic reflection considers neither abstract man nor the world without people, but people in their relations with the world. In these relations consciousness and world are simultaneous: consciousness neither precedes the world nor follows it.

The dialectic logic of the chapter will seek to explore the contradiction between 'humanization' and 'dehumanization', as Freire (1996: 25) has conceptualised it, and how social work education can through a process of critical reflection, confront contemporary reality with a view to changing it.

Critical theory

In Chapter Six, we argued that postmodernity has a profound impact on social work, which has been transformed by the neoliberal critique into a symbol of an overweening welfare state. Social work's purported regulatory power mechanisms have become reflexively categorised as 'authoritarian', although this perceived 'authoritarianism' emerges as an attempt to regulate behaviour considered to be 'illicit' by the predominant social-symbolic order, for example, child abuse. This paradox undermines the public view of the postmodern social worker because the mode of symbolic authority upon which the legitimacy of the profession rests has been culturally rejected. Ironically, the postmodern social order employs similar modes of symbolic authority to regulate vast areas of human behaviour, notably, restrictions on lifestyle: smoking, eating, sexuality and so on. Yet, postmodern society, immersed in consumer values, celebrates 'choice' as the guiding influence over symbolic law. Social work, in this postmodern civilisational configuration, is perceived as the antithesis of 'choice', since it is part of the apparatus of the enforcement state – Lacan's 'Big Other'.

The enforcement state conjures up the image of French philosopher Michel Foucault's concept of 'governmentality'. As a strategy of governance, the concept of 'governmentality' suggests organised practices (mentalities, rationalities and techniques) intended to produce citizens compliant within public policy. In Foucault's conceptualisation, social sites (schools, hospitals, psychiatric institutions) are part of the apparatus of power because they regulate citizens' behaviour through the internalisation of power. Social work emerges in the Foucauldian analysis as part of the enforcement state, seeking to promote behavioural norms that will make 'problem' citizens into dutiful citizens (Donzelot, 1997). However, social reality is more complex. Citizens are not simply 'subjects'. They actively contest for power over their lives. The Velvet Revolutions of 1989, the Arab Spring in 2011 and the Occupy movement in the West during 2011 all testify to citizens' capacity for agency (Powell, 2013). Freire (1996 [1972]: 29) observes in reference to citizen resistance to oppression as a reasoned and reflective response:

> To surmount the situation of oppression, people must first critically recognize its causes, so that through transforming action they can create a new situation, one which makes possible the pursuit of a fuller humanity. But the struggle to be more fully human has already begun in the authentic struggle to transform the situation. Although the situation of oppression is a dehumanized and dehumanizing totality affecting both the oppressors and those whom they oppress, it is the latter who must, from their stifled humanity, wage for both the struggle for a fuller humanity; the oppressor, who is himself dehumanized because he dehumanizes others, is unable to lead their struggle.

Freire is offering a message of hope in which he locates 'the oppressed' as potentially actors in their own liberation, but he does not underestimate the challenges:

> The oppressed, having internalized the image of the oppressor and adopted his guidelines, are fearful of freedom. Freedom would require them to eject this image and replace it with autonomy and responsibility. Freedom is acquired by conquest, not by gift. It must be pursued constantly and responsibly. Freedom is not an ideal located outside of

man; nor is it an idea which becomes myth. It is rather the indispensable condition for the quest for human completion. (Freire, 1996 [1972]: 29)

Freire's optimism of the will is reflected in Khaled Mattawa's (2012: xiii) poem celebrating the recent Arab Spring, called 'Now that we have tasted hope':

Now that we have tasted hope,
   Now that we have come out of hiding,
   Why would we live again in the tombs we'd made out of our souls?
   And the sundered bodies that we re-assembled with prayers and consolations,
   What would their torn parts be other than flesh?

As Dennis Saleeby (2011: 185) asserts: 'the heroism of everyday is all around us'. Barbara Fawcett (2011: 228), in an essay on postmodernism in social work, differentiates between 'postmodernity as a way of referring to the postmodern condition and postmodernism as a means of understanding the condition'. She further notes the impact of postmodernity on the construction and deconstruction of the 'self', arguing:

with regard to understanding the 'self', postmodern perspectives replace a modernist 'core' unitary 'self' that remains the same in all situations, with a fluid fragmented 'self', which is continually constructed and reconstructed by social practices and the interplay of dominant discourses. (Fawcett, 2011: 231)

Modernists have critiqued postmodernity as an epistemological project because of its perceived analytic despair and lack of emancipatory vision. Santos (2007: xix) views postmodernism as a form of 'epistemicide'. But critical social theory has arguably provided a conceptual bridge between modernism and postmodernism, allowing for the exploration of power relations and new empowering epistemological perspectives, influenced by feminism, queer theory and so on (Fraser, 1997).

Postmodern political consciousness has changed our understanding of what it means to be a citizen. Various strands within postmodern political life, such as feminism and disability rights, have challenged the precepts of liberalism and social democracy by reshaping the political agenda.

The personal has become political. The private spaces of social life, first opened to public scrutiny by pioneer social workers in the Victorian era, have become the battleground of cultural politics in the 21st century. Multiculturalism has had a major impact on social work theory and practice. Citizens are challenging experts and expert knowledge systems (Fisher, 2000). Radical democrats espousing participation through the fragmented causes of new social movements have been joined by neoliberals in challenging the hegemonic influences of liberalism, social democracy and the corporate state. The great meta-narratives of the pursuit of human emancipation through republicanism and socialism have lost their persuasive force in postmodern discourse. The politics of postmodernity has reshaped political discourse into an interplay between human subjectivities and the state. This reflexive process is continuously reinventing political issues into new forms, new debates and new subjectivities. Postmodern consciousness has transformed established meanings and relationships between the family, civil society and the state into an anti-bureaucratic and anti-clientist form, based upon the democratic value of the citizens' rights to participate. These opposed views of postmodernity mean transforming civil society into an ideological battlefield between neoliberalism and an emergent social Left (Powell, 2013). Connolly and Hourigan (2006) have demonstrated the growing importance of new social movements in reshaping Irish politics, including the possibilities for enhanced participation and the dangers of incorporation. Drawing on an Irish national survey of community workers, Powell and Geoghegan (2004) identified the problems of incorporation and the double-bind that social partnership imposes upon the community sector. Adapting social work to the social realities of the postmodern world is a key challenge for CPD since it goes to the core of the discipline's epistemological base and meaningful engagement with society.

We live in a society defined by risk, polarisation, global markets, chronic change and fragmentation. As Stokes and Knight (1997) have observed: 'today we seem to be plunging into a chaotic, privatised future, recapturing medieval extremes of wealth and squalor'. Ferguson et al (2002: 1) observe that in this new neoliberal order, 'social work is becoming more punitive, and social workers more stretched and stressed'. They conclude that placing profit before people 'has had a deleterious effect on the services provided for the working class, for the poor and for those in need' (Ferguson et al, 2002: 1). The austerity regime following the 2008 crash will have made things a lot worse.

According to postmodern theorists, including Anthony Giddens (1991) and Ulrich Beck (1992), our lives are no longer governed by nature or tradition. Instead, there is a socio-symbolic order (what Lacan calls the 'Big Other' – a kind of superego diffused throughout society) that regulates human behaviour in the postmodern world. Reflexivity 'colonises' the everyday aspects of lifestyle (including childcare, parenting, diet and leisure), which are habits to be learned and changed as the fashion of the time requires. Even the 'social' is now reflexively constructed. In vulgarised terms, the postmodernist version of reflexive society is that it is 'whatever we tell ourselves it is'. This gives us a sense of 'choice' over our lifestyles and identities, since we 'are' ultimately whoever we choose to 'be' – the products of our own narrative imagination.

On the face of it, our civilisation is both atomised and fractured. Yet, there is a paradox that confounds such conclusions. While the self, in the form of the independent citizen, may have become sovereign in the choice of lifestyles, solidarity is maintained by recognition-based social relations such as love, friendship, trust, empathy and compassion, charity, altruism and mutualism, and the willingness to make sacrifices for others. In short, as Berking (1996: 192) observes, 'these are cognitive, normative and emotional competencies which anything but reduce interest in the other to the mode of a merely strategic interaction'.

Boaventura de Sousa Santos has sought to confront the nihilism of postmodern theory in a project called 'Reinventing Social Emancipation', which has resulted in a series of challenging books. The third book in Santos's series, *Another knowledge is possible* (Santos, 2007) confronts Margaret Thatcher's 1980s' assertion that 'There is no alternative' with the proclamation by the World Social Forum that in the 21st century, 'Another world is possible'. Santos (2007: xix) links social justice to critical social theory and emancipatory practice:

> The main argument of this book is that there is no global social justice without global cognitive justice. Probably more than ever, global capitalism appears as a civilizational paradigm encompassing all domains of social life. The exclusion, oppression and discrimination it produces have not only economic, social, and political dimensions but also cultural and epistemological ones. Accordingly, to confront this paradigm in all its dimensions is the challenge facing a new critical theory and new emancipatory practices. Contrary to their predecessors, this theory and these practices must start from the premise that the epistemological diversity of the world is immense, as immense as its cultural diversity and that the recognition of such diversity must be

at the core of the global resistance against capitalism and of the formulation of alternative forms of sociability.

Dennis Saleeby (2011: 184–93), in his 'strengths perspective' in social work practice, is strongly influenced by Paulo Freire, arguing that his approach rests upon two philosophical principles: (1) liberation and empowerment; and (2) the combating of alienation and oppression in the lives of service users. Santos and Saleeby are reminding us that there are alternative epistemologies. These critical perspectives need to be at the centre of the CPD curriculum. They clearly have the capacity to breathe new life into social work theory and practice in what is increasingly called the 'Big Society'.

The 'Big Society', social work and postmodernity

Tony Judt (2012), in a valedictory testament, described social democracy as 'the banality of good'. He might have been talking about social work. In postmodern society, Judt (2012: 373) concludes, 'all that remains is the charitable impulse derived from a sense of guilt towards other suffering individuals'. Social suffering is an increasingly privatised experience. As the modernist sense of collective responsibility fades, we are left with a more atomised society in which the state is less supportive of the citizen and has re-situated itself towards the market in a project called 'Big Society, Small Government'.

Brodsgaard (2009: 113) observes that 'during the 1980s and most of the 1990s the critique of big government was the dominant theme of public policy and debate'. Conservative ideas in the form of neoliberalism re-emerged throughout most of the developed world and following the Thatcher and Reagan regimes, Western political-economic thinking shifted towards the Right, advocating 'small government, big society'. Remarkably, Brodsgaard, in his study of the Chinese island province of Hainan, also notes similar developments under an entirely different ideological regime, officially communist. The political theorist and reformer Liao Xun published a tract addressing Marx and Engels' purported view of 'small government' and also argued the case for economic liberalisation. Liao Xun's tract suggested that Marx and Engels (through their theory of 'the withering away of the state') favoured small government, unlike the big government of the Russian Soviet model. Liao Xun presented the case for downsizing bureaucracy and government as a key element in socialist reform (Brodsgaard, 2009: 86). In Liao Xun's view, the role of the state needed to be shrunk to the core functions: 'traffic cop', 'soccer referee' and 'firefighter'. The rest was up to civil society. However, his project in Hainan failed (partly because of a property bubble that collapsed the local economy in 1996) (Brodsgaard, 2009: 9). There is also a deeper problem in replacing politics with economic rationalism. It fails to connect with the public because it lacks a political imaginary (Robin, 2011: 162). Despite its failure in Hainan, the 'Big Society, Small Government' project was adopted by the Chinese Communist Party (CPC) as a national strategy in 2004 (Boychuk, 2007: 201). The adoption of the 'Big Society' model in China has coincided with a major expansion in social work training. This development of social work in China might be interpreted in two ways: as the personalisation of social problems; or as a growing recognition of civil society by the Chinese party-state. Either way, it indicates a role for social work in the 'Big Society'.

But what will social work in China be, a soccer referee, traffic cop or a firefighter? Or will it perform all three roles, as the state withdraws from the public sphere? Are these roles metaphors for the future of social work practice in postmodern society? Do they have application to Western society? Well, in a globalised world, Liao Xun's concept of 'Big Society, Small Government' is almost certainly going to be highly relevant to the rest of the world. It suggests a kind of ghost welfare state, where shadowy figures perform existential roles in a disaster society. Japanese novelist Haruki Murakami, in his recent novel *1Q84* (Murakami, 2011) (inspired by George Orwell's political parable *1984*), describes a counter-world of unreality – 'Big Society'?

'Big Society' is also a major policy issue in the West. Philip Blond's (2010) book *Red Tory* seeks to move British Conservative politics away from neoliberalism towards the 'Big Society' ideal, which combines economic equity with social conservatism in a new conservative narrative. Blondist conservatism is based on the disaggregation of civil society from the state in a social project that would ultimately replace the welfare state with charity, including faith-based charity. But there the problems begin. Bruce Anderson, writing in the *Financial Times* (2011) asserts: 'no one knows what "Big Society" means. The word "big" is vaguely threatening.' He concludes: 'the Big Society is not about coercion. It is about freedom, creativity and responsibility.' In reality, it is about civil society replacing the state as the 'first sector', rather than being the 'third sector'. It is manifestly a big political project, but, like Murakami's 'little people', the 'little platoons' of Cameron's 'Big Society' are by their nature invisible. They are more abstract ideas than real welfare programmes. That makes the concept of the 'Big Society' vaguely unsettling. The implications for social work are fundamental. It would be relocated from the welfare state back to voluntary organisations. It raises major questions about how professional social work can be funded in the future. That begs the question: 'Will professional social workers be replaced by "little platoons" of volunteers?'.

Arguably, the fallacy in the Conservative narrative for welfare reform, based upon the 'Big Society' project, is the fictional notion that is possible to roll back the state without running the risk of returning society to the Dickensian conditions of the Poor Law and reliance on charity for the 'deserving' poor. Blond's (2010: 206) citation of the 1890s' Primrose League directly connects the 'Big Society' project to its Victorian antecedents. Davis (2006) has compellingly demonstrated the abject quality of social life in states without state welfare, where slum conditions resemble the 19th-century England described by Engels in 1844 (Engels, 1993 [1844]). Civil society, in the neoliberal form of charity, arguably provides little in the way of solutions to structural poverty and weakens the bonds that hold democracy together because of its association with the welfare reform agenda that is driven by the political objective of ending social justice as the basis of political community. This suggests that the 'Big Society' project may turn out to be a political fiction rather than a new political narrative. Albeit, Jesse Norman (2010: 204), in presenting 'the contractual case', argues that the Big Society is ultimately about a new subjectivity, which he calls ICE – 'institutions, competition and entrepreneurship'. The archaic 18th-century image of Edmund Burke's 'little platoons' has done little to persuade the public that 'Big Society' is a positive political subject for the 21st century. There are too many unanswered questions. The imagery is wrong in a democracy. Social democrats have also been influenced by this 'Big Society' thinking, as they have re-situated their political project towards market capitalism in response to the dominance of neoliberal ideology. While the language is different, the policy substance is shared by conservatives and social democrats: shrink the state by transferring responsibility to civil society for its own welfare. New Labour's 'Third Way' in Britain epitomised its welfare reform strategy (Powell, 2013).

Kate Wilson et al (2011: 91), in a discussion of the implications of the 'Big Society' for social work in the UK, view it as transformative:

> the coalition Prime Minister, David Cameron, promoted
> his idea of 'Big Society' of locally organised voluntary effort
> and social entrepreneurship, at the same time many of the
> regulatory bodies and strategic organisations that shaped

health and social care provision over the previous decade were abolished or merged with other organisations.

As part of this process of rationalisation, the General Social Care Council, which had responsibility for the registration of the social work profession, was abolished in 2010 and its functions merged with a series of health organisations, inevitably weakening the profession's identity.

At the core of the 'Big Society' project is the objective of shrinking the state in line with its 'Big Society: Small Government' philosophy. Kate Wilson et al (2011: 91–2) conclude that these changes have significant political implications for the social work profession:

> They announced a vision of society in which strategic planning and central control of policy-making would be largely 'devolved' to local level, opening the way for more private and independent sector interests to flourish. However, a central function of strategic planning lies in its ability to redistribute resources and services to disadvantaged regions and localities, offsetting some of the 'structural' causes and effects of poverty.
>
> With fewer social work and social care 'support' services which are easy targets for savings, less strategic social care, education and health planning, and the likelihood of higher unemployment as the public sector contracts, localised poverty and disadvantage is certain to increase. Pressure on core, statutory social work services will mount as a result.
>
> The vision of a 'deregulated' society has other implications. The [Conservative–Liberal Democrat] coalition spoke often of the need to 'return power to professionals', and putting health planning in the hands of family doctors rather than 'bureaucrats' was one expression of this. Likewise the government's support for the emerging College of Social Work signalled their willingness to invest more autonomy and trust in the profession's own organisations. But the granting of greater 'autonomy' in a context of far more restricted opportunities and resources is a double-edged gift.

At a more fundamental level, the question arises as to whether the 'Big Society: Small Government' philosophy compatible with democracy? It is probably too early to say. But, so far, the omens are not propitious. The Conservative–Liberal Democrat Coalition government in the UK has sought to implement its 'Big Society' project through devolving policing to 41 new police and crime commissioners (PCCs) across England and Wales. However, elections in 2012 to the PCCs attracted little public participation, leading the *Guardian* (Travis and Wintour, 2012) to report that one of the signature elements of the 'Big Society' had failed to connect with the citizens in the eyes of its political critics. The connection between Michel Foucault's concept of 'governmentality' – meaning techniques and strategies by which a society is rendered governable – is very apparent in the PCCs as a signature policy of the 'Big Society'. If the 'Big Society' is intended to engage with citizens, it would appear that citizens are not cooperating with the government's attempts to draw them into a new project of governance.

The birth of the 'Big Society' has emerged in a world where politics is experiencing a restoration. The year 2011 witnessed the Arab Spring, the Occupy movement and *Los Indignados*. Civil society coexists in a triangular relationship with the state and the market. It is an uneasy relationship. Modernism resulted in a fusion between the state and civil society that produced the welfare state (Powell, 2013). Postmodernism has refocused that relationship into a growing fusion with the market. Civil society struggles to maintain its autonomy as a public sphere, where democratic association can flourish in sustainable communities. It is a contested role both in terms of the internal ethical goals of civil society to promote civic virtue and the external agendas of the state and the market to dominate society. But contestation defines civil society's role in the political order. Civic virtue rests on the idea of a virtuous state that ideally places equal value on the well-being of each of its citizens and their futures. This is the ideal of the welfare state. The reality invariable falls short of that ideal. Interests compete for the attention of the state. The more powerful the interest, the more likely it is to succeed in its goal of influencing the direction of policy. Civil society provides an ethical framework for social services because it represents the active voice of citizenship. Social work is deeply rooted in that ethical framework of society as the expression of the need for civic virtue in governance. How can social work contribute to a more ethical system of governance? That must be a core task of CPD, which will be challenged to consider the profession's ethical base in the shifting sands of the incoming postmodernist tide. How do we make society better when it is fragmenting into an atomised empty space? Santos (2007: xli) calls for 'revolutionizing the concept of social work'. Saleeby's (2006) *The strengths perspective in social work practice* seeks to address this task. Other social work theorists, such as Lena Dominelli (1998, 2002) have sought to re-imagine social work in a multicultural context. Bob Mullaly (1997) has articulated a social justice perspective that confronts the dehumanising effects of global capitalism. The critical social perspectives of these social work theorists and many others offer an important conceptual framework for CPD because this canon of knowledge interrogates social reality from alternative discursive perspectives based upon Freire's concept of 'humanisation'. The common sense that 'There is no alternative' (Margaret Thatcher and her ideological successors) to austerity, cultural domination and a market society are fundamentally questioned by these social work theorists. Their counter-vision of reality, predicated upon human agency, is important to discuss and consider in social work education. Equally, it is important to consider the arguments and positionality of dominant cultural and political discourses, if only to understand them.

Marketisation and managerialism: 'a new culture of social work'?

Another way of giving fresh definition to social work in postmodern society has been the adoption of market values, what has been described as 'a new culture of social work' (Wilson et al, 2011: 30). Nigel Horner (2012: 108) observes that 'the advent of the New Right policy under the Conservative Government after 1979 led to the development of business culture in the social services that was incorporated into New Labour's Third Way agenda'. The argument for change was couched in the postmodern language of greater choice and freedom. Kate Wilson et al (2011: 51) comment that:

> one of the ways in which market philosophy tempts us in pursuing solutions is by seeming to offer new freedoms. Often these are freedoms from the supposedly obstructive or constraining influence of the state and local authority regulation, bureaucracy, funding limits and so on.

This policy shift has led to the personal social services embracing a philosophy of marketisation and managerialism. The implications for social work are profound.

Marketisation has led to the emergence of quasi-markets in the public sector. This has given rise to the so-called 'new managerialism', which believes that good management can solve all problems and will make the public services more efficient and effective. The 'new managerialism' has created many new and prestigious positions for social workers. Undeniably, a welcome career structure has opened up for the social work profession. The downside is that the trend towards managerialism has been accompanied by devaluation of the traditional professional role of social workers in the public sector. Some social workers are seeking alternative futures in the voluntary sector, where humanistic values find a more congenial and respectful environment. Others have opted for private practice as therapists and counsellors. This shift to the voluntary and private sectors is being exacerbated by constant reorganisation within the public sector as the latest 'management fix' predictably fails 'to deliver the goods'. The problem is that human beings cannot be equated with 'goods'. The consequence for social workers of constant restructuring and organisational 'development' is the creation of an environment of permanent uncertainty and insecurity. This chronic instability saps the profession's morale. The impact on service users is rarely considered since management is governed by top-down administrative rationality rather than bottom-up democratic accountability – commodification rather than inclusion.

White (1999: 116) has noted that the 'new managerialism' is based upon three interlocking strategies of control:

1. decentralising operational units while achieving a greater degree of centralised control over strategy and policy;
2. establishing the principle of managed competition; and
3. developing processes of performance management and monitoring (audits, inspections, quality assessments, reviews), largely directed towards operationally decentralised units.

In Britain, the three strategic controls have impacted upon social work through the increasing privatisation of the National Health Service (NHS) and social care services that followed the election of the Conservative–Liberal Democrat Coalition government in 2010. But the fundamental step towards marketisation of social services began during the 1990s under the UK New Labour government. This change in public policy is not unique to any particular society. It is evident throughout the anglophone and European world and represented an ideological move towards marketisation following the collapse of communism in 1989. The limits of this model of capitalism, popularly referred to as 'neoliberalism', became evident with the global financial crisis in 2008. But the 'crash' has not led to a change in policy direction. The downsizing of the public sector continues unabated, driven by the imperative of profit, arguably at the expense of its humanistic value base. Nigel Horner (2012: 108), writing about 'the business of social work', views its commercialisation as transformative. But who benefits?

The power of central management has been increased at the expense of professionalism through labour market flexibility, which has created a 'contract culture' of temporary and part-time jobs. Mullender and Perrot (1998: 70) record that part-time employment in the general social services grew by 50% between 1988 and 1992, 'with women predominating at the flexible fringe'. Austerity policies, introduced in the wake of the 2008 crash, are likely to have a very serious impact on the social services labour market.

The community care reforms of the 1990s, with their emphasis on 'enabling authority' and 'the mixed economy of care', also impacted on the voluntary sector, which 'in many instances is being asked to become an alternative rather than supplementary or complementary provider' (Lewis, 1996: 108). Increasingly, funding-driven agendas influence policy and practice. The privatisation of social services is advancing. This has implications for both the statutory and voluntary sectors. Moreover, some professionals find their practice being transformed by 'professional' standards demanded by contract. Volunteers are sometimes faced with a stark choice to train as professionals or retire (Billis and Harris, 1996). In other instances, non-traditional organisations come under pressure to conform to the organisational and efficiency standards of the 'new managerialism' of the public sector. According to Mullender and Perrot (1998: 71): 'on a wider scale, voluntary agencies fear that competing for contracts to sustain their funding base will distance them from their pioneering roots and reduce their capacity for advocacy'. Essentially, the pragmatism of the managerialist ethos poses a major threat to both the ethical base of professional social work and the full independence and integrity of the voluntary and community sector. It is difficult to view such developments as other than deeply destructive for social work because they create a hostile environment for humanistic practice. It puts profit before people. That is very much at variance with the historic vision of social work and will challenge its ethical base and professional role in the future. It may also undermine social work through de-professionalisation, led by competency-based training.

Managerialism and de-professionalisation: the McDonaldisation of social work?

The intention of managerialism in the public sector is arguably to break the power of professional monopolies and trade unions, and to promote labour market flexibility. The recruitment of social work managers represents a move towards a performance-based labour force. On the positive side, a performance-led labour market opens up wider employment horizons to social workers and promotes choice and opportunity for many public servants. It also promotes professional diversity. At a more fundamental level, managerialism can be perceived as a threat to the core identity and future integrity of social work as a professional activity, since it incorporates a basic objective of professional 'flexibility' in the light of labour market rationality. Flexibility means performing whatever task an employer assigns regardless of professionalism. Managerialism occurs in a political context, which is intended to have political consequences. One such consequence would seem to be the de-professionalisation of social work by the redefinition of its ethos in terms of pragmatism rather than humanism.

Undoubtedly, in postmodern culture, the welfare crisis, burgeoning managerialism and a shift towards performance indicators and targets are radically changing social work. There are advantages in efficiency and in financial terms arising from this rationalisation of the personal social services, but, equally, rational systems have a tendency to dehumanise and be inhuman in practice: what Max Weber called the 'iron cage' of bureaucracy. Postmodernity, with its market orientation, seems to be weaving a seamless web of rationality, marginalising the human in favour of the pragmatic. George Ritzer (1993) has caricatured this process in *The McDonaldization of society*, which argues that we may be witnessing the McDonaldisation of the welfare state. The argument is that the welfare state is being existentially undermined by a business model, which is based on profit rather than people. The consequences for social work are potentially devastating. Ife (1997: 24) has commented:

> Many of the ideological and organisational foundations of social work practice, as traditionally understood, seem to be crumbling, and it is not clear whether what will take their place will be able to support the social work profession in anything like its present form.

Indeed, it is legitimate to ask whether the social work profession can survive the McDonaldisation of the welfare state. And what of its service-users?

The McDonaldisation of the welfare state, arguably, aims to turn the service-user into a consumer, and welfare into a product. Hughes et al (1998: 158) view this reinvention of the public sphere as an inevitable outcome of the neoliberal discourse on consumerism. On the positive side, the client-consumer is theoretically better placed than the service-user to choose rather than be dictated to by bureaucrats and professionals. New representational spaces may be opened up, giving service-users a right as reconfigured consumers to challenge 'Daddy knows best' elitism. But on the downside, the idea of 'consumer' narrows the concept of the public sphere to individualised users of services. Users of social work services are likely to be vulnerable people, already highly disempowered, and the symbolic 'dismantling of collective notions of the public' is likely to leave them even more vulnerable and unsupported. In reality, what has emerged is not a system characterised by choice and diversity, but one dominated by rationality and hierarchy. This has wrought a transformation in social work that undermines its humanistic value base. The emphasis on competencies leads to checklist practice so that managerial imperatives are met. Ife (1997: 78–80) calls it 'hierarchical practice' and concludes that it is simply a strategy to provide managers with more power and control.

Monediaire (1998) argues that both the theoretical and technical paradigms that have dominated social work discourse during the past 20 years have failed: 'The hypothesis is not exactly pleasant: considering the discrepancy between the dynamics of the global system and the means offered and held by social workers, their mission of seriously reducing contemporary poverty seems impossible' (Monediaire, 1998: 20). Instead of this 'Sisyphean task', Monediaire suggests a new paradigm: the adoption of the contemporary concept of 'sustainable development' based upon the discourse of international human rights conventions and national social rights and citizenship modalities. He sees this as a strategy of 'global social prevention'. Santos (2007: xxi) endorses this critical epistemological vision:

> Conceptions of knowledge, of what it means to know, of what counts as knowledge, and how that knowledge is produced are as diverse as the cosmologies and normative frameworks alluded to.... All social practices involve knowledge. The production of knowledge is, in itself, a social practice and what distinguishes it from other social practices is its self-reflexivity, which productively reshapes the context of practices in motive and engine of actions.

He adds:

> Self-reflexivity, viewed as the discovery of hetero-referentiality, is the first step towards the recognition of the epistemological diversity of the world. That latter, in turn, is inseparable from the diversity of cosmologies that

divide and organize the world in ways that differ from Western cosmology and its offshoot, modern science. Both the proposals for radicalizing democracy – which point towards post-capitalist horizons – and the proposals for decolonizing knowledge and power – which point towards post-colonial horizons – will be feasible only if the dominant epistemology is subject to a critique allowing for the emergence of epistemological options that give credibility to the forms of knowledge that underlie those proposals. (Santos, 2007: xxi)

Santos (2007: xli) concludes:

> The epistemic diversity of the world is open, since all knowledges are situated. There are neither pure nor complete knowledges; there are constellations of knowledges. The claim of the universal character of modern science is increasingly displayed as just one form of particularism, whose specificity consists of having the power to define all the knowledges that are its rivals as particularistic, local, contextual, and situational. The recognition of epistemological diversity is a highly contested terrain because in it converge not only contradictory epistemological and cultural conceptions but also contradictory political and economic interests.

The implications of both Monediaire's and Santos's analyses are radical, involving a fundamental change in professional culture, an opening of minds towards other professional cultures and processes of reasoning, and a thoroughgoing reform of professional training and education. The rationale that informs Monediaire's critique points towards more highly trained social workers becoming involved in the policymaking process, and community development, abandoning social care 'to poorly qualified people such as "family helpers", "environmental agents", "lay brothers"' (Monediaire, 1998: 21). CPD becomes highly relevant to this argument for more highly trained social workers. But there is a worryingly elitist tone to this credentialist approach. CPD needs to be about more than credentialism if it is to have legitimacy in the public mind. Santos (2007) suggests a more democratic and humanistic epistemological approach that evokes Freire's dualism of 'humanisation' versus 'dehumanisation'.

The highly respected critical theorist of postmodernity Zygmunt Bauman, in a paper given at the 100th anniversary of the Amsterdam

School of Social Work, commented on the future of social work. Observing that the impact of market values has transformed the social work landscape, Bauman (2000: 5) asserts:

> As social work, we are told, ought to be judged like any other human action by its cost and effects balance sheet, it does not, in its present form 'make economic sense'. It could justify its continued existence if it made dependent people independent and made lame people walk on their own feet.

Clearly, the achievement of the miraculous is beyond the powers of social work. However, its moral purpose may be its defining rationality. As Bauman puts it: 'The uncertainty which haunts social work is nothing more nor nothing less than the uncertainty endemic to moral responsibility'. He concludes:

> The future of social work and, more generally, of the welfare state, does not depend on classifications, on procedures, nor on reducing the variety and complexity of human needs and problems. It depends, instead, on the ethical standards of the society we all inhabit. It is those ethical standards which, much more than the rationality and diligence of social workers, are today in crisis and under threat. (Bauman, 2000: 10–11)

Social work exists in a cold climate dominated by the resurgence of the market and the hollowing out of the welfare state. But its ethical imperative and moral purpose have become more urgent than ever. However, it is essential to acknowledge its changed circumstances and the impact of postmodernity on its historic mission. The old paradigms that defined the role and task of social work are in doubt, if not eclipsed, but new paradigms are emerging that challenge social work to adapt or perish in the face of the deconstructive forces of the market. CPD will play an important part in enabling this professional reflexivity and action.

Trust, contractualism and social work

Trust is the basis of an inclusive society. The Irish *Green Paper on the Voluntary and Community Sector and its relationship with the state* (Department of Social Welfare, 1997: 25) observes that:

> It is important to create a culture and society which respects the autonomy of the individual. In such a society, individuals are given the opportunity to realise their potential and to take potential for themselves and others. This means creating a climate which supports individuals and groups to make things happen rather than have things happen to them. Such a culture respects diversity and community solidarity. Interdependence is built on trust and dialogue.... All people, but especially those who are at present excluded, must be facilitated to participate in dialogue about problems, policy solutions and programmes' implementation.

Paul Stepney and Keith Popple (2008: 3), in their book *Social work and the Community*, have sought to develop this perspective, declaring: 'this book offers a critically progressive and we hope inspiring, contribution to contemporary social work theory and practice'. They view community as a site of social change. For dialogue to take place with state agencies, officials must ensure that there is openness and trust and that there is flexibility towards new interactive ways of responding to the issues and concerns of those who are excluded. Social workers have unique skills that qualify them to play a defining role in rebuilding trust in society.

The Green Paper was part of Ireland's National Anti-Poverty Strategy, which sought to address the challenge of social exclusion. Whereas American and British discourse during the 20th century was grounded in the Anglo-Saxon belief that voluntary associations, Churches and communities should be free and autonomous, the Irish perspective has been more European: it views the relationship between the voluntary and community sector and the state as an essentially symbiotic one (Silver, 1996: 112; Powell and Guerin, 1997; Powell and Geoghegan, 2004).

During the 1990s, there were signs of a growing movement towards a partnership between the voluntary sector and the state in Britain (Lewis, 1999). It is notable that the New Labour government in Britain published a *Compact on relations between government and the voluntary and community sector in England* (Home Office, 1998). In recent years, the 'Big Society' concept has changed the narrative in a more radical direction, as the UK state divests itself of social responsibility. Social work in continental Europe is deeply embedded in the voluntary and community sector, with close links to the Churches, as well as having humanist and socialist associations. In the US, Canada and Australia, and most developing countries, the voluntary and community sector also plays a vital role in the delivery of personal social services, along with state agencies, for example, criminal justice, education, social assistance, special employment, health and housing. This organisational form is the global paradigm for social work (Jordan, 1997: 18). Global social work is situated within a mixed economy of welfare (Powell and Geoghegan, 2005).

British social work, on the other hand, has evolved as an integral part of the welfare state – the fifth social service. The particularism of British social work can be attributed to Lockean notions of contract based upon political and market relations. British social work in postmodern society therefore faces two profound dilemmas. First, its impulses are contradictory. Bill Jordan (1997: 10), writing in the British context, comments that 'there is a contradiction at the heart of social work, because it is spawned by market-oriented economic individualism, yet its values are those of caring, inclusive, reciprocal community that takes collective responsibility for its members'. Second, the emergence of the enforcement state has challenged the value base of social work. Bill Jordan (1997: 10) concludes: 'Social work is the spirit of community in the clothes of Hobbesian third party enforcement – a caring face in the service of Leviathan'. This is somewhat of a caricature. Government in Britain has thought it essential to decouple the Probation Service from social work, because it perceived the latter as subversive of retributive justice. Bill Jordan's analogy between social workers and 'blue helmeted UN troops serving as peacekeepers in a civil war' (1997) is more persuasive. The challenge is trust. The role is ambiguous: 'They [social workers] are often denounced, and sometimes attacked by both sides. They are open to manipulation and exploitation by the combatants, and their work is always morally compromised' (Jordan, 1997: 10).

Commercialisation, as already discussed, poses further challenges to social work, notably, in Britain and the US. The pressure to abandon the profession's historic mission to the poor in favour of managerialism is indicative of this growing influence. Moreover, the emergence of the 'contract culture', which turns welfare into a commodity to be bought and sold in the marketplace, threatens the very basis of trust. Commercialisation involves the privatisation of 'the social'. Solidarity is therefore removed from the provision of care. In an era of state enforcement and privatisation, it is difficult for social work to promote trust. To return to Jordan's blue-helmeted UN peacekeeper analogy, social work cannot afford to appear to stand by and adopt a position of neutrality in the face of exclusion and social injustice. Social work is challenged to negotiate between the state and civil society. This means renegotiating its own role and task in order to promote social cohesion, trust and social harmony. What does such renegotiation involve? How can CPD help? We hope this book will shed some light on these questions.

French social workers have demonstrated some of the possibilities. The French have developed their own version of 'the Third Way', reconciling socialist commitment to the value of solidarity with humanist concern for individual rights. Instead of the Lockean individualised contractualism that dominates British welfare discourse, the French emphasise the Durkheimian concept of the social bond between the state and the poor. The French have harnessed republican notions of fraternity to the working-class commitment to mutualism in order to forge the ideal of 'integration', 'cohesion' or 'solidarity' (Silver, 1996: 21). A policy of 'insertion', epitomised by the very popular guaranteed minimum income, *Revenue minimum d'insertion* (RMI), provides the necessary dynamic. Delahaye (1994: 245) defines insertion as 'the dynamic process by which an individual in a situation of exclusion acquires and finds a recognised place in the heart of the society while internalising the social functions whose mastery ensures autonomy'. Essentially, the policy of 'insertion' is about participation in society. While recipients of RMI are required to sign a *contrat d'insertion*, which frequently focuses upon employment, in some cases, the form of participation is negotiated with a social worker and involves issues of 'daily living, behaviour and family relationships' (Levitas, 1998: 22). The French approach underlines the importance of communitarianism in the practice of social work. The challenge of trust raises axial questions for social work education and practice regarding the tensions between individualism versus communitarianism. CPD is essential to addressing these issues. Social workers cannot find solutions on their own.

A heated debate took place in British social work on this issue of community responsibility following the publication of the Barclay Report in 1982. It concluded that:

> the Working Party believes that if needs of citizens are to be met in the last years of the twentieth century, the personal social services must develop a close partnership with citizens focussing more closely on the community and its strengths. (Barclay, 1982: 198)

Instead, a client-centred individualised approach emerged, geared towards a reactive service and preoccupied with risk management. No doubt the ascendancy of neoliberal thought in Britain during the 1980s played a key role in the rejection of the communitarianism espoused by the Barclay Report. A more atomised society had become preoccupied with risk. The UK Munro Report (2011) sought to counteract this reactive and proceduralised approach to social work by putting people and relationships back at the centre of professional social work. This provides social work education with a fundamental task. Munro's vision of social work invites us to move beyond personal competency-led training by re-imagining social work. Such a task evokes Santos's (2007) call for revolutionising social work. But what is the reality social work education should address in 'risk society'?

Social work in a 'runaway world'

Tony Giddens (1999), in his BBC Reith Lecture series 'Runaway world', made risk the theme of one of his lectures. For him, 'risk refers to hazards that are actively assessed in relation to future possibilities' (Giddens, 1999). The word 'risk' appears to be the product of modernity, being associated with the voyages of Western explorers in the 16th and 17th centuries. Risk, as Giddens points out, is 'inseparable from the ideas of probability and uncertainty'. In relation to social policy, Giddens (1999) comments: 'The Welfare State, whose development can be traced back to Elizabethan Poor Laws in England, is essentially a risk management system', and, he adds, 'those who provide insurance, whether in the shape of private or state welfare systems, are essentially redistributing risk'. Beck, in his influential book *Risk society* (1992), writes that what is new is not risk *per se* but our consciousness of risk and our capacity to control it. Parton (2011: 35) observes: 'increasingly, social workers and social welfare agencies are concerned in their day to day policies and practices with the issue of risk?'. He argues that risk is 'a way of thinking' in social work. This is a very helpful construct for CPD, since it seeks to relocate their social work imaginary within an unpredictable and uncertain world. It envisages moving beyond proceduralism and defensive social work. Jan Fook (2011: 31) observes that professional knowledge is uncertain in several ways:

- There may be inadequacy in addressing new and changing situations.
- Outcomes may be unpredictable since contexts (and factors involved in those contexts) change.
- Meaning is indeterminate – since there may be multiple differing interpretations which may change according to context.

- Meaning systems may become confused so that moral and technical realms overlap.

She contends that recognising these epistemological dilemmas is important in developing social work's characterisation of professionalism:

- We need a better understanding of how we work and develop knowledge in relation to specific contexts, as opposed to how we develop more abstract and generalised knowledge. I term this contextuality.
- As a result, we need to reconceptualise the nature of learning as contextual.
- We need to develop openness and tolerance for difference in the light of vulnerability – this is not only a challenge but also a necessity.
- We need to frame uncertainty and lack of control as positive opportunities.

Fook (2011: 32) envisages five core epistemological issues: contextuality (the ability to work with the whole context); transferability (the ability to create knowledge and theory relevant to contextuality); processuality (an ability to think and act methodically); critical reflexivity (the ability to critically reflect); and a transcendent vision.

Risk management is central to the idea of welfare and the practice of social work. Roche and Tucker (1997: 4) have observed that taking responsibility for someone else's welfare has traditionally involved a number of core activities with citizens:

1. Looking after them;
2. Making sure they are safe;
3. Meeting their physical needs for food, shelter and so on;
4. Supporting them in resolving their personal difficulties;
5. Teaching them appropriate forms of behaviour and discipline where necessary.

The emergence of risk has also been associated with the prediction of dangerousness in individuals and families. Child abuse enquiries frequently hinge on the calculus of risk (Munro, 2011). Yet, research into the prediction of violence does not inspire confidence, according to Parton (1995: 139): 'the empirical support for the prediction of violence is very poor'. He adds that 'such difficulties lead to the statistical problems of "false negatives" and "false positives"', which 'clearly ...

has enormous implications for civil liberties', and he concludes that 'those who oppose such developments generally stress the importance of individual rights of people likely to be subjected to intervention'. Dangerousness and desert have become reflexively connected in postmodern welfare discourse, justifying risk management strategies intended to control. Wilson et al (2011: 48) conclude that 'the crisis of risk is certain to continue' as a major challenge for both society and social work. CPD must address this core challenge.

Social work in postmodern society is engaged in risk management with a series of high-profile client groups, including children 'at risk', young offenders, the mentally ill in the community and the homeless and rough sleepers. These social groups challenge the limits of welfare and highlight the changing environment of risk and trust in which the perception of dangerousness has reframed both public policy and social work practice. Radical social work has pointed to the tradition of working with service users and poor people's movements in a manner where the latter become active citizens in their own self-directed welfare narrative (Mullaly, 1997; Beresford, 2007).

Active citizenship and the mobilised 'self': the co-production of 'social work'

Active citizenship has re-emerged in the transformed postmodern social landscape. It was initially promoted by neoliberals 'as an exhortation to discharge the responsibilities of neighbourliness, voluntary action and charity' in the context of 'the rundown public sector services, benefit cutbacks and privatised programme in which it was advanced' (Lister, 1997: 22). However, more radical democratic variants of active citizenship soon emerged in the form of community and service-user groups challenging paternalistic top-down relationships that disempower. These more democratic forms of active citizenship arguably indicate the emergence of new social movements among marginalised groups in a process of mobilising the 'self' through collective action. Active citizenship is here associated with demands for greater participation in the corporate state through the involvement of a burgeoning civil society as a partner. In this social reality, civil society is perceived as an alternative to state bureaucracy and professional elitism, and as a public space between the government and market. In its reinvigorated form, civil society is presented as a democratic community-based alternative to the dependent status imposed by social services upon the dispossessed. Under postmodern conditions, active citizenship in the form of volunteering is promoted as a more humane alternative to the Fordist philosophy of the 'one size fits all' welfare state. It is part of a wider critique of the modernist conception of entitled citizenship that has in part been induced by the consumerist philosophy of neoliberalism, but is also the product of a deeper social fragmentation connected to the rise of identity politics. Social politics, embodied in the institution of entitled citizenship, has consequently suffered in terms of public esteem. The growing disenchantment with this form of democracy and demands for greater public participation refocus attention away from the entitled to the active citizen. The core emphasis is on participation in the decision-making and service delivery processes of the state, leading to the empowerment of the citizen – 'the right to have rights' (Ramírez, 2009: 239). Active citizenship can be innovative (eg campaigns for migrant workers' rights), preservationist (protecting the environment) or remedial (helping the dispossessed) (Uprimmy and Garcia-Villegas, 2005: 84). Boaventura de Sousa Santos views the reconciliation of the confrontation between representative democracy and participatory democracy based upon active citizenship as the core challenge for late-modern society. In his book *Democratising democracy* (Santos, 2005: x), Santos declares:

> Such a confrontation, which derives from the fact that representative democracy has systematically denied the legitimacy of participatory democracy, will be resolved only to the extent to which such denial is replaced by the development of forms of complementarity between the two forms of democracy that may contribute to deepen one another. Such complementarity paves one of the ways to the reinvention of social emancipation.

In the reconstructed reality of postmodern society, the challenge facing social work is to respond reflexively to the changing needs of and demands for citizen participation. The challenge to the *zeitgeist* of the corporate state (social partnership, dutiful citizenship and centralisation) is manifest. If cultural agendas in the shape of identity politics and burgeoning social movements are to be the shape of things to come, where does that leave social work? Is it possible to practise social work in a polarised and fragmented social order? The answer is hopefully 'Yes, we can', through empowering service users in the co-production of social services (Skidmore and Craig, 2005). That imperative envisages the co-production of social services, in which social workers engage with active citizens.

President Obama, in the *Audacity of hope* (Obama, 2006), built a presidential political platform around the generation of a new kind of politics. This is a politics that draws upon the Ancient Greek tradition of civic republicanism, which is based upon the ideal of sustainable democratic communities. President Obama has utilised his experience as a community organiser in Chicago to reinvigorate the concept of citizenship. His slogan 'Yes, we can' invites the public to re-imagine its relationship with the polity. The extraordinary political success of the Obama campaigns in 2008 and 2012 was to create new political fiction at a time when Americans (and the rest of the world) were looking for change. It was viewed as a rejection of neoliberalism by supporters. President Obama, an advocate of reconciliation and participation, dreamt of a new Athens to replace the Sparta of austerity policies – revitalised global democracy versus imperial military hegemony. This may be a utopian vision that is at odds with *realpolitik*, but it resonates with global progressive opinion. Social work is challenged to reflect this optimism and harness it in the interests of service users. That means re-imagining the social work role and task in challenging times. CPD has a key role in enabling the profession to be reflexive towards change.

Citizenship and social work: 10 principles for civic social work

Social work has defined itself in two ways over time. First, those who advocate a social contract vision promote the state and traditional voluntary organisations as providing an enabling relationship in which the needy are helped. Second, those who seek to promote human emancipation believe that only by changing the social structure can the political and economic basis of inequality and injustice be successfully tackled. Postmodernism challenges the basis of both these visions of social work, inviting its reinvention in new reflexive forms of citizenship. The survival of social work in postmodern society is about a search for new paradigms, designed to empower the socially excluded, in a discursive shift that reconstructs practice as civic engagement and the client as citizen.

The concept of citizenship opens up a new site for social work practice. In this context, the traditional conflict between capitalism and socialism is moved on to new ground. In essence, the struggle of the poor and oppressed is against social exclusion, which can be defined as the absence of social, cultural and political rights. Civic social work is defined by a concern for the rights and needs of citizens. Ten core principles can be distilled from civic social work practice that promote citizenship as a site for practice:

1. Social inclusion: There needs to be a clear focus on social inclusion in social work practice that makes it the stated aim of the profession. Professional associations ought to place social inclusion at the heart of their agenda in a reconstructed value base grounded in the concept of civic engagement and citizen empowerment.

2. Redefining risk: Social work must reconstruct the language of risk from its current focus on danger and risk management into a vocabulary geared to the promotion of equal citizenship rights that balances rights and risks. This involves placing risk in its social and cultural context, challenging society's limited concept of victimhood.

3. Trust as symbolic practice: Social work should promote trust as a symbolic practice through the construction of relationships with service users based upon social inclusion. Trust is constructed through talk and action based upon the principle of equality. This means taking risks for trust. Casualties of misplaced trust will typically be referred to as 'innocent victims of social work incompetence by the media.

4. Dialogical relationship: Social workers committed to promoting trust as symbolic practice need to engage in a dialogical relationship with service users. Problem-solving is replaced by problem-posing in a reflective process, where critical reflection and action are unified in democratic praxis between equal citizens.

5. Justice, decency and social obligations: Social work represents a response to society's obligation to respond to the needs of its most vulnerable citizens. It can take both voluntary and professional forms and be pursued within a welfare pluralist context involving the state and civil society.

6. Promotion of civil society: Social work in postmodern society ought to be practised in a manner that harnesses community and voluntary initiative, with a view to promoting partnership and sustainable social development. Practitioners, managers and educators need to recognise and appreciate the scale and challenge of the task involved. It implies a discursive shift from individualisation (the basis of clientisation) towards communitarian approaches to practice that promote citizenship.

7. User participation and empowerment: The process of users participating as active citizens in shaping community-based initiatives and solutions is vitally important in an empowerment

strategy that aims to help the poor and oppressed. This is the essence of the historic mission of social work as civic engagement in a democratic society. It is the antithesis of the competency movement, which removes professional discretion in hierarchical management regimes detached from civic life.

8. Multiculturalism: New social movements have had a profound impact on society as a whole and social work in particular. The politics of recognition that lies at the core of a multicultural vision is essential to a social work practice that is genuinely transformative.

9. Poverty-proofing and social audits. Service providers need to continuously assess their policies and procedures to ensure that resources are employed in the most effective manner to benefit citizens and prevent social exclusion. They need to directly involve practitioners and service users in exercises that go to the heart of democratic accountability and civic engagement.

10. Public mandate: the onus is on the government and society to ensure that social work is supported with the necessary resources and given the legitimacy to carry out its public mandate: the civic nature of social work must be recognised. Without this endorsement, social work does not have a future. Similarly, if social work is perceived by service users as disempowering, its public mandate will be undermined, since it will have no legitimacy on the ground because its purpose and activities lack trust and community support. Social work requires not only top-down legitimacy, but also bottom-up legitimacy (Powell, 2001: 164–5)

These are the core principles required by civic social work. It is an invitation to reinvent the historic mission of social work in the vernacular of the times. Hugman (1998: 77) observes:

> Professionalism in this sense can be seen as 'ideas in conversation with context'. Values are the language of this conversation and fluency requires that such language is capable of grasping the complexities faced in practice. It is for this reason that decontextualised formal ethical codes are no longer seen as sufficient.

This observation goes to the core of the epistemological task in CPD. It should, as Hugman suggests, be about 'ideas in conversation with context'. Postmodernity has reshaped the context of social work education and practice. The challenge of CPD is to enable social work practitioners to re-imagine their professional context in ways that ensure that practice remains relevant to social reality and the ethical values that social work is defined by, both historically and in contemporary society.

Conclusion

In this chapter, we have sought to map the contours of contemporary social work in order to contextualise CPD. We stared with a consideration of the relationship between critical theory and social work. What emerges is a historic rupture – a meta-change – to the meaning and definition of social work. Critical theory will be a pivotal epistemology in any CPD curriculum, because it underpins the conceptual context in which social work is practised. Unless we can locate social work meaningfully in this fragmented world, it will slip into meaninglessness – as a shapeless activity in an uncertain world. The 'Big Society' offers a narrative, but it does not resonate with the public. Its 'little platoons' offer a poor substitute for social work. However, the 'Big Society' does envisage the downsizing of the state and its businessfication. We considered the related issues of managerialism and marketisation and their growing impact in commercialising social work. We raised existential considerations about whether it is possible to apply a business model to social work and retain its humanistic mission to the poor and the vulnerable? The emergence of competency-based training provides a pragmatism that appears to suit the business model. But does it suit the public? Is it compatible with the person-based approach of social work? We moved on to consider the two core paradigms of postmodernity – trust and risk – as architectonic ideas that will underpin any discourse about social work's future. We considered active citizenship, a concept favoured by all ideological shades of opinion, as a means to reconnect with the citizen. Finally, we identified 10 principles for a civic model of social work, based upon citizenship.

EIGHT

Conclusion: challenges and futurescapes

I hear that in New York
At the corner of 26th street and Broadway
A man stands every evening during the winter months
And gets beds for the homeless there
By appealing to passers-by.

It won't change the world
It won't improve relations among men
It will not shorten the age of exploitation
But a few men have a bed for the night
For a night the wind is kept from them
The snow meant for them falls on the roadway.

Don't put down the book on reading this, man.

A few people have a bed for the night
For a night the wind is kept from them
The snow meant for them falls on the roadway
But it won't change the world
It won't improve relations among men
It will not shorten the age of exploitation.
Bertolt Brecht (1931) *A bed for the night.*

This simple poem about the Great Depression starts a conversation about the relationship between altruism and social change. Brecht poses a profound social question. Should we be glad 'a few men have a bed for the night' or despairing that 'it will not shorten the age of exploitation'? The answer depends on how you read the poem and is ultimately shaped by your own subjectivity. The Project for Critical Reflection (no date), in a commentary on the poem, also poses a series of challenging questions that go to the core of the ethical purpose of social work. These questions provide the meta-themes for a continuing professional development (CPD) curriculum in social work: 'Is the service you provide changing the world?'; 'What kind of change is possible and how do you know whether you are achieving it or not?'; and 'How important is justice to service work and how do you know whether you are achieving it or not?'.

The writer J.G. Ballard remarked: 'Marxism is a social philosophy for the poor and what we need badly is a social philosophy of the rich' (quoted in *The Irish Times*, 2012). Quite so! Brecht's poem, *A bed for the night*, draws on his burgeoning Marxist world view but also that enduring civic virtue – altruism – about which he is deeply conflicted, as the poem reveals. Social work occupies the contested space between rich and poor, where altruism precariously coexists with consumerism, symbolised by the man in Brecht's poem, collecting at the corner of 26th Street and Broadway on a winter's evening in New York City. *A bed for the night* captures the multilayered complexity of what the social work role and task is and might be in the age of postmodernity. It is a parable for our times, when once again a global financial crash has imposed deep social suffering on the poor, homeless and vulnerable.

Our research into CPD suggests that social workers' views about what social work means to them are both practical and pragmatic. Yet, their reported experience in navigating the professional domains of social work practice exposes the organisational constraints that they operate within. It is a world in which the humanistic values of the social work profession are in a permanent tension with the bureaucratic world of the social service agency and the encroaching marketisation of society. In this concluding chapter, we hope to explore (as already suggested) some of the meta-themes that CPD curricula will need to address if social work as a professional activity is to retain its relevance in the uncertain landscape of postmodernity, including: its dual mandate; its role in civil society; its humanist legacy; and the challenges that will shape its future within a multicultural society – that is, characterised by deep social tensions and divisions.

Power and social work's dual mandate

The dual mandate defines the role and task of social work as promoting the interests of both the state and of the service user whom they are intended to help. This dual mandate makes social work by definition a politicised activity. For some practitioners, this has involved a high degree of sensitisation to the implications of the use of professional power. Others (the majority) prefer to avoid the implications of the dual mandate by adopting an individualised therapeutic approach that locates social work in the apolitical world of psychology and the personalisation of social problems. This was evident in our survey.

However, they are making an implicit choice that is itself political, since it assumes that the professional task of social work is neutral. Moreover, the individualised therapeutic approach seeks to ignore the social background that gives rise to the service user's request or referral for help in the first instance. Zavirsek (1999: 69) observes: 'For these social workers, power means something negative, always connected with manipulation and control, and social work remains defined as work that primarily requires "neutrality" towards people'. Powell (2001) has argued that social work is fundamentally shaped by politics.

Suzy Croft and Peter Beresford (1997: 273) have argued that 'social work is increasingly marginalised publically and politically, amid growing professional fears that it is tied to authoritarian welfare policies'. They argue the case for a user-led social work committed to the principles of autonomy, participation and inclusion. The emphasis on empowerment and participation advocated by the proponents of civil society offers a very positive agenda for addressing the problems of state bureaucracy and professional elitism that threaten the legitimacy of the welfare state in the eyes of its service users. Furthermore, the overextended welfare state can greatly benefit from the services of volunteers. The professional challenges of civil society, particularly the social movements it has generated, have been delineated for social work by Walter Lorenz (1994: 127):

> They call for limits to professionalism by putting the experienced volunteer, the use of 'the person who has been through it' against the power and elitism of certified experts. They value process and participation rather than technical efficiency and success as the key to self-directed learning and change. They search for identity, personally and collectively, by way of questioning the oppressive use of labels and attributes.

Given that social work is quintessentially a personal social service, located in the arena of community care, voluntarism in the context of a civil society that defines a social domain makes sense. However, the volunteer cannot be a substitute for a well-trained professional in a risk society, any more than charity can be a substitute for state welfare benefits. What civil society can offer is greater participation and the recognition of the rights of the service user. Lorenz's emphasis on participation goes to the core of the imperative to democratise the personal social services and make them inclusive of user and community organisations. Co-production has emerged as an alternative to top-down social work, advocated by progressive think tanks, such as Demos, in the UK.

The challenge for the social work CPD curriculum is to help devise an approach for practitioners in defining civic virtue that is sufficiently robust to protect the rights of the service user – while not becoming so robust that it amounts to the imposition of a particular version of 'the good' – in a multicultural world where diverse moral and social perspectives define reality. In practice, this balance is not easy to strike, as the line between domination and non-domination is a thin one. It requires civic skills and political awareness. The dual mandate of social work raises the dilemma between domination and non-domination that go to the core of social work practice in a democratic society.

Social work and civil society in changing times

Kate Wilson et al (2011: 47, emphasis added), reflecting upon the challenges facing social work in the second decade of the 21st century, identify the 'political responses to the consequences of the global financial crises of 2008–2009' and predict that:

> it is likely that new and unfamiliar contexts of *social spaces* will evolve in which social work can play a role. These might include new forms of voluntary and community based organisation funded from a variety of sources – social enterprises.

They appear to be speculating about social work's potential future relationship with civil society, which will need to form a core focus of a reflective and discursive process in CPD.

There is nothing new in the link between social work and poverty. It is a perennial theme traceable from the Settlement movement of the late 19th century, through the role of social work during the Great Depression of the 1920s and 1930s, and the radical social work movement of the 1960s and 1970s, to the emergence of anti-oppressive and anti-discriminatory practice in the late 20th century. Social work practice has always been reflexive towards social change. What is new is that poverty in post-2008 crash conditions is once again a major social challenge and is exacerbated by growing anti-immigrant sentiment that is undermining multicultural society in Europe, North America and Australia. Culture wars, epitomised by the rise of the Tea Party in the US, increasingly define the political, cultural and social landscape as unstable. The fragmentation of the economy is mirrored in the fragmentation and polarisation of society, accompanied by extreme political parties vocalising increasingly angry feelings towards diversity and immigration.

Civil society, communitarianism and social work

Civil society is challenged to respond. Cohen and Arato (1994: ix) define civil society 'as a sphere of social interaction between the economy and the state, composed above all of the intimate sphere (especially the family), the sphere of associations (especially voluntary associations), social movements and forms of public communication'. Put simply, civil society is our collective self. It is us: our civic narrative – encompassing our families, communities, life worlds, forms of communication (personal and virtual) and value orientations. It is as diverse as people are, reflecting their hopes, aspirations and prejudices. Within social policy discourse, civil society has a more restrictive meaning. It refers to the voluntary and community sector (Powell and Guerin, 1997). This is the arena in which much of social work practice is conducted in postmodern society.

Not surprisingly, in postmodern society, a new debate has begun about the values of civic trust. In this debate, the good society has been recast as civil society. This development essentially represents a swing back towards collectivism, since it promotes a new form of communitarianism (Etzioni, 1994; Fukuyama, 1995). However, to describe this trend as a reassertion of the collectivist values of the welfare state would be simplistic. What the 'new communitarianism' of the exponents of civil society seeks to do is reconcile the globalised market with a form of active citizenship in which the individual seeks to achieve a moral commitment through involvement in the community. In a sense, this is a cross-cutting definition that defies the distinction between individualism and collectivism. This is both its strength and its weakness.

The exponents of civil society in the contemporary debate about the moral economy of welfare view reciprocal responsibility and social well-being as the basis of 'social capital'. Fukuyama (1995: 26) asserts:

> Social capital is a capability that arises from the prevalence of trust in society or certain parts of it. It can be embodied in the smallest and most basic social group, the family, as well as the largest of all groups, the nation, and in all other groups between. Social capital differs from all other forms

of human capital insofar as it is usually transmitted through cultural mechanisms like religion, tradition or habitual habit.

Social capital, therefore, comprises the institutional relationships of vibrant civil society, based on a 'solidary individualism' and active citizenship, from extended families to neighbourhood networks, community groups to religious organisations, youth clubs to parent–teacher associations, local businesses to local public services, playgroups to the police on the beat (Borrie Report, 1994: 307–8). At the heart of civil society is empathy, compassion, trust and participation. This is the basis of the 'good society' that we all yearn to belong to in the midst of uncertainty, scepticism, disillusionment and institutional fragmentation. Consequentially, the pluralisation of lifestyles and the search for meaning in the midst of uncertainty has stimulated a revitalisation of the concept of civil society as a means for resolving the problems of contemporary society.

The renewal of civil society has been associated with demands for a larger role for voluntary welfare provision in both Western society and the former Soviet Bloc. The voluntary sector is perceived as: (1) an alternative to state bureaucracy and professional elitism; and (2) a public space between state and market. In its reinvigorated form, civil society is presented by its advocates as a democratic movement based on the concept of active citizenship of the welfare state. The emphasis of active citizenship is on participation in the decision-making process leading to empowerment of the citizen (Etzioni, 1994).

According to the concept of civil society, communities, neighbourhoods, voluntary associations and Churches are the basic building blocks of society because they teach civic virtues such as trust and cooperation (Keane, 1988; Putnam, 1993, 2000; Etzioni, 1994; Fukuyama, 1995). These 'new communitarians' promote the fostering of intermediate institutions, that is, families, neighbourhoods and schools, in civil society. They view these intermediate institutions as a source of moral and social cohesion in the globalised market society. At the same time, they regard the revitalised civil society as a bulwark against an overweening welfare state that, in their view, has lost its legitimacy because of its remote bureaucratic structure and domination by professional elites. The renewal of interest in community raises the prospect of social work education and practice rediscovering its relationship with community as one of its core methods – a task to be addressed within a reflexive CPD curriculum.

Social work, community development and political ideology

Community development, like the camel, is easier to describe than define. It is a discourse of action informed by communitarian values that aims to promote social inclusion and democratic participation. 'People power' or 'Power to the people' are popular slogans associated with community development, emphasising its rootedness in concepts of empowerment. Equally, consciousness-raising, what the Brazilian community educator Paulo Freire (1972) called 'conscientisation', is a core construct, linking power to knowledge in the manner of the French structuralist philosopher Michel Foucault (eg 1972, 1977). However, it is more Freirian than Foucauldian because of its subscription to humanist values and its abiding belief in the possibility of societal transformation and human emancipation from poverty and oppression.

The authoritative British source Keith Popple (1995: 4) has acknowledged the problems inherent in defining community development: 'the term community work is likewise a contested concept and there is no universally agreed meaning ... the fluidity in its definition presents particular problems and challenges'. Popple suggests that there is an intimate connection between community development (community work in his parlance) and political values. He points out that some community development theorists employ a democratic pluralist model: Goetschius (1969), Thomas (1980, 1983) and Twelvetrees (1991). Others take a distinctly radical and socialist line: Craig et al (1982), Dominelli (1990) and Stepney and Popple (2008). Powell and Geoghegan (2004) examined the relationship between community development and social partnership in Ireland.

Popple's distinction ultimately rests on the issue of ideology. The pluralists (or, perhaps more accurately, 'pragmatists') share a general opposition to ideological politics, which they view as being overly preoccupied with political abstractions. Pluralists reject 'abstract' political doctrines (eg Marxism, feminism, environmentalism, anti-racism) concerned with the promotion of universal and immutable rights or a universal form of political institutions. On the other hand, Marxist, feminist, environmentalist and anti-racist approaches to community development are rooted in emancipatory political traditions that subscribe to the fundamental transformation of the political and social order, based upon the principles of equality, solidarity, social justice and human rights. The influence of the American radical community activist Saul Alinsky (1969, 1972) on the latter approach is beyond doubt, but their ideas have also been shaped by the poverty programmes of the 1960s and 1970s, as well as the emergence of multiculturalism in recent decades. Radical community educators, notably, Freire (1996 [1972]), Lovett (1975; Lovett et al, 1983) and Mezirow (1991), have furthermore been seminal influences in terms of orienting community development towards a radical transformative agenda geared towards changing people's consciousness of the causes of their poverty and oppression.

Latterly, following the emergence of a post-welfare state world order, the hope invested in emancipatory politics has dimmed. The dominance of a neoliberal political agenda has redefined politics in the form of an ideological victory for global conservatism, epitomised by the neoliberal project. Opponents of global conservatism have fallen back upon classical political concepts such as citizenship, civil society and human rights in their struggle to articulate an alternative political agenda.

Where does postmodern social work locate itself within this critical debate? The evidence from our survey suggests that social workers are largely depoliticised. Their preoccupation is the everyday reality of their practice with individuals and families. What has changing the world got to do with their professional brief? An answer has been suggested by Stepney and Popple (2008: 3) in the introduction to their book *Social work and the community*, in which they assert that 'it is written and published at a significant time in the development of UK social work, and social work education, which in our view has much to gain from community-based approaches'. Stepney and Popple (2008: 4) note that the importance of CPD in the development of social work has coincided with a step-change in social policy: 'at the same time government social policy has focused on social inclusion, community regeneration and sustainability, partnership working, multidisciplinary collaboration and the development of responsible citizenship'. They conclude that there is a need to 'discuss and reflect upon the contemporary situation, and consider the future of social work ... and how it might gain from a re-examination of its role and purpose' (Stepney and Popple, 2008: 4). In the wake of the 2008 global financial crisis and the emerging emphasis on communitarianism and active citizenship, CPD offers an opportunity for reflection on and discussion of the role and task of social work in uncertain times.

The role and task of social work in a multicultural society

Kate Wilson et al (2011) have discussed the conceptual challenges that multiculturalism poses for universalism. This debate must be central to any CPD curriculum that seeks to address the challenges and futurescapes of social work in the 21st century. Wilson et al (2011: 96) have posed a seminal question about the intellectual coherence of the multicultural perspective:

> Political thinkers and social work theorists in the late twentieth and early twenty-first centuries have sometimes welcomed this new political landscape, and sometimes bemoaned the loss of old univeralist frameworks. Identity politics, or a preoccupation with single issue political campaigns, have been criticised precisely because they seem to detract from a fully 'structural' analysis, and focus attention on just one dimension of the production of oppression, marginalisation and discrimination. How can negative aspects of the situation of black women in Britain, for example, be adequately grasped through theories or movements that concern themselves only with gender, or only with race?

They conclude that the epistemological tensions between multiculturalism and universalism are very challenging for social work practice and its underpinning values:

> Thus the problem of hierarchies of oppression – questions about who is more oppressed than whom, and according to what criteria – have often dogged this new political culture. Universalists point to this fragmentation and say that the whole strength of an inclusive, single framework of political analysis is that it promotes solidarity; pluralists, on the other hand, and proponents of the value of identity politics have stressed how personal experience and the subjective dimensions of political life are more easily linked and assimilated to one another within an approach to politics that makes more room for subjectivity and is thus less 'totalising' or 'objectifying' of the very people that political and value-driven movements are claiming to emancipate. (Wilson et al, 2011: 97)

However, Gould (1996: 33–4) notes that multiculturalism is a 'devalued norm' in social work, which implicitly endorses the value of 'Anglo-conformity'. She concludes:

> Despite the fact that the profession, in principle, has endorsed the value of implementing a multicultural curriculum, there was always an unease involving the mission of social work – whether social work education was trying to achieve a kind of a rainbow collectivist society by teaching required courses. (Gould, 1996: 39)

The experience of implementing an 'anti-racist' practice curriculum in the UK underlines the complexity of addressing multiculturalism in social work education and training. Dominelli (1997: 162–70) has charted the failure of this initiative, despite well-intentioned support. Interest in multiculturalism arose from anti-racist and anti-sexist programmes promoted by the Greater London Council (GLC) during the 1980s. Minority ethnic and women's groups felt empowered to campaign for fundamental attitudinal change, based upon the politics of recognition.

Problems quickly emerged in terms of the inability of universities to successfully negotiate this multiculturalist educational task. In part, there was a lack of resources. There was also often a lack of comprehension about what was required in terms of curriculum design and content. At a deeper level, there were profound epistemological problems, common to cultural studies in general in universities. Anti-racist practice challenges some of the most hallowed principles of liberal humanism, upon which the idea of the university in Western society rests. Social work courses in the UK are often short (eg three-year undergraduate courses); 50% of the course is spent in practice and the curriculum is already overcrowded. Preparation for anti-racist practice requires considerable theoretical input that seeks to explore the cultural complexities of its underlying principles. Simplistic understanding is open to the charge of propaganda. CPD will play a potentially important part in exploring and explaining the dynamics of multicultural society and the challenges it poses for social work.

Conclusion

CPD faces profound challenges in enabling social workers to meet the demands of contemporary social work practice during the 21st century. We have explored some of the meta-themes of social work in this chapter, starting with the dual mandate of social work and controversies about power and its uses and abuses. We employed Bertolt Brecht's poem *A bed for the night* to set social work in the context of the times we live in and the challenges it poses for the profession. Our argument is that CPD will needs to grapple with these bigger questions, as well as providing practical knowledge about practice with individuals and families. While Brecht challenges the assumption that it is possible to help individuals without changing the system that underpins their circumstances, social work exists in that space between the individual and society. Vulnerability demands a humanistic response, whatever the system. Social work is that humanistic response.

References

AASW (Australian Association of Social Workers) (2012) *The AASW campaign to achieve registration of social workers in Australia: frequently asked questions*. Available at: http://www.aasw.asn.au/document/item/1818 (accessed August 2012).

Agbim, K. and Ozanne, E. (2007) 'Social work educators in a changing higher education context: looking back and looking forward 1982–2005', *Australian Social Work*, 60(1): 68–82.

Alinsky, S. (1969) *Reveille for radicals*, New York, NY: Vintage.

Alinsky, S. (1972) *Rules for radicals*, New York, NY: Vintage.

Alsop, A. (2000) *Continuing professional development: a guide for therapists*, Oxford: Blackwell Science.

Anderson, B. (2011) 'Cameron's "little platoons" get lost in the woods', *Financial Times*, 9 February.

Argyris, C. and Schön, D. (1978) *Organisational learning: a theory of action perspective*, Reading, MA: Addison-Wesley.

Argyris, C. and Schön, D. (1996) *Organisational learning 11: theory, method and practice*, Reading, MA: Addison-Wesley.

Baldwin, M. (2004) 'Critical reflection: opportunities and threats to professional learning and service development in social work organizations', in N. Gould and M. Baldwin (eds) *Social work, critical reflection and the learning organization*, Aldershot: Ashgate.

Banks, S. (2006) *Ethics and values in social work* (3rd edn), Basingstoke: Palgrave Macmillan.

Barber, J.G. and Cooper, L. (1997) 'Current trends in the education of Australian social workers', in B. Lesnik (ed) *Change in social work*, Aldershot: Arena.

Barclay, P. (1982) *Social workers: their role and tasks*, London: National Institute of Social Work/Bedford Square Press.

Bauman, Z. (2000) 'Am I my brother's keeper?', *European Journal of Social Work*, 2(1): 5–11.

Beck, U. (1992) *Risk society: towards a new modernity*, London: Sage.

Beck, U. (1999) *World risk society*, Cambridge: Polity Press.

Beddoe, L. (2006) 'Registration and continuing education for social work in New Zealand – what about the workers?', *Social Work Review*, 18(4): 100–11.

Beddoe, L. (2007) 'Change, complexity, and challenge in social work education in Aotearoa, New Zealand', *Australian Social Work*, 60(1): 46–55.

Beddoe, L. (2009) 'Creating continuous conversation: social workers and learning organisations', *Social Work Education*, 28(7): 722–36.

Beddoe, L. and Duke, J. (2009) 'Registration in New Zealand social work: the challenge of change', *International Social Work*, 52(6): 785–97.

Beresford, P. (2007) 'User involvement, research and health inequalities', *Health and Social Care in the Community*, 15(4): 306–312.

Berking, H. (1996) 'Solidarity individualism', in S. Lash, B. Szersnyski and B. Wynne (eds) *Risk, environment and modernity*, London: Sage.

Billis, D. and Harris, M. (1996) *Voluntary agencies: challenges of organisations and management*, London: Macmillan.

Blewett, J. (2011) 'Continuing professional development: enhancing high-quality practice', in J. Sedan, S. Matthews, M. McCormick and A. Morgan (eds) *Professional development in social work*, Oxon: Routledge.

Blond, P. (2010) *Red Tory*, London: Faber and Faber.

Borrie Report (1994) *Commission on social justice*, London: Vintage.

Boud, D., Keogh, R. and Walker, D. (eds) (1985) *Reflection: turning experience into learning*, London: Kogan Page.

Boulet, J., Diemer, K. and MacLaren, S. (2007) *Needs and expectations of AASW-Vic. membership for continuing professional education (CPD)*, report produced by the Borderlands Co-operative on behalf of the Victorian Branch of the AASW.

Boychuk, T. (2007) 'Big society, small government', *Macalester International*, 18: 201–13.

Brecht, B. (1931) All Poems of Bertolt Brecht, Available at: http://www.poemhunter.com.

Brockbank, A. and McGill, I. (1998) *Facilitating reflective learning in higher education*, Buckingham: SRHE and Open University.

Brodsgaard, K.E. (2009) *Hainan-state, society, and business in a Chinese province*, London: Routledge.

Brookfield, S. (1995) *Becoming a critically reflective teacher*, San Francisco, CA: Jossey-Bass.

Brookfield, S. (2009) 'The concept of critical reflection: promises and contradictions', *European Journal of Social Work*, 12(3): 293–304.

Bubb, S. and Earley, P. (2007) *Leading & managing continuing professional development: developing people, developing schools*, London: Sage.

Buchanan, I. (2011) 'Policy swings and roundabouts: social work in shifting social and economic contexts', in J. Seden, S. Matthews, M. McCormick and A. Morgan (eds) *Professional development in social work: complex issues in practice*, Abingdon: Routledge.

Burns, K. (2012) 'Moving beyond "case-management": social workers' perspectives on professional supervision in child protection and welfare', in D. Lynch and K. Burns (eds) *Children's rights and child protection: critical times, critical issues in Ireland*, Manchester: Manchester University Press.

Cervero, R. (2000) 'Trends and issues in continuing professional education', *New Directions for Adult and Continuing Education*, 86: 3–12.

Clarke, N. (2001) 'The impact of in-service training within social services', *British Journal of Social Work*, 31: 757–74.

Coffield, F. (2002) 'Breaking the consensus: lifelong learning as social control', in R. Edwards, N. Miller, N. Small and A. Tait (eds) *Supporting lifelong learning, Vol 3: Making policy work*, Routledge Falmer: London, pp 174–200.

Cohen, J. and Arato, A. (1994) *Civil society and political theory*, Cambridge, MA: MIT Press.

Connolly, L. and Hourigan, N. (2006) *Social movements and Ireland*, Manchester: Manchester University Press.

CORU (2011) *Code of Professional Conduct and Ethics for Social Workers*, Dublin: CORU. Available at: http://www.coru.ie/uploads/documents/typeset_Social_Worker_Code_Feb_2010.pdf

CORU (2013) *Frequently asked questions – general*. (Available at: http://www.coru.ie/en/faq, accessed 14/08/2013.)

Coulshed, V. and Mullender, A. (2001) *Management in social work* (2nd edn), Basingstoke: Palgrave.

Craig, G., Derricourt, N. and Loney, M. (eds) (1982) *Community work and the state: towards a radical practice*, Routledge and Kegan Paul: London.

Cree, V.E. (2009) 'The changing nature of social work', in R. Adams, L. Dominelli and M. Payne (eds) *Social work: themes issues and critical debates* (3rd edn), Basingstoke: Palgrave Macmillan.

Cree, V. (2011) *Social work: a reader*, Oxon: Routledge.

Cree, V. and Wallace, S. (2005) 'Risk and protection', in R. Adams, L. Dominelli and M. Payne (eds) *Social work futures: crossing boundaries, transforming practice*, Basingstoke: Palgrave Macmillan

Croft, S. and Beresford, P. (1997) 'Service user's perspectives', in M. Davies (ed) *The Blackwell companion to social work*, Oxford: Blackwell.

Davis, M. (2006) *Planet of slums*, London: Verso.

Davy, A. and Beddoe, L. (2010) *Best practice in professional supervision: a guide for the helping professions*, London: Jessica Kingsley.

Delahaye, V. (1994) *Politique Lutte Contre le Chomage et l'exclusion et mutation de l'action Sociale*, Paris: Ecole National d'Administration.

Dempsey, M., Halton, C. and Murphy, M. (2001) 'Scaffolding reflective learning in social work education', *Journal of Social Work Education*, 20(6): 631–41.

Dempsey, M., Murphy, M. and Halton, C. (2008) 'Introducing tools of reflective learning into peer supervision groups in a social work agency: an action research project', *The Journal of Practice Teaching & Learning*, 8(2): 25–43.

Department of Children and Youth Affairs (2011) *Children first: national guidance for the protection and welfare of children*, Dublin: Government Publications.

Department of Social Welfare (1997) *Green Paper on the voluntary and community sector and its relationship with the state*, Dublin: Government Publications.

Dewey, J. (1933) *How we think*, Boston, MA: D.C. Heath & Co.

Doel, M., Nelson, P. and Flynn, E. (2008) 'Experiences of post-qualifying study in social work', *Social Work Education*, 27(5): 549–71.

Dominelli, L. (1990) *Women and social action*, Birmingham: Venture Press.

Dominelli, L. (1996) 'Deprofessionalising social work: anti-oppressive practice, competencies and post-modernism', *British Journal of Social Work*, 26: 153–7.

Dominelli, L. (1997) *Sociology for social work*, London: Macmillan.

Dominelli, L. (1998) *Anti-racist social work*, London: Macmillan.

Dominelli, L. (2002) *Feminist social work: theory and practice*, London: Palgrave.

Dominelli, L. (2004) *Social work: theory and practice for a changing profession*, Cambridge: Polity Press.

Dominelli, L. (2007) 'Contemporary challenges to social work education in the United Kingdom', *Australian Social Work*, 60(1): 29–45.

Dominelli, L. (2010) *Social work in a globalizing world*, Cambridge: Polity.

Donzelot, J. (1997) *The politics of families*, Baltimore, MD: Johns Hopkins University Press.

Engels, F. (1993 [1844]) *The condition of the working class in England*, Oxford: Oxford University Press.

Ennis, E. and Brodie, I. (1999) 'Continuing professional development in social work: the Scottish context', *Social Work Education*, 18(1): 7–18.

Eraut, M. (1994) *Developing professional knowledge and competence*, London: Falmer Press.

Eraut, M. (2001) 'Learning challenges for knowledge based organisations', in J. Stevens (ed) *Workplace learning in Europe*, London: Chartered Institute of Personnel and Development (CIPD).

Etzioni, A. (1994) *The spirit of community*, New York, NY: Touchstone.

Fawcett, B. (2011) 'Post-modernism in social work', in V. Cree (ed) *Social work: a reader*, London: Routledge.

Featherstone, B, Broadhurst, K and Holt, K (2012) 'Thinking systemically – thinking politically: building strong partnerships with children and families in the context of rising inequality', *British Journal of Social Work*, 42(4): 618–33.

Ferguson, H. (2001) 'Social work, individualisation and life politics', *British Journal of Social Work*, 31(1): 41–55.

Ferguson, I., Lavalette, M. and Mooney, G. (2002) *Rethinking welfare: a critical perspective*, London and New Delhi: Sage.

Ferguson, I., Lavalette, M. and Whitmore, E. (2005) 'Introduction', in I. Ferguson, M. Lavalette and E. Whitmore (eds) *Globalisation, global justice and social work*, Abingdon: Routledge.

Fisher, F. (2000) *Citizens, experts and the environment: the politics of local knowledge*, Durham, NC, and London: Duke University Press.

Fitzgerald, W. (2012) *Probation and social work on trial: violent offenders and child abusers*, Basingstoke: Palgrave.

Fook, J. (1999) 'Critical reflectivity in education and practice', in B. Pease, and J. Fook (1999) *Transforming social work practice*, London: Routledge.

Fook, J. (2002) *Social work: critical theory and practice*, London: Sage.

Fook, J. (2004) 'What professionals need from research: beyond evidence-based practice', in D. Smith (ed) (2004) *Social work and evidence-based practice*, London: Jessica Kingsley.

Fook, J. (2011) 'Uncertainty: the defining characteristic of social work', in V. Cree (ed) *Social work: a reader*, London: Routledge.

Fook, J., Ryan, M. and Hawkins, L. (2000) *Professional expertise: practice theory and education for working in uncertainty*, London: Whiting and Birch.

Foucault, M. (1972) *The archaeology of knowledge*, London: Tavistock.

Foucault, M. (1977) *Discipline and punish*, London: Allen Lane.

Franklin, B. and Parton, N. (eds) (1991) *Social work, the media and public relations*, London: Routledge.

Fraser, N. (1997) *Justice interruptus*, London: Routledge.

Freidus, H. (2001) 'Culture and contexts in reflective teacher education', presentation at International Portfolio Conference, U.C.C., Ireland.

Freire, P. (1996 [1972]) *Pedagogy of the oppressed*, New York, NY: Seabury.

Fukuyama, F. (1995) *Trust: the social virtues and the creation of prosperity*, London: Hamish Hamilton.

Galpin, D. (2009) 'Who really drives the development of post-qualifying social work education and what are the implications of this?', *Social Work Education*, 38(1): 65–80.

Garrett, P.M. (2010) 'Examining the "conservative revolution": neoliberalism and social work education', *Social Work Education*, 29(4): 340–55.

Gaughan, L. and Garrett, M. (2012) 'The "most twisted and unaccountable force in the state"? Newspaper accounts of social work in the Republic of Ireland in troubled times', *Journal of Social Work*, 12(3): 267–86.

General Social Care Council (2010) *Raising standards: social work education in England, 2008–09*, London: GSCC.

Gibbons, N. (2010) 'Roscommon Child Care Case: report of the inquiry team to the Health Service Executive'. Available at: http://www.oneinfour.ie/content/resources/RoscommonChildCareCase.pdf (accessed May 2011).

Giddens, A. (1991) *Modernity and self identity*, Cambridge: Polity.

Giddens, A. (1999) *Runaway world*, London: BBC Reith Lectures.

Goetschius, G. (1969) *Working with community groups*, London: Routledge and Kegan Paul.

Gough, J. (2012) 'A sharp and provocative visionary', *Irish Times Weekend Review*, 22 December.

Gould, K. (1996) 'The misconstruing of multiculturalism: the Stanford debate and social work', in P. Ewalt, E. Freeman, S. Kirk and D. Poole (eds) *Multicultural issues in social work*, Washington, DC: NASW Press.

Gould, N. (2004) 'Introduction: the learning organisation and reflective practice – the emergence of a concept', in N. Gould and M. Balwin (eds) *Social work, critical reflection and the learning organization*, Aldershot: Ashgate Publishing.

Gould, N. and Baldwin, M. (eds) (2004) *Social work, critical reflection and the learning organisation*, Aldershot: Ashgate.

Gould, N. and Taylor, I. (eds) (1996) *Reflective learning for social work*, Aldershot: Ashgate.

Green, L.C. (2006) 'Parriah profession, debased discipline? An analysis of social work's low academic status and the possibilities for change', *Social Work Education*, 25(3): 245–64.

Halton, C. (2007) 'Innovative course developments in the Department of Applied Social Studies: experienced social work practitioners undertake practice research on a new masters course', *UCC: Arts Faculty Research Journal*, (3): 32–35.

Halton, C. (2010) 'Fostering reflective practice in the public service: a study of the probation service in the Republic of Ireland', in N. Lyons (ed) *Handbook of reflection and reflective inquiry: mapping a way of knowing for professional reflective inquiry*, New York, NY: Springer.

Halton, C. (2011) 'Postgraduate diploma in advanced fieldwork practice and supervision (social work): follow up study of graduates of the programme 2001–2010', unpublished study.

Halton, C. and Lyons, N. (2007) 'Educating practitioners for reflective inquiry: the contribution of a portfolio process to new ways of knowing', in C. O'Farrell (ed) *Teaching portfolio practice in Ireland: a handbook*, Dublin: HEA.

Halton, C., Murphy, M. and Dempsey, M. (2007) 'Reflective learning in social work education: researching student experiences', *Reflective Practice Journal*, 8(4): 511–22.

Harris, J. (2005) 'Globalisation, neo-liberal managerialism and UK social work', in I. Ferguson, M. Lavalette and E. Whitmore (eds) *Globalisation, global justice and social work*, Abingdon: Routledge.

Harris, P. (1997) 'Power', in M. Davies (ed) *The Blackwell companion to social work*, Oxford: Blackwell.

Hawkins, P. and Shohet, R. (2000) *Supervision in the helping professions*, Buckingham: Open University Press.

Hawkins, P. and Shohet, R. (2006) *Supervision in the helping professions*, 3rd edn, Buckingham: Open University Press.

HCPC (Health and Care Professions Council) (2012) *Continuing professional development and your registration*, London: HCPC.

Health & Social Care Professionals Council (2012a) 'Protection of professional titles'. Available at: http://www.coru.ie/registration-section/protection-of-titles/ (accessed November 2012).

Health & Social Care Professionals Council (2012b) 'Social workers – approved qualifications'. Available at: http://www.coru.ie/education-section/alias-41/alias-42/ (accessed November 2012).

Healy, K. (2000) *Social work practices: contemporary perspectives on change*, London: Sage.

Healy, K. (2005) *Social work theories in context: creating frameworks for practice*, Basingstoke: Palgrave Macmillan.

Healy, K. (2012) *Social work methods and skills: the essential foundations of practice*, London: Palgrave Macmillan.

Higham, P. (2009) *Post-qualifying social work practice*, London: Sage.

Home Office (1998) *Compact on relations between the government and the voluntary and community sector in England* (Cmnd 4100), London: HMSO.

Horner, N. (2012) *What is social work?*, London and New York, NY: Sage.

Houle, C.O., Cyphert, F. and Boggs, D. (1987) 'Education for the professions', *Theory into Practice*, 26(2): 87–93.

HSE (Health Service Executive) (2010) *Report of the task force for children & families social services: principles and practices*, Dublin: HSE.

Hughes, G., Clarke, J., Lewis, G. and Mooney, G. (1998) *Imagining welfare futures*, London: Routledge.

Hugman, R. (1998) *Social welfare and social value*, London: MacMillan.

Hugman, R. (2001) 'Post-welfare social work? Reconsidering post-modernism, post-Fordism and social work education', *Social Work Education*, 20(3): 321–33.

Hustler, D., McNamara, O., Jarvis, J., Londra, M., Campbell, A. and Howson, J. (2003) *Teachers' perceptions of continuing professional development*, Norwich: HMSO.

Ife, J. (1997) *Rethinking social work: towards critical practice*, Melbourne: Longman.

Jennings, C. and Kennedy, E. (1996) *The reflective professional in education*, London: Jessica Kingsley.

Joint Committee on the Family (1996) *Kelly: a child is dead. Interim report of the Joint Committee on the Family*, Dublin: Government of Ireland.

Jones, M. (2004) 'Supervision learning and transformative practices', in N. Gould and M. Baldwin (eds) *Social work, critical reflection and the learning organization*, Aldershot: Ashgate.

Jordan, B. (1997) 'Social work and society', in M. Davies (ed) *The Blackwell companion to social work*, Oxford: Blackwell.

Judt, T. (with Snyder, T.) (2012) *Thinking the twentieth century*, New York, NY: Penguin.

Kadushin, A. (1992) *Supervision in social work* (3rd edn), New York, NY: Columbia University Press.

Karvinen-Niinikoske, S. (2004) 'Social work supervision: contributing to innovative knowledge production and open expertise', in N. Gould and M. Baldwin (eds) *Social work, critical reflection and the learning organization*, Aldershot: Ashgate.

Keane, J. (1988) *Democracy and civil society*, London: Verso.

Keville, H. (2002) 'Doomed to drop out?', *Community Care*, 28 November, no 1450: 36–7.

Khinduka, S.K. (2007) 'Towards rigor and relevance in US social work education', *Australian Social Work*, 60(1): 18–28.

Kroll, B. (2004) 'The challenge of post qualifying child care award teaching: reflexivity and the role of books and biscuits', *Social Work Education*, 23(6): 653–66.

Laming, H. (2003) 'The Victoria Climbié inquiry: report of an inquiry', presented to Parliament by the Secretary of State for Health and the Secretary of State for the Home Department by Command of Her Majesty, January (Cm 5730).

Laming, H. (2009) *The protection of children in England: a progress report*, London: The Stationery Office.

Langer, E.J. (1989) *Mindfulness*, Reading, MA: Addison-Wesley.

Leinster, J. (2009) 'Identifying the education and training needs of social work managers in Ireland', M.Litt thesis, National University of Galway.

Leinster, J. (2010) 'Social work management in Ireland: time for education and training', *Social Work & Social Sciences Review*, 14(2): 73–94.

Lester, S. (1999) 'Professional bodies, CPD and informal learning: the case of conservation', *Continuing Professional Development*, 3(4): 110–21.

Levitas, R. (1998) *The inclusive society? Social exclusion and New Labour*, London: Macmillan.

Lewis, J. (1996) 'What does contracting do to voluntary organisations?', in D. Billis and M. Harris (eds) *Voluntary agencies: challenges of organisation and management*, London: Macmillan.

Lewis, J. (1999) 'Reviewing the relationship between the voluntary sector and the state in Britain in the 1990s', *Voluntas*, 10(3): 225–70.

Lister, R. (1997) *Citizenship: a feminist perspective*, London: Macmillan.

Lorenz, W. (1994) *Social work in a changing Europe*, London: Routledge.

Loughran, J. (2006) *Developing a pedagogy of teacher education*, New York, NY: Routledge.

Lovett, T. (1975) *Adult education, community development and the working class*, London: Ward Lock.

Lovett, T., Clarck, C. and Kilmurray, A. (1983) *Adult education and community action*, London: Croom Helm.

Lymbery, M. (2001) 'Social work at the crossroads', *British Journal of Social Work*, 31(3): 369–84.

Lymbery, M. (2003) 'Negotiating the contradictions between competence and creativity in social work education', *Journal of Social Work*, 3(1): 99–117.

Lynch, K. (2006) 'Neo-liberalism and marketisation: the implications for higher education', *European Educational Research Journal*, 5(1): 1–17.

Lyons, N. (1998) *With portfolio in hand: validating the new teacher professionalism*, New York, NY: Columbia Press.

Lyons, N. (2002) 'The personal self in a public story: the portfolio presentation narrative', in N. Lyons and V.K. LaBoskey (eds) *Narrative inquiry in practice: advancing the knowledge of teaching*, New York, NY: Teachers College Press.

Lyons, N. (ed) (2010) *Handbook of reflection and reflective inquiry: mapping a way of knowing for professional reflective inquiry*, New York, NY: Springer.

Madden, C.A. and Mitchell, V.A. (1993) 'Professions, standards and competence: a survey of continuing education for the professions', University of Bristol, Department of Continuing Education.

Marsh, P. and Doel, M. (2005) *The task-centred book*, London: Routledge.

Mathiason, N. (2007) 'Children's homes hit by buyout fears', *The Observer*, 14 October.

Mattawa, K. (2012) 'Now that we have tasted hope', in M. Kaldor, H. Moore and S. Selchow (eds) *Global civil society: ten years of critical reflection*, London: Palgrave MacMillan.

McCarthy, A. and Evans, D. (2003) 'A study on the impact of continuing education for nurses and midwives who completed post registration courses', The Nursing and Midwifery Planning and Development Unit, Western Health Board.

McGuinness, C. (1993) *Kilkenny incest investigation: report presented to Mr. Brendan Howlin T.D., Minister for Health by South Eastern Health Board*, Dublin: Stationery Office.

Megginson, D. and Whitaker, V. (2007) *Continuing professional development* (2nd edn), London: Chartered Institute of Personnel Development.

Mezirow, J. (1991) *Transformative dimensions of adult learning*, San Francisco, CA: Jossey Bass.

Monediaire, G. (1998) 'The social status of social service occupations', *Social Work in Europe*, 5(3): 19–24.

Morgan, A., Cullinane, J. and Pye, M. (2008) 'Continuing professional development: rhetoric and practice in the NHS', *Journal of Education and Work*, 21(3): 233–48.

Morrison, T. (2001) *Staff supervision in social care: making a real difference for staff and service users*, Brighton: Pavilion.

Mullalay, B. (1997) *Structural social work*, Oxford: Oxford University Press.

Mullender, A. and Perrot, S. (1998) 'Social work and organisations', in R. Adams, L. Dominelli and M. Payne (eds) *Social work: themes, issues and critical debates*, London: Macmillan.

Munro, E. (2011) *The Munro review of child protection, final report: a child-centred system* (Cm 8062), London: The Department of Education.

Murakami, H. (2011) *1Q84*, London: Harvil Secker.

Murphy, M., Halton, C. and Dempsey, M. (2008) 'A study of the transfer of reflective engagement from social work education into the workplace', *Irish Educational Studies*, 27(1): 71–80.

Murphy, M., Dempsey, M. and Halton, C. (2010) 'Reflective inquiry in social work education', in N. Lyons (ed) *Handbook of reflection and reflective inquiry: mapping a way of knowing for professional reflective inquiry*, New York, NY: Springer.

Nakkula, M.J. and Ravitch, S.M. (1998) *Matters of interpretation: reciprocal transformation in therapeutic and developmental relationships with youth*, San Francisco, CA: Jossey Bass.

Nash, M. and Munford, R. (2001) 'Unresolved struggles: educating social workers in Aotearoa New Zealand', *Social Work Education*, 20(1): 21–34.

National Council for the Professional Development of Nursing and Midwifery (2004) *Report on the continuing professional development of staff nurses and staff midwives*, Dublin: National Council for the Professional Development of Nursing and Midwifery.

Noble, C. and Irwin, J. (2009) 'Social work supervision: an exploration of the current challenges in a rapidly changing social, economic and political environment', *Journal of Social Work*, 9(3): 345–58.

Norman, J. (2010) *The big society*, Buckingham: University of Buckingham Press.

NSWQB (National Social Workers Qualifications Board) (2006) *Social work posts in Ireland*, Dublin: NSWQB.

Obama, B. (2006) *The audacity of hope*, Random House: New York.

O'Hagan, K. (1996) 'Social work competence: an historical perspective', in K. O'Hagan (ed) *Competence in social work practice: a practical guide for professionals*, London: Kingsley Publishers.

OMCYA (Office of the Minister for Children and Youth Affairs) (2009) *Report of the Commission to Inquire into Child Abuse, 2009: implementation plan*, Dublin: The Stationery Office.

O'Sullivan, J. (2006) 'Continuing professional development', in R. Jones and F. Jenkin (eds) *Developing the allied health professional*, Oxon: Radcliffe Publishing.

O'Toole, F. (2012) *Up the republic!*, London: Faber.

Page, S. and Wosket, V. (1994) *Supervising the counsellor: a cyclical model*, London: Routledge.

Parsloe, P. (2001) 'Looking back on social work education', *Social Work Education*, 20(1): 9–19.

Parton, N. (1995) *The politics of child abuse*, London: MacMillan.

Parton, N. (2011) 'Social work, risk and "the blaming system"', in V. Cree (ed) *Social work: a reader*, Oxon: Routledge.

Parton, N. and O'Byrne, P. (2000) *Constructive social work: towards a new practice*, Basingstoke: Macmillan.

Payne, M. (1994) 'Supervision in social work', in A. Connor and S.E. Black (eds) *Performance review and quality in social care*, London: Jessica Kingsley.

Payne, M. (2002) 'Management', in R. Adams, L. Dominelli and M. Payne (eds) *Critical practice in social work*, Basingstoke: Palgrave.

Payne, M. (2005) *Modern social work theory* (3rd edn), Basingstoke: Palgrave.

Pease, B. and Fook, J. (1999) *Transforming social work practice*, London: Routledge.

Peet, S. and Jennings, O. (2010) 'Examining social workers' views of supervision', *The Irish Social Worker Journal*, Summer 2010: 12–15.

Phillipson, J. (2002) 'Supervision and being supervised', in R. Adams, L. Dominelli and M. Payne (eds) *Critical practice in social work*, Basingstoke: Palgrave.

Popple, K. (1995) *Analysing community work: its theory and practice*, Milton Keynes: Open University Press.

Postle, K., Edwards, C., Moon, R., Rumsey, H. and Thomas, T. (2002) 'Continuing professional development after qualification – partnerships, pitfalls and potential', *Social Work Education*, 21(2): 157–69.

Powell, F. (2001) *The politics of social work*, London: Sage.

Powell, F. (2013) *The politics of civil society: big society, small government*, Bristol: Policy Press.

Powell, F. and Geoghegan, M. (2004) *The politics of community development*, Dublin: AA Farmar.

Powell, F. and Geoghegan, M. (2005) 'Reclaiming civil society: the future of global social work', *European Journal of Social Work*, 8(2) 129–144.

Powell, F. and Guerin, D. (1997) *Civil society and social policy: voluntarism in Ireland*, Dublin: AA Farmar.

Preston-Shoot, M. (2007) 'Engaging with continuing professional development: with or without qualification?', in W. Tovey (ed) *The post-qualifying handbook for social workers*, London: Jessica Kingsley Publishers.

Project of Critical Reflection (no date) 'Discussion of a bed for the night'. Available at: www.civicreflection.org

Putnam, R. (1993) *Making democracy work: civic tradition in modern Italy*, Princeton, NJ: Princeton University Press.

Putnam, R. (2000) *Bowling alone: the collapse and revival of American community*, London and New York, NY: Simon & Schuster.

Ramirez, M. (2009) 'The politics of recognition and citizenship' in B. de Sousa Santos (ed) *Democratising democracy*, London: Verso.

Rath, A. (2000) 'Reflective practice: mapping a pedagogy for transformation', in A. Hyland (ed) *Multiple intelligences curriculum and assessment project*, Cork: Education Department UCC.

Rath, A. (2010) 'Reflective practice as conscious geometry: portfolios as a tool for sponsoring, scaffolding and assessing reflective inquiry in learning to teach', in N. Lyons (ed) *Handbook of reflection and reflective inquiry: mapping a way of knowing for professional reflective inquiry*, New York, NY: Springer.

Ritzer, G. (1993) *The McDonaldization of society*, Thousand Oaks, CA: Pine Forge Press.

Robin, C. (2011) *The reactionary mind*, Oxford: Oxford University Press.

Roche, J. and Tucker, S. (1997) *Welfare in introduction to social work*, Milton Keynes: Open University.

Rosenman, L. (2007) 'Social work education, the university and the state', *Australian Social Work*, 60(1): 5–17.

Ruch, G. (2002) 'From triangle to spiral: reflective practice in social work education, practice and research', *Social Work Education*, 21(2): 199–216.

Ruch, G. (2005) 'Reflective practice in contemporary child care social work: the role of containment', *British Journal of Social Work*, 37(4): 659–80.

Saleeby, D. (2006) *The strengths perspective in social work practice*, Boston, MA: Pearson Education.

Saleeby, D. (2011) 'Power to the people', in V. Cree (ed) *Social work: a reader*, London: Routledge.

Santos, B. (2005) *Democratising democracy: beyond the liberal democratic canon*, London: Verso.

Santos, B. (2007) *Another knowledge is possible: beyond Northern epistemologies*, London: Verso.

Schön, D.A. (1983) *The reflective practitioner: how professionals think in action*, New York: Basic Books.

Schön, D.A. (1987) *Educating the reflective practitioner: toward a new design for teaching and learning in the professions*, San Francisco, CA: Jossey-Bass.

Schön, D.A. (1991) *The reflective practitioner: how professionals think in action*, Aldershot: Ashgate.

Scottish Executive (2005) *National strategy for the development of the social service workforce in Scotland: a plan for action 2005–2010*, Edinburgh: Scottish Executive.

Seden, J. and McCormick, M. (2011) 'Caring for yourself, being managed and professional development', in J. Sedan, S. Matthews, M. McCormick and A. Morgan (eds) *Professional development in social work*, Oxon: Routledge.

Shulman, L.S. (1994) 'Portfolios in historical perspective', presentation at the Portfolios in Teaching and Teacher Education Conference, Cambridge, MA, USA.

Shulman, L.S. (2005) 'Signature pedagogies in the professions', *Daedalus*, 134(3): 52–59.

Silver, H. (1996) 'National discourses on the new urban poverty', in E. Mingione (ed) *Urban poverty and the underclass*, Oxford: Blackwell.

Skehill, C. (1999) *The nature of social work in Ireland: a historical perspective*, Lewiston, NY: Edwin Mellen Press.

Skidmore, P. and Craig, J. (2005) *Start with people*, London: Demos.

Skinner, K. (2005) *Continuing professional development for the social services workforce in Scotland*, Dundee: Scottish Institute for Excellence in Social Work Education.

Social Work Reform Board (2010) website, www.education.gov.uk/swrb

Social Workers Registration Board (2010) *Continuing professional development for registered social workers*, Wellington, New Zealand: SWRB.

SSSC (Scottish Social Services Council) (2004) *Continuing professional development for the social service workforce*, Dundee: SSSC.

SSSC (2011) *Post registration training and learning requirements for social workers: guidance notes*, Dundee: SSSC.

Stepney, P. and Popple, K. (2008) *Social work and the community: a critical context for practice*, London: Palgrave.

Stokes, P. and Knight, B. (1997) 'A citizen's charter to save our cities', *Independent*, 1 January.

SWTF (Social Work Task Force) (2009) *Building a safe, confident future: the final report of the Social Work Task Force, November 2009*, London: DCSF. Available at: http://webarchive.nationalarchives.gov.uk/+/www.dh.gov.uk/en/SocialCare/DH_098322

SWTF (2010) *Social workers' workload survey: messages from the frontline. Findings from the 2009 survey and interviews with senior managers.* Available at: https://www.gov.uk/government/uploads/system/uploads/attachment_data/file/221950/social_20workers_20workload_20survey_202009.pdf

Taylor, B.J., Mullineux, J.C. and Fleming, G. (2010) 'Partnership, service needs and assessing competence in post qualifying education and training', *Social Work Education*, 29(5): 475–89.

Thomas, D.N. (1980) 'Research and community', *Community Development Journal*, 15(1): 30–40.

Thomas, D.N. (1983) *The making of community work*, London: Allen and Unwin.

Thompson, N. (1995) *Theory and practice in health and social welfare*, Buckingham: Open University Press.

Thompson, N. (2002) *People skills* (2nd edn), Basingstoke: Palgrave.

Thompson, N. (2005) *Understanding social work: preparing for practice* (2nd edn), Basingstoke: Macmillan.

Thompson, N. (2006) *Promoting workplace learning*, Bristol: BASW/Policy Press.

Tovey, P. (1994) *Quality assurance in continuing professional education: an analysis*, Routledge: London.

Travis, A. and Wintour, P. (2012) 'None of the above: electorate spurns David Cameron's police polls', *Guardian*, 17 November.

Twelvetrees, A. (1991) *Community work* (2nd edn), London: Macmillan.

Uprimmy, R. and Garcia-Villegas, M. (2005) 'The Constitutional Court and emancipation in Columbia', in B. Santos (ed) *Democratising democracy*, London: Verso.

Vurtel, I. (2008) 'CPE needs analysis and expectations of AASW Victorian membership', *AASW Victorian Branch Newsletter*, 2(1): 2–3.

West, D., Heath, D. and Ennis, G. (2009) 'Northern Territory social work: views and approaches', *Australian Social Work*, 62(1): 74–89.

White, S. (2011) 'Fabled uncertainty in social work', in L. Bondi, D. Carr, C. Clark and C. Clegg (eds) *Towards professional wisdom: practical deliberation in the peoples professions*, Surrey: Ashgate.

White, V. (1999) 'Feminist social work and the state', in B. Lesnik (ed) *Social work and the state*, Brighton: Pavilion Publishing.

Williams, C.C. (2007) 'Mixed-method evaluation of continuing professional development: applications in cultural competence training', *Social Work Education*, 26(2): 121–35.

Wilson, G. and Kelly, B. (2010) 'Evaluating the effectiveness of social work education: preparing students for practice learning', *British Journal of Social Work*, 40(8): 2431–49.

Wilson, G., Hamilton, B., Britton, F., Campbell, J., Hughes, P. and Manktelow, R. (2005) 'Approved social work training in Northern Ireland: using research to examine competence-based learning and influence policy change', *Social Work Education*, 24(7): 721–36.

Wilson, K., Ruch, G., Lymbery, M. and Cooper, A. (2011) *Social work: an introduction to contemporary practice* (2nd edn), Harlow: Pearson.

Winter, R., Buck, A. and Sobiechowaska, P. (1999) *Professional experience and the investigative imagination: the art of reflective writing*, London: Routledge.

Yelloly, M. and Henkel, M. (eds) (1995) 'Introduction', in *Learning and teaching in social work: towards reflective practice*, London: Jessica Kingsley.

Yuen, A.W.K. and Ho, D.K.L. (2007) 'Social work education in Hong Kong at the crossroads: challenges and opportunities amidst marketization and managerialism', *Social Work Education*, 26(6): 546–59.

Zavirsek, D. (1999) 'Civil society, memory and social work', in B. Lesnik (ed) *Social work and the State*, Brighton: Pavilion Publishing.

Index

Page references for notes are followed by n